The Sport of Grilling

by

Grilling Coach Big Bob Snoor

authorHOUSE®

AuthorHouse™
1663 Liberty Drive, Suite 200
Bloomington, IN 47403
www.authorhouse.com
Phone: 1-800-839-8640

First published by AuthorHouse 9/30/2007

ISBN: 978-1-4343-1569-4 (sc)

Library of Congress Control Number: 2007904253

Printed in the United States of America
Bloomington, Indiana

This book is printed on acid-free paper.

ACKNOWLEDGMENTS

Special Thanks to:

My Wife Cynthia & My Daughter Elizabeth

My Mom & Dad

My Sister Diane & her husband Jeff

My In-Laws John & Lena

My Sister In-Law Elaine, John, Sarah & Johnny

My Sister Connie, Ric, Tyler & Travis

Christina, Russ, Ryan & Lauren

Dan & Dana

My Brother Roger & His Son JR

My Entire Family & Friends

In Memory of:

Our Angel Katie Cassidy

My Grandmother Pearl Snoor

My Grandfather Paul Snoor, Who gave me a love for baseball on the Radio.

My Grandfather John Rusk, Who gave me my love of the Great Outdoors

My Aunt Donna

Norm Nixon

Earl Drake

FOREWORD

Webster's Dictionary: Defines Sport as; A game; a merrymaking: out-of-door recreation, as shooting, horse-racing, etc....To play, to frolic, to practice the diversions of the field.

Growing up my favorite form of recreation was eating. I still enjoy eating as my favorite type of recreation (Sport), along with grilling and golf.

When we go to a bowling alley, I can drink a beer, while we bowl a few frames. On the golf course from a cart, I can buy a candy bar and a coke, to eat while we play our round. Who is the true athlete in horse racing the Jockey -OR- the Horse? In auto racing who is the super star, a new super fast Race Car and Great Crew -OR- the Driver? If these are sports, as I've been told! Then how can you tell me that Iron Chef America is not a Sporting Event and Bobby Flay is not an athlete. I watched a lady on TV win a $1,000,000.00 for cooking a chicken recipe. A guy grilled the perfect burger for the prize of $10,000.00. I watch the big time great Barbecue Champs on TV all the time winning prize money and a trophy. We in the food business work long hard hours perfecting are craft. We even have a Sports Event called the Culinary Olympics, which is held in Germany. To be an athlete whether it's golf, bowling, horse racing, auto racing, grilling, cooking -OR- barbecue, you must have talent, skill, pride, knowledge, be hard working and practice your trade.

So the next time your standing at that hot grill, drinking a cold one. Remember my friend you are an athlete and Grilling is a Sport.

Big Bob's Top 10 Most Important Things in Life!

Your Top 10 List:

#1. My Wife Cynthia & My Daughter Elizabeth _____

#2. Family & Friends _____

#3. Country (USA) & Freedom _____

#4. Ohio State Buckeye Fan _____

#5. Faith _____

TIE #6. Love _____

TIE #6. Health _____

#7. Happiness _____

#8. Grilling & Eating BBQ _____

TIE #9. Writing this Book _____

TIE #9. Success in a Career _____

TIE #10. Golf & Being a Sports Fan _____

TIE #10. Bacon & Steak _____

Your Top 10 List of the Most Important Things in Your Life, will be different than mine. That's the way it should be. It's good to do a gut check from time to time.

Golf Club, Golf Ball & Flag

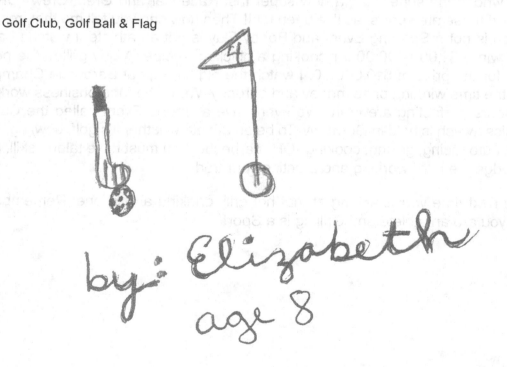

by: Elizabeth age 8

Table of Contents

CHAPTER #1

Basic Grilling 101

COLLEGE FOOTBALL

Notes

The Difference Between Barbecue & Grilling

People often use the word barbecue when referring to meats that where grilled.

However, barbecue and grilling are two completely different cooking methods.

Barbecuing:

1. Barbecuing refers to foods that are cooked with a long, slow process using indirect low heat generated by smoldering logs or wood chips that smoke cook the meat.
2. The fuel and heat source are separate from the cooking chamber, the cooking heat source contains enough heat to properly cook the meat over a period of time.
3. The cooking chamber fills with smoke, giving the meat it's characteristic smoked flavor which varies depending on the type of wood that is used for the fuel.
4. The best temperature for barbecue is between 200 degrees F. and 300 degrees F.. If the temperature is above 300 degrees F., it is considered to be grilling.

Grilling:

1. Grilling refers to foods that are cooked (fast) quickly and directly over high heat.
2. Grilling temperatures typically reach 500 degrees F. or higher, however any temperature above 300 degrees F. is considered to be a grilling temperature.
3. The heat of grilling sears the surface of the meat, forming a very flavorful browned crust covering.

Barbecue: Kinds of Woods to use for Smoking

A very wide range of woods can be used for smoking. Hardwoods are much better than softwoods, because hardwoods burn longer and produce more heat. Hardwoods will also add more flavors to foods through the smoke that is produced as the wood burns. Softwoods burn fast and will add very little flavor to foods.

Big Bob's Top 10 Best Woods for Barbecuing (Smoking)

#1. Hickory: Hickory is big in the South, but is popular in many regions. It is used just as often, if not more than Oak. Hickory creates a very strong smoked bacon flavor and can be used for all types of meats. Hickory is the best for pork and ribs.

#2. Oak: Oak is one of the most common woods used in many regions of the country. It provides a good flavor without overpowering the food. It can be used with all types of meat and fish.

#3. Maple: Maple provides a mild, smoky and sweet flavor to foods and can be used with pork, poultry and small game birds.

#4. Mesquite: Mesquite wood burns very hot and gives a strong flavor to foods. It is very popular in Texas and the Southwestern U.S. and gives great results when used with cuts of beef.

#5. Apple: Apple wood provides a sweet, fruity taste to most meats, poultry and small game birds. Apple is really good for smoking bacon and ham.

#6. Birch: Birch provides a flavor very similar to maple wood. Birch wood is best used with cuts of pork and poultry.

#7. Alder: In the Northwest Region of the U.S. where smoked salmon is common, alder wood is the most popular choice. It can also be used for poultry and small game birds. Alder provides a subtle and sweet taste to the meat.

#8. Pecan: Pecan is big in Louisiana and other Gulf Coast States. It has a flavor similar to hickory, but is not as strong in flavor. It can be used with most cuts of meats.

#9. Cherry: Cherry can be used to smoke all types of meats. Like apple, cherry provides a subtle sweet and fruity flavor to foods.

#10. Walnut: Walnut is best used for red meats and strong tasting heavy game meat. Because of the strong and somewhat bitter flavor the Walnut provides. Walnut is often mixed with other woods, that have milder flavors in order to produce more subtle flavors to smoked foods.

FOOD SAFETY

Cooking Tips for Food Safety:

One of the critical points in controlling bacteria in food is to control the temperature.

Pathogenic microorganisms will grow slowly at low temperatures, multiply rapidly in middle range temperatures and are killed at high temperatures. For your safety, foods should be held at the proper cold temperatures in refrigerators or freezers and they must be cooked thoroughly to proper temperatures. It is important to use a thermometer when cooking meat and poultry to prevent undercooking and will prevent food borne illness.

Use a Thermometer for Food Safety:

Using a thermometer is the best way to ensure food safety and to determine the proper "doneness" of most grilled and barbecue foods. To be safe, a food product must be cooked to an internal temperature that is high enough to destroy any harmful bacteria that may have been in the food.

Doneness refers to a food being cooked to the desired state and indicates the sensory aspects of grilled foods such as appearance, texture and the juiciness. Unlike taking the temperature required for food safety, the sensory aspects are always subjective.

Meat & Poultry Grilling Chart:

Use this chart as a general guide for proper grilled food temperatures. All temperatures listed are final target temperatures. To prevent overcooking and dryness to the beef, lamb, veal and pork, stop the grilling 5 degrees below your target temperature and always let the meat rest for 5-10 minutes. This does not apply to ground meat or grilled poultry.

Final cooked target internal temperature & description of doneness:

Item:	Rare:	Medium:	Well:
	(very red, warm center)	(pink, warm center)	(pink, warm center)
Beef	125-130 degrees	130-145 degrees	145 degrees & above
Lamb		130-145 degrees	145 degrees & above
Pork	Cook to 150 degrees or over		
Ground Beef	Cook to 160 degrees		
Poultry	Cook to 170 degrees or above		

Hand-Washing

Hand-washing is a easy and very effective way to prevent diseases, such as food poisoning, flu and colds.

When to Wash Your Hands:

1. Before and after preparing or serving food reduces your risk of catching and spreading bacteria that may cause food poisoning. Make sure to wash your hands before and after preparing meat, seafood, poultry -OR- raw eggs.

2. After going to the bathroom or changing diapers reduces your risk of catching or spreading infectious diseases such as Hepatitis A -OR- Salmonella.
3. Washing your hands often, during cold and flu season, can reduce your chance of catching or spreading a cold or the flu.

Wash your hands after:

#1. Taking out the garbage
#2. Eating -OR- Snacking
#3. Smoking
#4. Touching your pets
#5. Using the bathroom
#6. Blowing your nose, coughing or sneezing.
#7. Touching your ears, nose or mouth.
#8. Touching money
#9. Touching different types of raw -OR- cooked meats.
#10. Any kind of contact with a dirty work surface.
#11. Any contact with dirty equipment

Proper hand-washing:

1. Use warm -OR- hot water for killing bacteria on your hands.
2. Under running water, wet your hands and wrists completely.
3. If you use a bar of soap, rinse it off before using it. Apply a small dab of liquid soap, if using liquid soap.
4. Always work up a good lather, by rubbing your hands together. Wash all the surfaces of your skin, including your wrists, palms, fingers, fingernails and backs of your hands. Wash your hands for at least 20 seconds.
5. Rinse your hands thoroughly.
6. Dry your hands. Always use paper towel to turn off the water, when you have finished.

Hand Sanitizing Tips for Backyard Grilling

If soap and water are not available, use gel hand sanitizers -OR- alcohol based hand wipes.

If using the gel sanitizer, rub your hands together until the gel is dry. You don't need to use water, the alcohol in the gel kills the germs on your hands.

Big Bob's Outdoor Cooking & Grilling Basics

Safety:

Following a few outdoor cooking methods will ensure your safety. Your food will be prepared correctly and you, your family and friends will enjoy some very delicious food.

These are just really basic steps, but they must be told. Make sure your grill is always on a flat level surface, it should be a concrete or a blacktop surface. A level surface will keep your grill from tipping over accidentally. Don't put your grill in a grass area. A concrete -OR- blacktop surface is safer from fire, than a grass surface. You should always have a fire extinguisher near by at all times.

You will need a good set of grilling tools. Such items as all long handled utensils, long oven mitts -OR- heavy duty pot holders. A good quality long heavy-duty manly apron, to protect you from the heat and the spills. Something else you should consider is the safety of your feet and legs. Always be careful if you wear shorts and/or sandals when cooking on the grill outdoors.

Direct Heat Cooking Method:

Direct heat is simply cooking directly over the coals -OR- flame if using a gas grill. This method of outdoor cooking is used for small cuts of meats such as burgers, hot dogs, steaks and cut up chicken parts. Grilled Foods should always be cooked with the grill lid on to minimize flareups. Take off or open the grill lid only to turn the meat and to remove the meat from the grill to serve.

Indirect Heat Cooking Method:

To use this method of outdoor cooking with charcoal. Place the coals around the edges of the grate and place a drip pan in the center. Place the food to be cooked over the drip pan. The grill lid should always be closed and only opened to baste or mop, turn the food -OR- take the food off of the grill rack. This cooking method is used to cook larger cuts of meats such as beef, pork roasts, whole chickens and turkey.

If you are using a gas grill, turn the center burner off and place a drip pan under the grill rack.

Do you Want to Live Longer ?

(YES)

* Answer: Eat More Barbecue!!!!

XXXXXXXXXXXXXXXXXXXXX

This

Pit Master

Makes

Pit Stops

Big Bob's Top 35 College Football Rivalries List

I Love College Football, I'm a Lifetime Ohio State Buckeye Fan!!!!!

Your Top 35 List:

#1. Ohio State-Michigan   1._____

#2. Army-Navy   2._____

#3. Notre Dame-USC   3._____

#4. USC-UCLA   4._____

#5. Harvard-Yale   5._____

#6. Texas-Oklahoma   6._____

#7. Auburn-Alabama   7._____

#8. Florida-Florida State   8._____

#9. Stanford-California   9._____

#10. Texas-Texas A&M   10._____

#11. Michigan State-Michigan   11._____

#12. Georgia-Georgia Tech   12._____

#13. Oregon-Oregon State   13._____

#14. Amherst-Williams   14._____

#15. Wabash-Depauw   15._____

#16. Lehigh-Lafayette   16._____

#17. Purdue-Indiana   17._____

#18. Minnesota-Michigan   18._____

#19. Pittsburgh-Penn State   19._____

#20. Tennessee-Vanderbilt   20._____

#21. Louisiana State-Tulane   21._____

#22. Missouri-Kansas   22._____

#23. Alabama-Georgia   23._____

#24. Oklahoma-Nebraska   24._____

#25. Notre Dame-Army   25._____

#26. Mississippi-Mississippi State   26._____

#27. North Carolina-North Carolina State   27._____

#28. Cornell-Colgate   28._____

#29. Texas-Arkansas   29._____

#30. Clemson-South Carolina   30._____

#31. Washington-Washington State   31._____

#32. Bates-Colby   32._____

#33. North Dakota-South Dakota   33._____

#34. Kansas-Kansas State   34._____

#35. Cincinnati-Miami (OHIO)   35._____

I received NO MONEY for making this list, sorry if your team and your rival didn't make the list.

Big Bob's Top 30 Best College Football Players All-Time

Your top 30 list:

#1. Red Grange HB Illinois

1._____

#2. Sammy Baugh QB/DB/P TCU

2._____

#3. George Gipp HB Notre Dame

3._____

#4. Herschel Walker RB Georgia

4._____

#5. Bronko Nagurski FB/T Minnesota

5._____

#6. Hugh Green DB Pitt.

6._____

#7. Dick Butkus LB/C Illinois

7._____

#8. Jim Thorpe HB Carlisle

8._____

#9. Deion Sanders CB FSU

9._____

#10. Nile Kinnick HB Iowa

10._____

#11. Archie Griffin RB Ohio State

11._____

#12. O. J. Simpson RB USC

12._____

#13. John Hannah OL Alabama

13._____

#14. Ron Dayne RB Wisconsin

14._____

#15. Tommy Nobis LB/G Texas

15._____

#16. Jim Brown RB Syracuse

16._____

#17. Barry Sanders RB Okla. State

17._____

#18. Bubba Smith DL Mich. State

18._____

#19. Archie Manning QB Ole Miss

19._____

#20. Doak Walker RB SMU

20._____

#21. Charles Woodson CB/WR/KR
      Michigan

21._____

#22. Keith Jackson TE Oklahoma

22._____

#23. Orlando Pace OT Ohio State

23._____

#24. Lee Roy Jordan LB/C Alabama

24._____

TIE #25. Bo Jackson RB Auburn

25._____

TIE #25. Lawrence Taylor LB/DE UNC

25._____

#26. Tony Dorsett RB Pitt.

26._____

#27. Ricky Williams RB Texas

27._____

#28. Bennie Onsterbaum End Michigan

28._____

#29. Don Hudson End Alabama

29._____

TIE #30. Brain Bosworth LB Oklahoma

30._____

TIE #30. Earl Campbell RB Texas

30._____

This list is just my opinion, it is for sure not shared by many.

Big Bob's Top 25 Greatest College Football Teams All-Time

My favorite is #8 the 1968 Ohio State Buckeyes!!!!

Your Top 25 List:

#1. Nebraska 1971   1._____
#2. USC 1972   2._____
#3. Army 1945   3._____
#4. Nebraska 1995   4._____
#5. Miami 2001   5._____
#6. Notre Dame 1947   6._____
#7. Michigan 1947   7._____
#8. Ohio State 1968   8._____
#9. Oklahoma 1956   9._____
#10. Alabama 1961   10._____
#11. Oklahoma 1974   11._____
#12. Notre Dame 1949   12._____
#13. Notre Dame 1988   13._____
#14. Army 1944   14._____
#15. USC 1962   15._____
#16. Oklahoma 2000   16._____
#17. Michigan 1948   17._____
#18. Texas 1969   18._____
#19. TCU 1938   19._____
#20. Pittsburgh 1976   20._____
#21. Florida State 1999 21._____
#22. Florida 1996   22._____
#23. Minnesota 1940   23._____
#24. Oklahoma 1955   24._____
#25. Notre Dame 1930   25._____

So many great college football teams to pick from, only 25 make the list.

Big Bob's Top 7 College Football Perfect Teams

(This seven went an entire season without losing a game and had no points scored on them all season)

It's tough to have a perfect season in College Football!!!!

#1. 1901 Michigan (11-0)
#2. 1919 Texas A&M (10-0)
#3. 1939 Tennessee (10-0)
#4. 1932 Colgate (9-0)
#5. 1938 Duke (9-0)
#6. 1917 Texas A&M (8-0)
#7. 1911 Utah State (5-0)

This list was fun & easy, no money changed hands and it's one mans opinion!

Big Bob's Top 35 College Football Coaches of All Time

My all-time favorite is Woody Hayes of Ohio State !!!!!

Coach:	Notable College:
#1. Frank Leahy	Notre Dame
#2. Knute Rockne	Notre Dame
#3. Paul "Bear" Bryant	Alabama
#4. Fielding Yost	Michigan
#5. Glenn S. "POP" Warner	Carlisle, Cornell, Pitt. & Stanford
#6. Amos Alonzo Stagg	Chicago
#7. Percy Haughton	Harvard
#8. Howard Jones	Iowa
#9. Ara Parseghian	Notre Dame
#10. Bobby Bowden	Florida State
#11. Joe Paterno	Penn State
#12. Woody Hayes	Ohio State
#13. Barry Switzer	Oklahoma
#14. Tom Osborne	Nebraska
#15. Fritz Crisler	Michigan
#16. Andy Smith	Penn
#17. Bob Devaney	Nebraska
#18. Jock Sutherland	Layfayette & Pittsburgh
#19. Bo Schembechler	Michigan

Coach:	Notable College:
TIE #20. Steve Spurrier	Florida
TIE #20. Bud Wilkinson	Oklahoma
#21. Eddie Robinson	Grambling
#22. Bernie Bierman	Minnesota
#23. Bob Neyland	Tennessee
#24. Wallace Wade	Alabama & Duke
#25. Earl "RED" Blaik	Army
#26. John McKay	USC
#27. Dennis Erickson	Miami-Florida
#28. Darrel Royal	Texas
#29. Lou Holtz	Notre Dame
#30. Frank Thomas	Alabama
#31. Pete Carroll	USC
#32. Phil Fulmer	Tennessee
#33. Jimmy Crowley	Fordham
#34. Bob Zuppke	Illinois
#35. Henry Williams	Minnesota

Notes

CHAPTER #2

Grilling Tools

The Right Tools for Grilling

PRO FOOTBALL

Notes

Getting Started:

Great grilled meals start with a little bit of planning. Chefs call it mise en place. It's a French cooking term that means "everything in its place". This means organizing yourself, do you have fuel for the grill, your meal ingredients, accompaniments, wood chips or cedar wood plank (If needed) and all your grilling tools.

Big Bob's Top 20 Most Important Grilling Tools

You will need the right grilling tools for the job!

Your Top 20 List:

#1. This Book: "The Sport of Grilling"
#2. A grill & fuel
#3. Metal grill brush
#4. Long handle barbecue fork
TIE #5. Long handle barbecue tongs
TIE #5. Long handle slotted spatula
#6. Digital thermometer
#7. Basting brush
#8. Sharp knives
#9. Cutting board
TIE #10. Wood chips -OR- chunks
TIE #10. Heavy-duty hot pads
#11. Brush -OR- soft cloth for oiling grill racks
#12. Prep & serving platter
#13. Nonstick grilling foil
#14. Smoker box for a gas grill
TIE #15. Mixing Bowls
TIE #15. Wire whip
#16. A good hand held can opener
#17. Garlic press
#18. Vegetable brush
#19. Measuring cups
TIE #20. Strainer
TIE #20. Juicer

OUTDOOR GRILL

CAST IRON GRILL

CAST IRON GRIDDLE

OAK CHIPS

CAST IRON SMOKER BOX

GRILL BRUSH

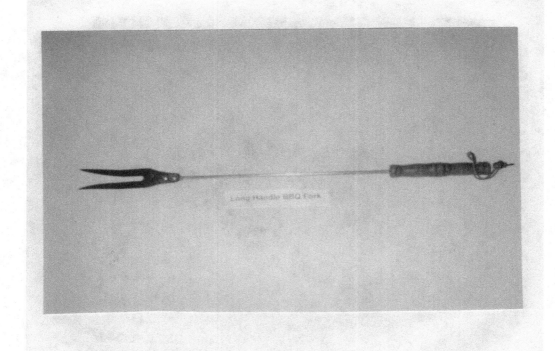

LONG HANDLE BBQ FORK

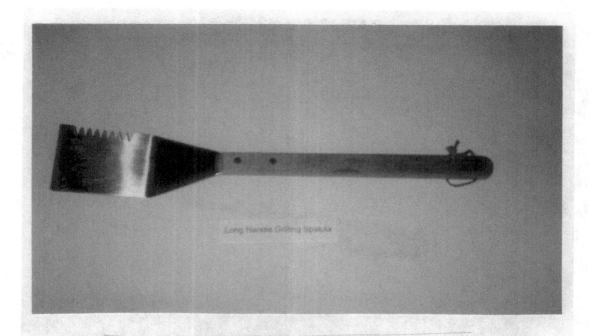

LONG HANDLE GRILLING SPATULA

CEDAR GRILLING PLANKS

GARLIC PRESS

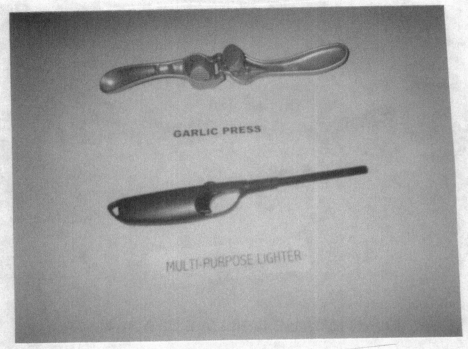

GARLIC PRESS

MULTI-PURPOSE LIGHTER

MULTI-PURPOSE LIGHTER

LONG HANDLE GRILLING SPATULA

STRAINER

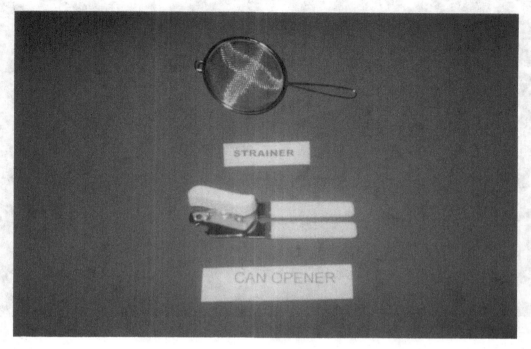

CAN OPENER

BOTTLE OPENER

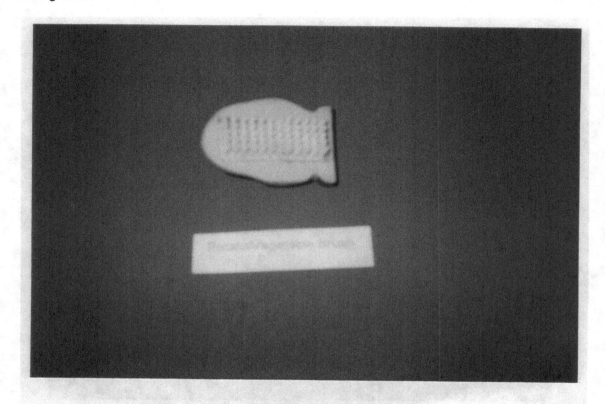

POTATO / VEGETABLE BRUSH

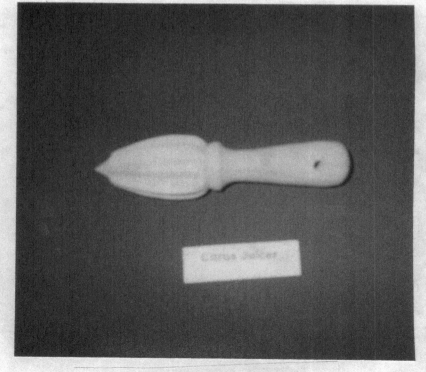

CITRUS JUICER

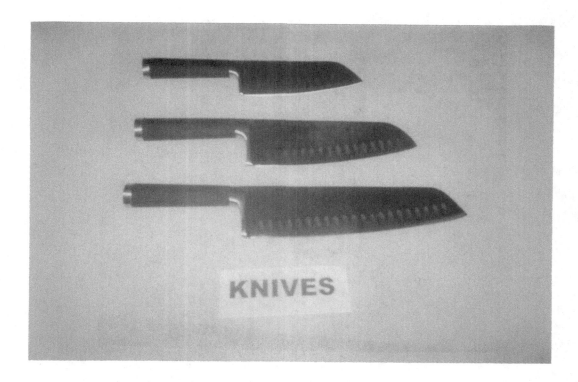

KNIVES

CHEF'S KNIFE

PRO MADOLINE SLICER

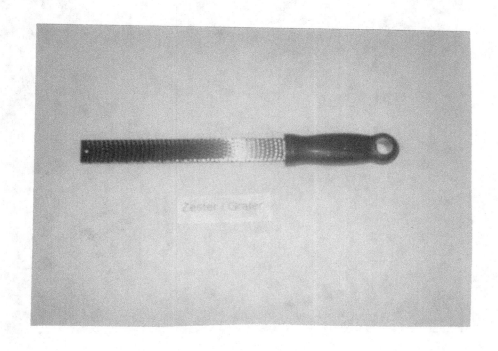

ZESTER / GRATER

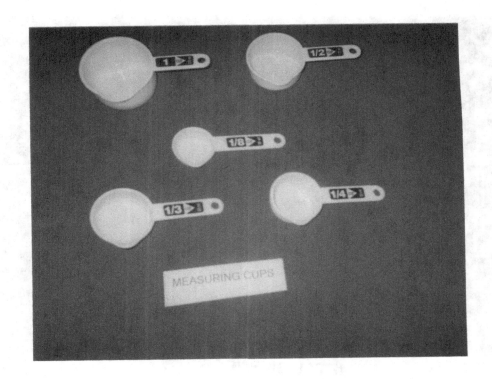

MEASURING CUPS

MIXING BOWL   **WIRE WHIP**

METAL SKEWERS

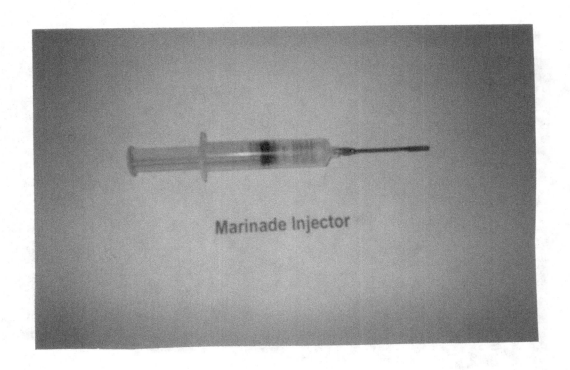

MARINADE INJECTOR

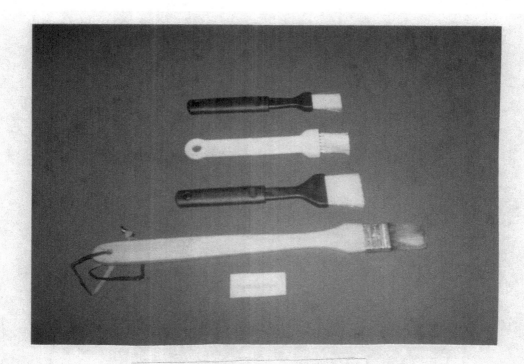

BASTING BRUSHES

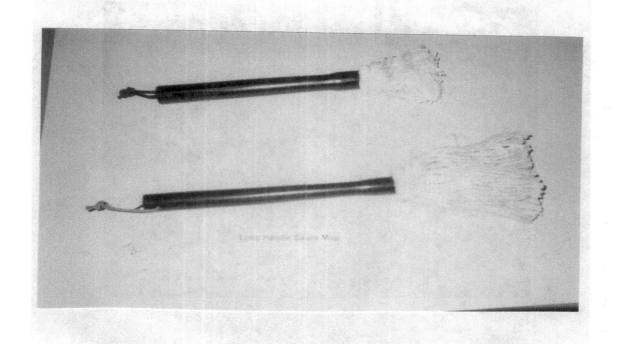

LONG HANDLE SAUCE MOPS

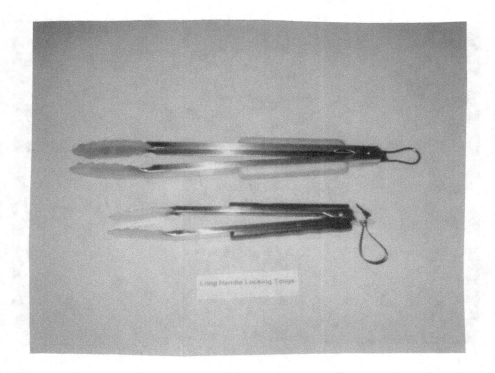

LONG HANDLE LOCKING TONGS

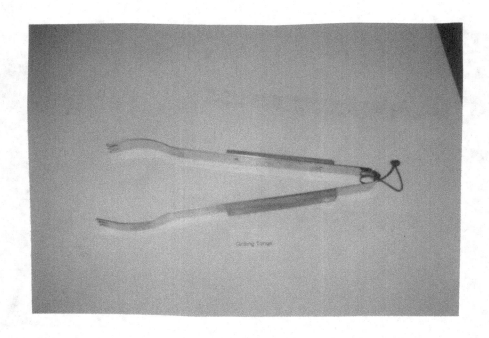

GRILLING TONGS

King
OF
THE
Grill

XXXXXXXXXXXXXXXXXXXXXXXXXXXXXX

A CLEAN
GRILL
Is A
HAPPY
GRILL

Big Bob's Top 25 Greatest NFL Coaches All Time

Your Top 25 List:

#1. Vince Lombardi

#2. Don Shula

#3. Tom Landry

#4. Paul Brown

TIE #5. George Halas

TIE #5. Chuck Noll

#6. Earl "Curly" Lambeau

#7. Bill Walsh

#8. Hank Stram

#9. John Madden

TIE #10. Bill Belichick

TIE #10. Bill Parcells

#11. Joe Gibbs

#12. Dan Reeves

#13. Bud Grant

TIE #14. Chuck Knox

TIE #14. Marty Schottenheimer

TIE #15. Sid Gilman

TIE #15. George Allen

#16. George Seifert

#17. Don Coryell

TIE #18. Ray "Buddy" Parker

TIE #18. Mike Ditka

#19. Marv Levy

#20. Tom Flores

#21. Weeb Ewbank

#22. Jim Mora

#23. Bill Cowher

#24. Mike Holmgren

#25. Dennis Green

Big Bob's Top 20 Greatest NFL Quarterbacks All Time

Your Top 20 List:

#1. Johnny Unitas

#2. Bart Starr

#3. Terry Bradshaw

#4. Joe Montana

#5. Bob Griese

#6. John Elway

TIE #7. Peyton Manning

TIE #7. Dan Marino

#8. Otto Graham

TIE #9. Roger Staubach

TIE #9. Fran Tarkenton

#10. Sid Luckman

#11. Sammy Baugh

#12. Joe Namath

#13. Troy Aikman

#14. Brett Farve

TIE #15. Steve Young

TIE #15. Dan Fouts

#16. Lenny Dawson

#17. Kenny "The Snake" Stabler

#18. Y.A. Tittle

#19. Phil Sims

TIE #20. Tom Brady

TIE #20. Kurt Warner

Big Bob's NFL Top 10 QB-WR Combinations of All Time

Your Top 10 List:

#1. Joe Montana-Jerry Rice 49ers

#2. Johnny Unitas-Raymond Berry Colts

#3. Terry Bradshaw-Lynn Swann Steelers

#4. Peyton Manning-Marvin Harrison Colts

#5. Joe Namath-Don Maynard Jets

#6. Troy Aikman-Micheal Irvin Cowboys

#7. Steve Young-Jerry Rice 49ers

#8. Jim Kelly-Andre Reed Bills

#9. Dan Marino-Mark Clayton Dolphins

#10. Dan Fouts-Charlie Joiner Chargers

Big Bob's Favorite Top 25 NFL QB's All Time

Your Top 25 List:

#1. Daryle Lamonica _____

#2. Terry Bradshaw _____

#3. Kenny "The Snake" Stabler _____

#4. Jim Plunkett _____

#5. Fran Tarkenton _____

#6. Bart Starr _____

#7. Roger Staubach _____

#8. Joe Montana _____

TIE #9. John Brodie _____

TIE #9. Kenny Anderson _____

TIE #10. Doug Flutie _____

TIE #10. Bob Griese _____

#11. George Blanda _____

#12. Billy Kilmer _____

#13. Sonny Jurgenson _____

#14. John Hadl _____

#15. John Elway _____

#16. Boomer Esiason _____

#17. Joe "Willie Namath _____

#18. Johnny Unitas _____

#19. Jim McMahon _____

TIE #20. Peyton Manning _____

TIE #20. Archie Manning _____

TIE #21. Tom Brady _____

TIE #21. Warren Moon _____

#22. Dan Pastorini _____

TIE #23. Dandy Don Meredith _____

TIE #23. Brian Sipe _____

TIE #24. Dan Fouts _____

TIE #24. Lynn Dickey _____

TIE #25. Dan Marino _____

TIE #25. Lenny Dawson _____

TIE #25. Phil Sims _____

These are my favorite NFL QB's of all-time, I'm sure if you are a NFL fan you have your own favorite all-time QB's.

Big Bob's Top 40 Greatest Pro Running Backs All Time

Your Top 40 List:

#1. Jim Brown

#2. Walter Payton

#3. Emmit Smith

#4. O.J. Simpson

#5. Barry Sanders

#6. Marshall Faulk

#7. Gale Sayers

#8. Hugh McElhenny

#9. Tony Dorsett

TIE #10. Tiki Barber

TIE #10. Eric Dickerson

#11. Marcus Allen

#12. Earl Campbell

#13. Curtis Martin

#14 Marion Motley

#15. Larry Csonka

#16. Terrel Davis

#17. Frank Gifford

#18. Thurman Thomas

#19. Franco Harris

TIE #20. Bronko Nagurski

TIE #20. John Riggins

#21. Clarke Hinkle

#22. O.J. Anderson

#23. Floyd Little

#24. Jim Taylor

#25. Joe Perry

#26. Paul Hornung

#27. Priest Holmes

#28. Bo Jackson

#29. Herschel Walker

#30. Steve Van Buren

#31. Carlton "COOKIE" Gilchrist

#32. Orban "SPEC" Sanders

#33. Larry Brown

#34. Ken Willard

#35. Ollie Matson

#36. Emerson Boozer

#37. Billy Sims

#38. Eddie George

#39. Leroy Kelly

#40. Ahman Green

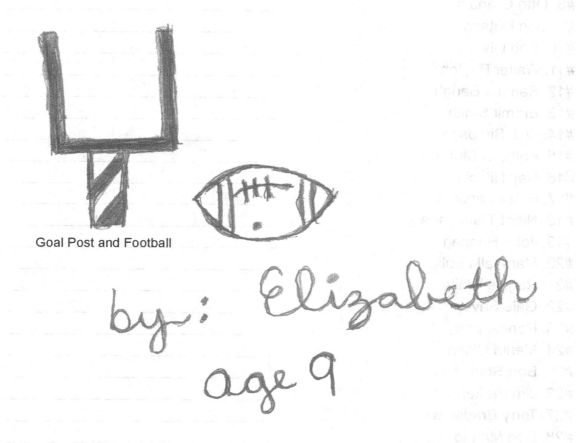

Goal Post and Football

by: Elizabeth

age 9

Big Bob's Top 70 Greatest NFL Players All Time

Your Top 70 List:

#1. Jim Brown

#2. Jerry Rice

#3. Johnny Unitas

#4. Lawrence Taylor

#5. Dick Butkus

#6. John Elway

#7. Joe Montana

#8. Otto Graham

#9. Don Hutson

#10. Bob Lily

#11. Walter Payton

#12. Sammy Baugh

#13. Emmit Smith

#14. O.J. Simpson

#15. Anthony Munoz

#16. Ray Nitschke

#17. Barry Sanders

#18. Night Train Lane

#19. John Hannah

#20. Marshall Faulk

#21. Reggie White

#22. Gale Sayers

#23. Ronnie Lott

#24. Merlin Olsen

#25. Bart Starr

#26. Jim Parker

#27. Terry Bradshaw

#28. Dan Marino

#29. Joe Greene

#30. Deacon Jones

#31. Gino Marchetti

#32. Deion Sanders

#33. Jack Ham

#34. Roger Staubach

#35. Jack Lambert

#36. Lance Alworth

#37. Raymond Berry _____

#38. Willie Lanier _____

#39. Larry Nelson _____

#40. Herb Adderley _____

#41. Bronko Nagurski _____

#42. Alan Page _____

#43. Steve Largent _____

#44. John Mackey _____

#45. Bill George _____

#46. Forrest Gregg _____

#47. Tony Dorsett _____

#48. Eric Dickerson _____

#49. Marcus Allen _____

TIE #50. Tiki Barber _____

TIE #50. Marion Motley _____

#51. Earl Campbell _____

#52. Joe "Willie" Namath _____

#53. Frank Gifford _____

#54. Mel Blount _____

#55. Sid Luckman _____

#56. Willie Brown _____

TIE #57. Peyton Manning _____

TIE #57. Bruce Smith _____

#58. Dave Casper _____

#59. George Blanda _____

#60. Jim Otto _____

#61. Larry Csonka _____

#62. Y.A. Tittle _____

#63. Lynn Swann _____

#64. Chuck Bednarik _____

#65. Dwight Stephenson _____

#66. John Riggins _____

#67. Troy Aikman _____

TIE #68. Steve Young _____

TIE #68. Sam Huff _____

TIE #69. Junior Seau _____

TIE #69. Mike Singletary _____

TIE #70. Red Grange _____

Grilling Tools

TIE #70. Jim McMahon   _____

TIE #70. Curtis Martin   _____

CHAPTER #3

Marinades

and

Mop Sauces

BOXING

Tiger Marinade

1 cup fresh orange juice

2 tablespoons fresh lime juice

2 tablespoons fresh lemon juice

2 tablespoons soy sauce

4 teaspoons fresh tarragon, chopped

3 garlic cloves, crushed in a garlic press

1/2 cup canola -OR- olive oil

ground black pepper - to taste

Great for chicken -OR- meaty fish (fresh tuna -OR- salmon)

In a bowl, whisk together the orange juice, lime juice, lemon juice, soy sauce, tarragon, garlic and black pepper to taste. Very Slowly whisk in the oil. Best to use right away.

Roma Marinade

1/4 cup olive oil -OR- canola oil

2 tablespoons fresh lime juice

grated zest of 1 fresh large lime

2 teaspoons fresh basil, chopped

pinch sea salt -OR- kosher salt

pinch crushed hot red pepper flakes

Great for grilled chicken -OR- fish.

In a bowl, whisk together the lime juice, lime zest, basil, salt and red pepper flakes. Slowly whisk in the oil in a stream. Best to use right away.

Honey-Mustard Sauce

1 tablespoon canola oil or olive oil

3 tablespoons shallots, chopped

1 cup whole grain mustard -OR- spicy brown mustard

1/2 cup honey

1 tablespoon soy sauce -Or- teriyaki sauce

Great for grilled chicken, fish -OR- pork.

In a saucepan, heat the oil over medium heat. Add the shallots, COOK uncovered, stirring often, until the shallots are tender, around 3-4 minutes.

Remove the saucepan from the heat, stir in the mustard, honey and soy sauce -OR- teriyaki sauce. You can make this sauce 4-5 days in advance, place in a covered container and refrigerate.

High-5 Marinade

1/2 cup store bought bottled Teriyaki Marinade and/or Sauce

1/2 cup store bought bottled Italian Salad Dressing

2 garlic cloves, crushed in a garlic press juice of 2 fresh limes

Best Marinade for pork, beef, chicken, salmon -OR- vegetables.

In a bowl, combine all of the ingredients, mix well. Best to use right away!

*Tip: This recipe will marinate 1-2 pounds of pork, beef, chicken -OR- salmon. Place the meat or salmon in a large resealable plastic bag, pour in the marinade. Place in the refrigerator.

Marinate the salmon 2-4 hours and the meat 6 hours -OR- overnight. Marinate 4 cups of zucchini, eggplant -OR- whole mushrooms 2-6 hours. Place the vegetables in a large resealable plastic bag, pour in the marinade. Seal the bag and place in the refrigerator.

Always let what you are grilling come up to room temperature. Grill until done, turning once and basting with more marinade.

Fajita Marinade

1/2 cup olive oil -OR- canola oil

1/2 cup red wine vinegar

4 teaspoons fresh oregano leaves

2 teaspoons chili powder

2 teaspoons granulated sugar

1 teaspoon garlic powder

1 teaspoon onion powder

1 teaspoon kosher salt -OR- sea salt

1/2 teaspoon ground black pepper

Great Marinade for boneless chicken, beef, pork -OR- shrimp.

In a large resealable plastic bag, mix all of the ingredients. Add 1-2 pounds boneless chicken, beef -OR- pork; turn to coat. Seal the bag and refrigerate, turning often. Marinate for at least 8-24 hours, don't go over 24 hours. For the shrimp, add about 1-1 1/2 pounds shrimp to marinade seal the bag and refrigerate, turning the shrimp often. Marinate the shrimp for 2-6 hours, don't go over 6 hours. Take the meat or shrimp out of the marinade, keep the marinade. Heat the marinade over medium heat to a boil, COOL before using. Grill the meat or shrimp until done, brushing occasionally with the marinade. Serve food right away and throw out any leftover marinade.

Johnny is the Man Marinade

1/4 cup fresh orange juice

5 garlic cloves, crushed in a garlic press

2 tablespoons fresh thyme, chopped

1 tablespoon freshly grated lime zest

1 tablespoon prepared mustard

1 teaspoon kosher salt -OR- sea salt

1/2 teaspoon ground black pepper

1/4 cup olive oil -OR- canola oil

Great marinade for kabobs using boneless lamb, chicken -OR- pork cubes.

In a bowl, whisk together the orange juice, garlic, thyme, lime zest, mustard, salt & pepper, mix well. Keep whisking don't stop, pour in the oil in a steady stream; don't stop until it is emulsified.

*Tip: This recipe is good for 1 1/4 pounds of boneless meat. Add the meat, cover, marinate for 30 minutes at room temperature. Then place meat on skewers; grill over medium-high heat to desired doneness. Serve right away.

Lizzies Honey Marinade and Sauce
(My daughter Elizabeth created this marinade and sauce.)

1 1/2 cups store bought Italian salad dressing

3 tablespoons honey

Juice of 1 fresh large lime

Juice of 1 fresh large lemon

1 1/2 tablespoons freshly grated lime zest

Best marinade in the world for boneless chicken breast on the grill.

In a bowl, whisk together the Italian dressing, honey, lime juice, lemon juice and lime zest, mix well. *Tip: For Best results; This recipe is for 1 3/4 pounds of boneless chicken breast. Add the meat to the marinade, cover, refrigerate and marinate for 2-6 hours. (Don't marinate for over 6 hours). Grill over direct medium-high heat, until COOKED to the desired doneness.

Big Bob's Mustard Marinade & Baste

1 1/2 cups store bought bottled Italian dressing

3 tablespoons prepared mustard

2 garlic cloves, crushed in a garlic press

1 1/2 tablespoons fresh tarragon leaves, chopped

juice of 1 fresh lime

Best marinade for pork, chicken, lamb, salmon -OR- fresh tuna.

In a bowl, whisk together the Italian dressing, mustard, garlic, fresh tarragon and lime juice, mix well. Use right away!

*Tip: This recipe is for 1 1/2 pounds of meat -OR- fish. Add meat -OR- fish to the marinade, cover, let stand for 30 minutes at room temperature. Grill over medium-high heat until done.

Teriyaki Marinade W/ Wine

1/2 cup White Wine

1/2 cup Store Bought Bottled Teriyaki Marinade & Sauce

1/2 cup Fresh Orange Juice

Great marinade for savory fresh pineapple slices, pork, chicken, fish -OR- steak.

In a bowl, whisk together the wine, teriyaki marinade & sauce and orange juice, mix well.

Best to use right away!

*Tip: This is a very easy recipe to increase -OR- decrease.

Red Wine Marinade

1 cup good quality red wine

1/3 cup balsamic vinegar

1 tablespoon fresh rosemary, chopped

1 tablespoon fresh sage, chopped

1 tablespoon fresh basil, chopped

2 garlic cloves, crushed in garlic press

1/2 teaspoon kosher salt -OR- sea salt, to taste

1/2 teaspoon crushed hot red pepper flakes, to taste

1/2 cup canola oil -OR- olive oil

Great marinade for beef, lamb, pork -OR- vegetables (Example: fresh mushrooms)

In a bowl, whisk together the wine, balsamic vinegar, rosemary, sage, basil, garlic, salt and red pepper flakes, mix well. Slowly whisk in the oil in a steady stream. Use right away!

White Wine Marinade

1 cup dry white wine

1/4 cup fresh lime juice

1 tablespoon fresh basil, chopped

1 tablespoon fresh thyme, chopped

1 tablespoon fresh oregano, chopped

1/2 teaspoon onion powder

3 garlic cloves, crushed in a garlic press

1/2 teaspoon kosher salt -OR- sea salt

1/2 teaspoon crushed hot red pepper flakes, to taste

1/2 cup canola oil -OR- olive oil

Great marinade for fish, shrimp, chicken -OR- pork.

In a bowl, combine the wine, lime juice, basil, thyme, oregano, onion powder, garlic, salt and hot red pepper flakes, mix well. Slowly whisk in the oil in a steady stream.

Slam Dunk Baste

3/4 cup store bought bottled Italian dressing

1/4 cup Worcestershire Sauce

2 garlic cloves, crushed in a garlic press juice of 1 fresh lime

1/4 teaspoon ground black pepper, to taste

Great Basting Sauce for beef, pork, chicken, fish -OR- vegetables!

In a bowl, combine the Italian dressing, Worcestershire Sauce, garlic, lime juice and pepper to taste, mix well. Best to use right away.

*Tip: This recipe will baste 1-2 pounds of beef, pork, chicken or fish -OR- 4 cups of sliced onions, eggplant, zucchini, whole mushrooms -OR- other vegetables. When grilling brush baste generously on both sides of beef, pork, chicken, fish -OR- vegetables. Let stand for 30 minutes at room temperature. Grill over medium-high heat, COOK until done, turning only once and keep brushing with more baste.

Down Home Mop Sauce

2 large fresh limes (juice & rind)

1 quart distilled white vinegar

1/3 cup ketchup

1/2 cup sweet paprika

3 tablespoons kosher salt

2 tablespoons ground black pepper

1 tablespoon hot red (cayenne) pepper

1 tablespoon garlic powder

1 tablespoon onion powder

Best mop for pork shoulder, ribs, beef briskets -OR- whole chickens.

Squeeze the limes through your fingers into a big bowl, catching the seeds in your fingers.

Add the lime rinds, vinegar, ketchup, paprika, black pepper, red pepper, garlic powder and onion powder and stir in the salt until it dissolves. The mop sauce will keep in a covered container in the refrigerator for 1-2 weeks, however remove the lime rinds after 3-4 hours or they'll make the mop bitter.

*Tip: 1 cup of mop for 2 pounds of meat. This recipe makes enough mop sauce for 8 pounds of meat. When making pulled pork you can use the mop as your sauce for the meat.

Java & Beer Mop Sauce

1 cup (8 ounce) Beer

1 cup apple cider -OR- apple juice

1/3 cup brewed strong good quality coffee

1/3 cup apple cider vinegar

1/3 cup beef -OR- chicken broth

1/4 cup canola oil -OR- vegetable oil

1/4 cup Worcestershire Sauce -OR- Soy Sauce

2 tablespoons hot red pepper sauce kosher salt, to taste

1 teaspoon ground black pepper

Best for Beef Brisket, also for pork shoulder, ribs -OR- chicken on the bone.

In a bowl, combine the beer, apple cider or juice, coffee, vinegar, broth, oil, Worcestershire Sauce or soy sauce, red pepper sauce, salt to taste and black pepper, mix with a whisk. Taste, add more salt if needed.

*Tip: Use 1 cup of mop for every 2 pounds of meat. This recipe will mop 5-6 pounds of meat.

For the Best meat you have ever ate use the following; Buckeye Rub on the meat first. Brush on the Java & Coffee Mop sauce several times during the grilling so the meat won't dry out.

At the very end of the grilling brush on the Woody's BBQ Sauce.

Beer Mop Sauce

1 cup (8 ounces) Beer

1/4 cup Worcestershire Sauce

1/4 cup canola oil -OR- vegetable oil

1/4 cup apple cider vinegar

2 teaspoons any hot style mustard

bottled hot red pepper sauce, to taste

Super mop for beef brisket, pork chops, ribs, pork shoulder -OR- poultry.

In a bowl stir together the beer, Worcestershire Sauce, oil, vinegar, mustard and hot red pepper sauce to taste.

*Tip: This recipe is enough mop for 10-12 pounds of meat.

Longhorn Beer Mop Sauce

2 cans (12 ounces each) Regular Beer

12 ounces store bought Hickory Smoke barbecue sauce (I like Kraft)

1 cup Worcestershire Sauce

1/2 cup yellow mustard

1/2 cup apple cider vinegar

1/4 cup honey dash hot red pepper flakes, to taste

1 onion, very finely chopped

2 large fresh limes, sliced

This is the World's Best Mop for Beef Brisket !!!

In a big bowl, whisk together all of the ingredients, mix very well. Use right away -OR- cover and refrigerate for at least 2-4 hours to let the flavors blend.

Great also for pork, ribs, game -OR- whole chickens!!!

FIRE-UP THE GRILL IT'S SHOWTIME

Big Bob's Top 75 Greatest Boxers All Time

Being a huge boxing fan, this might be my toughest list to decide on so far!

Your Top 75 List:

#1. Muhammad Ali

#2. Jack Johnson

#3. Sugar Ray Robinson

#4. Joe Louis

#5. Rocky Marciano

#6. Archie Moore

#7. Jack Dempsey

#8. Roy Jones Jr.

#9. Sugar Ray Leonard

#10. Pernell Whitaker

#11. Julio Cesar Chavez

#12. Marvin Hagler

#13. Benny Leonard

#14. Henry Armstrong

#15. Aaron Pryor

#16. Ricardo Lopez

#17. Roberto Duran

#18. Jimmy Wilde

#19. Willie Pep

#20. Harry Greb

#21. Carlos Monzon

#22. Ezzard Charles

#23. Eder Jofre

#24. Alexis Arguello

#25. Thomas "The Hit Man" Hearns

#26. Gene Tunney

#27. Larry Holmes

#28. Evander Holyfield

#29. Sandy Sandler

#30. John L. Sullivan

#31. Salvador Sanchez

#32. Barney Ross

#33. Ike Williams

#34. Mickey Walker

#35. Ruben Olivares

#36. Emile Griffth _____

#37. Bernard Hopkins _____

#38. Felix Trinidad _____

#39. Mike Tyson _____

#40. Lennox Lewis _____

#41. Pascual Perez _____

#42. Miguel Canto _____

#43. Manuel Ortiz _____

#44. George Foreman _____

#45. Joe Frazier _____

#46. Oscar De La Hoya _____

#47. Jake LaMotta _____

#48. Wilfred Benitez _____

#49. Sonny Liston _____

#50. Michael Spinks _____

#51. Carmen Basilio _____

#52. Charles Burley _____

#53. Khaosai Galaxy _____

#54. Kid Chocolate _____

#55. Tiger Flowers _____

#56. Fernando Fargas _____

#57. Meldrick Taylor _____

#58. Floyd Mayweather Jr. _____

#59. Sugar Shane Mosley _____

#60. Floyd Patterson _____

#61. Jim Jeffries _____

#62. James J. Corbett _____

#63. Jersey Joe Walcott _____

#64. Riddick Bowe _____

#65. Virgil Hill _____

#66. Ken Norton _____

#67. Max Schmeling _____

#68. Panama Al Brown _____

#69. Joe Brown _____

TIE #70. Howard Davis Jr. _____

TIE #70. Lazlo Papp _____

#71. Joe Calzaghe _____

#72. Sam Langford _____

#73. Leon Spinks   _____

TIE #74. Tony Craig "TNT" Tucker   _____

TIE #74. James "Buster" Douglas   _____

TIE #75. Teofilo Stevenson   _____

TIE #75. Felix Savon   _____

Big Bob's Top 25 Greatest "POUND 4 POUND" Boxers All Time

Your Top 25 List:

#1. Sugar Ray Robinson   _____

#2. Muhammad Ali   _____

#3. Jack Johnson   _____

#4. Joe Louis   _____

#5. Julio Cesar Chavez   _____

#6. Roy Jones Jr.   _____

#7. Marvin Hagler   _____

#8. Archie Moore   _____

#9. Roberto Duran   _____

#10. Aaron Pryor   _____

#11. Sugar Ray Leonard   _____

#12. Mike Tyson   _____

#13. Meldrick Taylor   _____

#14. George Foreman   _____

#15. Rocky Marciano   _____

#16. Lennox Lewis   _____

#17. Bernard Hopkins   _____

#18. Thomas "The Hit Man" Hearns   _____

#19. Floyd Mayweather Jr.   _____

#20. Evander Holyfield   _____

#21. Joe Frazier   _____

#22. Oscar De La Hoya   _____

#23. Felix Trinidad   _____

TIE #24. Sugar Shane Mosley

TIE #24. Fernando Fargaz   _____

TIE #25. Eder Jofre

TIE #25. Willie Pep

Big Bob's Top 28 Greatest Heavyweight Boxers All Time

Your Top 28 List:

#1. Muhammad Ali

#2. Jack Johnson

#3. Joe Louis

#4. Rocky Marciano

#5. Jack Dempsey

#6. Gene Tunney

#7. Larry Holmes

#8. John L. Sullivan

#9. Mike Tyson

#10. Lennox Lewis

#11. George Foreman

#12. Ezzard Charles

#13. Joe Frazier

#14. Sonny Liston

#15. Floyd Patterson

#16. Evander Holyfield

#17. Michael "Jinx" Spinks

#18. Jim Jeffries

#19. James J. Corbett

#20. Jersey Joe Walcott

#21. Riddick Bowe

#22. Ken Norton

#23. Max Schmeling

#24. Leon Spinks

#25. Tony Craig "TNT" Tucker

#26. James "Buster" Douglas

#27. Teofilo Stevenson

#28. Felix Savon

Notes

CHAPTER #4

Everything

Rubs

GOLF

Anytime Rub

6 tablespoons paprika

2 tablespoons coarse-ground black pepper

2 tablespoons kosher salt

1 tablespoon chili powder

2 teaspoons onion powder

2 teaspoons garlic powder

pinch -OR- more of ground hot red (cayenne) pepper

Great all purpose grill rub, always have some on hand for adding flavor to a quick and easy Dinner.

*Tip: When using a dry rub always brush oil on the grill.

In a bowl, stir in the spices, mix well. Store the rub in a air tight container (aka: jar W/ lid), place in a cool dry pantry -OR- in a resealable plastic bag and freeze.

Cajun Rub

4 tablespoons sweet paprika

2 tablespoons dried basil

2 tablespoons dried thyme

2 teaspoon s onion powder

2 teaspoons garlic powder

1 teaspoon ground black pepper

1/2 teaspoon ground hot red (cayenne) pepper

Great for steaks, burgers, chicken, tuna steaks -OR- try it on popcorn.

In a bowl, stir in all of the ingredients, mix well. Will store for months in a air tight container in a cool dry dark place -OR- pantry.

To use the rub; toss the meat -OR- fish in canola oil -OR- olive oil, use around 1-2 tablespoons of oil for every 1 pound of meat -OR- fish. Sprinkle a lot of rub on both sides and toss well to evenly coat the meat -OR- fish with rub. You can let stand for 1 hour at room temperature.

*Tip: When using a dry rub always brush the grill with oil!!!

Tex Mex Rub

1/2 cup chili powder

4 tablespoons garlic powder

4 tablespoons onion powder

4 tablespoons ground black pepper

4 tablespoons sweet paprika

1 teaspoon ground hot red (cayenne) pepper

Great rub for beef brisket, pork, ribs -OR- grilled chicken.

In a bowl, mix all of the ingredients together. Use right away !

Use 2 tablespoons of rub per pound of meat -OR- poultry. Brush the meat with oil, sprinkle with rub. Great mixed with ground meat for spicy burgers. Grill over medium-high heat until done.

Tuscan Rub

4 tablespoons dried oregano

4 tablespoons dried basil

2 teaspoons dried thyme

1 teaspoon dried sage

1 teaspoon garlic powder

1 teaspoon onion powder

1 teaspoon crushed hot red pepper flake

Great robust rub for grilled lamb, pork -OR- chicken on the bone.

In a bowl, mix all of the ingredients together, until well blended. Use right away -OR- store in a cool, dry and dark pantry in a air tight container.

*Tip: Use about 1-2 tablespoons of rub for every 1 pound of meat. Brush the meat with olive oil, sprinkle with rub. Great if mixed with ground meat for Tuscan Burgers.

Sweet-N-Spicy Rub

4 tablespoons butter

2 teaspoons cinnamon

1 teaspoon salt

1 teaspoon turmeric

1 teaspoon ground cumin

1 teaspoon hot red (cayenne) pepper

1 teaspoon ground black pepper

1/2 teaspoon ground cardamom

1/4 teaspoon curry powder

1/4 teaspoon ground cloves

1/4 teaspoon ground nutmeg

2 tablespoons sugar

Great Rub for a Whole Grilled Chicken.

In a saucepan, melt the butter. Stir in cinnamon, salt, turmeric, cumin, red pepper, black pepper, cardamon, curry powder, cloves and nutmeg. Remove from the heat. Stir in the 2 tablespoons of sugar, COOL. Rub the mixture evenly onto the chicken. Cover and chill the chicken in the refrigerator for 4 hours -OR- overnight before grilling. Grill using indirect heat, until done.

Spicy Cajun Rub

3 teaspoons black pepper

1 teaspoon ground hot red (cayenne) pepper

1 teaspoon kosher salt -OR- sea salt

1 teaspoon ground cumin

1 teaspoon ground nutmeg

2 tablespoons olive oil -OR- canola oil

Great rub for chicken, pork -OR- beef

In a bowl, stir in all of the ingredients together, except the oil. Brush the oil on both sides of 2 pounds of meat (chicken, pork -OR- beef). Spread the rub evenly on both sides of the meat.

Grill the meat to desired doneness.

Cowboy Rub

2 tablespoon chili powder

2 tablespoons canola oil -OR- olive oil

2 teaspoons ground cumin

2 teaspoons onion powder

1/2 teaspoon kosher salt

1/2 teaspoon ground hot red (cayenne) pepper

2 large garlic cloves, crushed in a garlic press

Great "Wet Rub" for chicken, pork -OR- beef.

In a bowl, mix all the ingredients together, Spread the rub evenly onto 2 pounds of meat (chicken, pork and beef). Grill the meat to the desired doneness.

"Fact: Because this rub has oil in it, it is called a "Wet Rub" rather than the more common Dry Rub".

Spicy Mustard Rub

1/3 cup dry mustard

1/3 cup sweet paprika

1/4 cup kosher salt -Or- sea salt

1 tablespoon onion powder

1 tablespoon garlic powder

1 tablespoon ground black pepper

Great rub for steaks, pork chops, ribs -OR- burgers.

In a bowl, stir to mix all the ingredients together. Your hands will work better than a spoon -OR- or whisk for mixing a dry rub. Store the rub in a air tight container (aka: jar) in a cool, dark, dry pantry.

It will keep for at least 4-6 months.

*Tip: Use 1-2 tablespoons of dry rub per 1 pound of meat.

Big Bob's Rub

2 tablespoons sweet paprika

2 tablespoons chili powder

2 tablespoons ground coriander

2 tablespoons kosher salt

4 teaspoons ground cumin

4 teaspoons dried thyme

2 teaspoons dried basil

2 teaspoons dry mustard

2 teaspoons onion powder

2 teaspoons garlic powder

1/4 teaspoon allspice

1/4 teaspoon ground black pepper

1/4 teaspoon hot red (cayenne) pepper

Perfect rub for pork, chicken, beef -OR- lamb.

In a bowl, stir to mix all of ingredients together. Your fingers will work better to mix the rub than a spoon -OR- a whisk.

Store the rub in a airtight container (aka: clean jar). It will keep for at least 4-6 months in a cool, dry and dark pantry.

*Tip: Use 1-2 tablespoons of rub for every 1 pound of meat.

**Fact: Don't forget to brush oil on the grill when using a dry rub.

Buckeye Dry Rub

1/4 cup sweet paprika

1/4 cup packed brown sugar

1/4 cup kosher salt -OR- sea salt

2 tablespoons ground black pepper

2 tablespoons chili powder

1 tablespoon garlic powder

1 tablespoon onion powder

1/2 teaspoon dried oregano

Best for Beef Brisket, also for pork shoulder, ribs -OR- chicken on the bone.

In a bowl, combine the paprika, brown sugar, salt, black pepper, chili powder, garlic powder, onion powder and oregano, stir to mix. Your fingers will be better at mixing the rub than a spoon or whisk. This rub will keep for several months in a air tight container (aka: clean jar), kept in a cool, dry and dark pantry.

*Tip: Use 3 tablespoons of rub on each side of a 5-6 pound center-cut beef brisket, pat it into the meat with your finger tips. Use 1-2 tablespoons of rub per 1 pound of other meats.

After you apply the rub to the meat let it set in the refrigerator, covered for 6-24 hours, don't go over 24 hours.

Java Rub

1/2 cup coarse-ground coffee beans (use your favorite coffee)

1/4 cup coarse-ground black pepper

1 1/2 tablespoons kosher salt -OR- sea salt

1 tablespoon ground cinnamon

1 tablespoon packed brown sugar

1 tablespoons chili powder

1/2 teaspoons ground allspice

1/4 teaspoon ground ginger

1/4 teaspoon ground nutmeg

Great rub for game birds (aka: quail) -OR- pork.

In a bowl, mix the spices. Store the rub in a air-tight container (aka: jar -OR- resealable bag) in a cool, dark pantry -OR- freezer.

*Tip: Use 1-2 tablespoons of rub per 1 pound of meat. When using a dry rub always brush oil onto the grill rack.

Java Steak Rub

1/4 cup ground coriander

1/4 cup kosher salt -OR- sea salt

3 tablespoons finely ground dark roast coffee

3 tablespoons freshly ground black pepper

1 tablespoon ground cloves

Best rub for steaks, also for lamb, pork -OR- poultry.

In a bowl, stir to mix all the ingredients together. Store the rub in a air tight container (aka: jar) in a cool and dark pantry for 3-4 months.

*Tip: Use 1-2 tablespoons of rub per 1 pound of meat. Always brush oil on the grill rack when using a dry rub on meat.

Big Bob's Top 10 Male Golfers of the 20th. Century

Your Top 10 List:

#1. Jack Nicklaus _____
#2. Ben Hogan _____
#3. Bobby Jones _____
#4. Walter Hagan _____
#5. Sam Snead _____
#6. Byron Nelson _____
#7. Arnold Palmer _____
#8. Gary Player _____
#9. Harry Vardon _____
#10. Tom Watson _____

*Tiger Woods will be the Greatest Golfer of the 21st. Century & maybe All-Time.

Big Bob's Top 10 Female Golfers of the 20th. Century

Your Top 10 List:

#1. Mickey Wright _____
#2. BABE Zaharias _____
#3. Kathy Whitworth _____
#4. Nancy Lopez _____
#5. Joyce Wethered _____
#6. Glenna Collett Vare _____
#7. Louise Suggs _____
#8. Patty Berg _____
#9. JoAnn Carner _____
#10. Betsy Rawls _____

Big Bob's Top 60 Greatest Male Golfers All Time

Your Top 60 List:

#1. Jack Nickalus

#2. Tiger Woods

#3. Ben Hogan

#4. Bobby Jones

#5. Walter Hagan

#6. Sam Snead

#7. Byron Nelson

#8. Arnold Palmer

#9. Gary Player

#10. Harry Vardon

#11. Tom Watson

#12. Lee Trevino

#13. Gene Sarazan

#14. Billy Casper

#15. Raymond Floyd

#16. Nick Faldo

#17. Seve Ballesteros

#18. Greg Norman

#19. Hale Irwin

#20. Gary Middlecoff

#21. Jimmy Demaret

#22. Willie Anderson

#23. Gene Littler

#24. Johnny Miller

#25. Tommy Armour

#26. Julius Boros

#27. Henry Picard

#28. Tom Kite

#29. Ben Crenshaw

#30. Peter Thomson

#31. Larry Nelson

#32. Nick Price

#33. Payne Stewart

#34. Curtis Strange

#35. Ernie Els

#36. Mark O'Meara

#37. Jack Burke Jr _____

#38. Lenny Wadkins _____

#39. Hubert Green _____

#40. Fred Couples _____

#41. Tom Weiskopf _____

#42. Phil "Lefty" Mickelson _____

#43. Jose-Maria Olazabal _____

#44. Doug Ford _____

#45. Vijay Singh _____

#46. Tony Jacklin _____

#47. Ken Venturi _____

#48. Craig Stadler _____

#49. Fuzzy Zoeller _____

#50. Bernhard Langer _____

#51. Davis Love III _____

#52. David Stockton _____

#53. Ian Woosman _____

#54. Sandy Lyle _____

#55. Corey Pavin _____

#56. David Graham _____

#57. Bob Charles _____

#58. Lee Janzen _____

#59. Doug Sanders _____

#60. John Daly _____

I left the golf course for this?

Big Bob's Top 7 Best Golf Movies All Time

Your Top 7 List:

#1. Tin Cup

#2. Dead Solid Perfect

#3. Caddyshack

#4. The Legend of Bagger Vance

#5. Happy Gilmore

#6. Follow the Sun

#7. Bobby Jones-Stoke of Genius

If a lot people gripped a knife and fork as poorly as they do a golf club, they'd starve to death.

by: Sam Snead

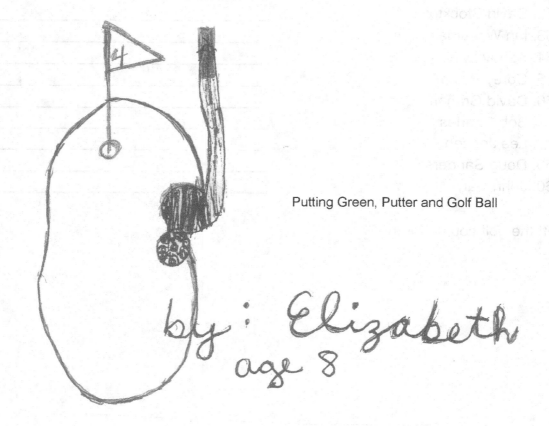

Putting Green, Putter and Golf Ball

by: Elizabeth age 8

CHAPTER #5

BBQ Sauce

BASEBALL

Chocolate BBQ Sauce
(Mole BBQ Sauce)

1/4 cup olive oil -OR- canola oil

1 small sweet onion

2 garlic cloves, crushed in a garlic press

1 tablespoon lime juice

1 tablespoon prepared yellow mustard

1/2 tablespoon freshly ground black pepper

1 teaspoon kosher salt -OR- sea salt - to taste

1 teaspoon paprika

1/2 teaspoon hot red pepper sauce - to taste

1 1/2 cups ketchup (I like Heinz Ketchup)

1/4 cup Hershey's Special Dark Chocolate Syrup

1/4 cup apple cider vinegar

Best Mole BBQ Sauce for Chicken -OR- Pork!!!

In a saucepan, add the olive oil, heat, sauté the onions & garlic, COOK until tender. Stir in lime juice, mustard, black pepper, salt, paprika and hot sauce, mix well. SIMMER for 5-6 minutes, reduce the heat. Stir in the ketchup, dark chocolate syrup and cider vinegar. SIMMER on low heat for 15-20 minutes, stir often. Use right away -OR- COOL, pour into a covered container and store in the refrigerator for 1-2 weeks. Always warm the BBQ Sauce back up to room temperature before using.

*Note: Always brush this sauce on the meat during the last 5-10 minutes of grilling. It's also great as a condiment on the side.

Easy Chocolate (Mole) BBQ Sauce

1 1/2 cups store bought Original barbecue sauce (I like Kraft BBQ Sauce)

2 1/4 tablespoons unsweetened cocoa powder

2 1/4 tablespoons honey

1 1/4 teaspoons chili powder - to taste

Great mole BBQ Sauce for Barbecue Chicken.

In a saucepan, combine all of the ingredients, mix well with a spoon. COOK, over medium heat for 5-6 minutes -OR- until sauce bubbles, it will begin to darken slightly, stir often. Use right away -OR- COOL, pour into a covered container and place in the refrigerator for up to 1 week.

Brush the BBQ sauce on the chicken during the last 10-15 minutes of the grilling time.

Dr. Bob's BBQ Sauce

1 bottle (18 ounces) store bought Original barbecue sauce (I Like Kraft)

1/3 cup store bought bottled chili sauce

1/3 cup brown sugar

2 teaspoons prepared yellow mustard

dash of hot red pepper sauce (aka: Tabasco Sauce)

Good Sauce for grilling pork, chicken -OR- beef.

In a bowl, combine all of ingredients together, mix well. This is a great mop sauce -OR- can be used as a condiment. Use right away -OR- cover, store in the refrigerator for 1-2 weeks (no more than 2 weeks).

Always brush on the BBQ sauce during the last 10-15 minutes of the grilling time.

Out of BBQ Sauce?

1 jar (26 ounces) store bought traditional pasta sauce (whatever you have in the pantry)

2 tablespoons Worcestershire Sauce

2 tablespoons honey

1 tablespoon brown sugar

1 tablespoon prepared yellow mustard

1 tablespoon chili powder

1 teaspoon apple cider vinegar

Good for barbecue chicken -OR- pork.

In a big saucepan -OR- small pot, combine the pasta sauce, Worcestershire Sauce, honey, brown sugar, yellow mustard, chili powder and vinegar. Over medium-high heat bring the sauce to a boil and lower the heat. SIMMER for around 15 minutes, stir often. You can reserve 1/2 of the BBQ sauce for mopping during the grilling. Set aside the other 1/2 of the BBQ sauce for serving on the side.

Always brush the BBQ sauce on the meat during the final 10-15 minutes of grilling.

Big Bob's 911 Honey/Mustard BBQ Sauce

1 1/2 cups store bought Hickory Smoke barbecue sauce (I like Kraft)

2 tablespoons Honey - to taste

2 tablespoons prepared mustard (yellow -OR- spicy brown) - to taste

hot red pepper sauce - to taste

apple cider vinegar - to taste

Great BBQ Sauce for pork -OR- chicken.

In a saucepan, combine the barbecue sauce, honey, mustard, hot sauce to taste and vinegar to taste. Over medium heat slowly bring to a boil, stir often. Reduce the heat, Simmer on low for 10 minutes, stir often. Use right away !

Always brush BBQ sauce on the meat during the last 10 minutes of grilling.

Woody's BBQ Sauce

1 cup store bought bottled barbecue sauce (aka: Open Pit, Bull's Eye -OR- KC Masterpiece)

1 cup store bought (aka: jar) red salsa, mild -OR- hot

2 tablespoons -OR- more apple cider vinegar - to taste

kosher salt -OR- sea salt - to taste

freshly ground black pepper - to taste

Best for Beef Brisket, also for pork shoulder, ribs -OR- chicken on the bone.

In a saucepan, combine the barbecue sauce, red salsa and vinegar over medium heat, bring to a SIMMER. SIMMER until thick and flavorful, COOK 6-8 minutes. Season to taste with salt and pepper. The sauce can be served hot -OR- at room temperature. You can make it in advance and keep it covered in the refrigerator for up to 2 days.

Always warm BBQ sauce back up to room temperature before using.

Best sauce to serve with Beef Brisket -OR- pulled pork sandwiches.

Fast Break Beer BBQ Sauce

1-2 tablespoons canola oil -OR- olive oil

1/4 cup onion, very finely chopped

2 fresh garlic cloves, crushed in a garlic press

1 fresh jalapeno pepper, seeded, ribs removed & very finely chopped

2 cups store bought Hickory Smoke barbecue sauce (I like Kraft)

1 cup (8 ounces) regular beer

Easy & fast to make for a killer sauce on pork, ribs, beef, game -OR- poultry.

In a saucepan, heat the oil over a medium flame, add the onions, garlic and jalapeno. COOK, for 4-5 minutes, stir often. Stir in the barbecue sauce and the regular beer, reduce the heat.

SIMMER on low heat for 7-10 minutes, stir often. Serve right away!

Always brush sauce on during the last 10-15 minutes of grilling.

Spicy Beer BBQ Sauce

2 tablespoons olive oil -OR- canola oil

1 small sweet onion, finely chopped

1 garlic clove, crushed in garlic press

1/2 cup ketchup

2 tablespoons brown sugar

2 teaspoons chili powder

2 chipotle peppers in abobo sauce, canned, finely chopped

1 teaspoon prepared yellow -OR- spicy brown mustard

1/2 teaspoon salt - to taste

1/2 teaspoon ground black pepper

BBQ Sauce

1 can beer (12 ounces), the best is pilsner beer

1/2 cup tomato juice

1/4 cup soy sauce -OR- teriyaki marinade and/or sauce

1 tablespoon fresh lime juice

Great BBQ Sauce for Ribs -OR- Chicken on the Bone!

In a big saucepan, heat the oil over medium heat, until hot, add the onions and garlic.

COOK and stir often, until the onions are tender, don't burn the garlic.

In a bowl, combine the ketchup, brown sugar, chili powder, chipotle peppers, mustard, salt and black pepper. Add beer, tomato juice, soy sauce -OR- teriyaki sauce and lime juice; whisk to mix well. Add beer mixture to the onions and garlic mixture. COOK, until sauce is reduced to 2 cups. COOL, place in a covered container and refrigerate for 6 hours -OR- overnight.

Always warm BBQ Sauce back up to room temperature before using!

*Tip: This sauce will cover (2-each); 3-3 1/2 pound chickens; cut-up. When grilling baste with sauce during the last 10 minutes of grilling. Also warm up some of the sauce and serve with the chicken as a condiment on the side.

***Note: Just as a reminder when dealing with hot peppers, like chipotles you might want to wear plastic gloves to protect your hands.

MOJO's Java BBQ Sauce

1 cup ketchup

1/2 cup brewed strong black coffee (any dark roast coffee)

1/2 cup apple cider vinegar

1/2 packed brown sugar

1 Vidalia -OR- Sweet Onion, chopped (1 cup)

2 garlic cloves, crushed in a garlic press

1-3 jalapeno peppers, cut in half, seeded & ribbed, for heat (1-2 ounces)

2 tablespoons prepared brown spicy mustard -OR- yellow mustard

2 tablespoons Worcestershire Sauce -OR- Soy Sauce

2 tablespoon chili powder

2 tablespoons dark molasses

1-2 tablespoon cumin seeds, to taste

Great sauce for Buffalo, Pork, Game -OR- Black Angus Beef Cuts.

In a saucepan, combine all of the ingredients together, mix well. Bring to a light boil over medium heat. Reduce the heat and SIMMER over low heat for 20-25 minutes, stir often.

Let the sauce COOL. Then puree in a food processor -OR- blender until smooth and then strain.

Store in a covered container in the refrigerator for weeks.

Red-Eye BBQ Sauce
(Coffee Barbecue Sauce)

2 tablespoons olive oil -OR- canola oil

1/2 cup onions, finely chopped

1-2 teaspoons garlic cloves, crushed garlic press

1/2 cup store bought chicken broth

1/4 cup ketchup

1/4 cup store bought -OR- homemade steak sauce

1 tablespoon soy sauce -OR- teriyaki sauce and/or marinade

1 tablespoon flat leaf parsley, finely chopped

2 teaspoons coffee, finely ground

1/2 teaspoon ground black pepper, to taste

In a saucepan, heat the oil over medium-high heat. Add onion and garlic, sauté until soft, COOK, around 5 minutes. Add all the ingredients together, mix well. Bring up to a boil slowly over medium heat. Reduce the heat to low, SIMMER for 10-12 minutes, stir often. Let COOL.

Puree in a blender -OR- a food processor until smooth. Cover and refrigerate 2-6 hours to let the flavors blend.

Always let the BBQ sauce warm back up to room temperature before using.

Best coffee BBQ sauce for pork, chicken, tuna -OR- beef.

In a Flash Java BBQ Sauce

1 tablespoon olive oil -OR- canola oil

1/4 cup onion, finely chopped

2 garlic cloves, crushed in a garlic press

2 cups store bought Original barbecue sauce (I like Kraft)

1/2 cup Brewed very strong good quality coffee

Great for pork, poultry, beef, burgers, lamb -OR- game.

In a saucepan, heat the oil over medium-high heat. Add onion and garlic, sauté until soft around 5 minutes. Add all the remaining ingredients. Reduce the heat to low and SIMMER for 8-10 minutes, stir often. COOL, store in a covered container and refrigerate until use.

Always warm BBQ sauce back up to room temperature before using.

Bourbon-Java BBQ Sauce

1 cup (8 ounces) Your favorite brewed strong black coffee

1/2 cup good quality Bourbon

1/2 cup light brown sugar

1/2 cup store bought soy sauce -OR- teriyaki sauce

2 tablespoons apple cider vinegar

2 garlic cloves, crushed in a garlic press

1 tablespoon stone ground mustard

1 tablespoon ketchup

1 teaspoon Worcestershire Sauce

In a heavy saucepan -OR- small pot (2-3 qt's), combine all of the ingredients together, mix well. SIMMER, uncovered, 15-20 minutes, stir often, reduce to around 1 cup. Use this sauce at room temperature and use as a marinade -OR- baste.

Always brush BBQ sauce on the meat during the last 10-15 minutes of grilling.

Great BBQ Sauce for Chicken, Certified Angus Beef Steaks -OR- Burgers.

So Good Bourbon BBQ Sauce

1/4 cup butter

1 medium onion, finely chopped

2 garlic cloves, crushed in a garlic press

1-2 jalapeno peppers, seeded, ribbed & finely chopped (adjust the heat, to taste)

2 cups ketchup

1/2 cup brown sugar

2 tablespoons soy sauce -OR- teriyaki marinade and/or sauce

1 tablespoon apple cider vinegar

1 tablespoon honey

1/2 teaspoon prepared yellow mustard ground black pepper, to taste

1/4 cup Good Quality Bourbon, to taste

So Good for pork, BBQ pulled pork, ribs, chicken -OR- beef.

In a big saucepan -OR- small pot, melt the butter over medium heat, add the onions, garlic and jalapeno peppers, sauté for 4-5 minutes, stir often and don't burn. Lower the heat, add all the other ingredients, except the bourbon, give a stir after adding each ingredient. SIMMER for around 10 minutes, stir often, then add the Bourbon. Stir in the Bourbon, COOK for 3-5 minutes -OR- more. COOL down the sauce, use right away -OR- store in the refrigerator in a covered container.

Warm the BBQ sauce back to room temperature before using.

Pepsi BBQ Sauce

1 can (12 ounces) Pepsi -OR- any brand Cola (1 1/2 cups)

1 1/2 cups Ketchup

1 cup onions, finely chopped

1/4 cup apple cider vinegar

1/4 cup soy sauce -OR- teriyaki sauce

1 teaspoon chili powder

1 teaspoon salt - to taste

hot red pepper sauce - to taste, to adjust the heat

Great for pork, pulled pork, chicken, game, beef, burgers -OR- franks.

In a saucepan, combine all of the ingredients, mix well. Bring to a boil over medium-high heat, reduce the heat to low, cover. SIMMER for 30-45 minutes, stir often. Serve right away or COOL, store in a covered container in the refrigerator for up to 6 weeks.

Always brush BBQ sauce on the meat during the final 10-15 minutes of grilling.

Joe's Cola BBQ Sauce

3/4 cup Coca Cola -OR- any brand Cola

3/4 cup ketchup

1/2 cup onions, finely chopped

2 tablespoons teriyaki sauce -OR- soy sauce

2 tablespoons apple cider vinegar

1/2 teaspoon chili powder

1/3 teaspoon salt-to taste hot red pepper sauce - to taste

Best Cola sauce for pork, ribs, game, burgers, franks -OR- chicken on the bone.

In a saucepan, combine all of the ingredients together, mix well. Bring to boil over medium-high heat, cover. Reduce the heat to low, SIMMER for 35-45 minutes, stir often. COOK, until the sauce is very thick.

Use right away!

Easy Rider Cola BBQ Sauce

2 cups store bought Original barbecue sauce (I like Kraft)

1 can (12 ounces) Coca Cola -OR- any brand Cola

2 tablespoons soy sauce -OR- teriyaki sauce

2 tablespoons Steak Sauce (aka: A1 Steak Sauce)

1 teaspoon liquid smoke

Very Good Sauce for Chicken, Pork, Beef, Game, Franks -OR- Burgers.

In a saucepan, combine all of the ingredients together, mix well. Slowly bring to boil over med- ium heat, reduce the heat to low. Cover the pan, SIMMER for 7-10 minutes -OR- until thick. Stir Often, use right away -OR- store in a covered container in the refrigerator for up to 6 weeks.

Always brush sauce on the meat during the last 10-15 minutes of grilling.

Mean Joe's Cola BBQ Sauce

1 cup Coca Cola -OR- any brand Cola

1 cup ketchup

1/2 cup Steak Sauce (aka: A1 steak Sauce)

3 tablespoons Worcestershire Sauce - to taste

1 teaspoon liquid smoke

1/2 teaspoon garlic powder

1/2 teaspoon onion powder

1/2 teaspoon ground black pepper - to taste

Great sauce for pork shoulder, ribs, beef brisket, burgers -OR- chicken on the bone.

In a saucepan, combine all the ingredients together, mix well. Slowly bring to a boil over medium heat, stir often. Reduce the heat to low, SIMMER for 7-10 minutes, stir often. COOK until thick. Use right away -OR- COOL, store in a covered container in the refrigerator for up to 8 weeks.

Big Bob's Ginger Ale Barbecue Sauce

2 cups store bought Hickory Smoke barbecue sauce

3/4 cup Ginger Ale Soda Pop - to taste

2 tablespoons molasses

1 teaspoon prepared mustard

Best for pork, ribs, chicken, game, steaks -OR- burgers.

In a bowl, whisk together the barbecue sauce, ginger ale, molasses and mustard, mix well.

Use right away -OR- cover and refrigerate for up to 2 weeks.

Always let sauce warm to room temperature before serving.

Dr. Pepper is in the House BBQ Sauce

1 cup Dr. Pepper Soda Pop

1 cup of ketchup

1/2 cup onions, finely chopped

3 tablespoons Worcestershire Sauce

2 tablespoons Steak Sauce (aka: A1 Steak Sauce)

2 tablespoons fresh lime juice

1-2 tablespoons fresh lime zest - to taste

1 tablespoon hot red pepper sauce -OR- more to taste

1 tablespoon apple cider vinegar

2 garlic cloves, crushed in a garlic press

1 teaspoon liquid smoke

1/2 teaspoon ground black pepper kosher salt -OR- sea salt - to taste

Great sauce for pork, ribs, chicken, beef brisket, steaks -OR- burgers.

In a heavy big saucepan, combine the Dr. Pepper, ketchup, onion, Worcestershire sauce, steak sauce, lime juice, lime zest, hot sauce, vinegar, garlic, liquid smoke and black pepper, mix - well. Slowly bring to boil over medium heat, reduce the heat to low, cover the pan. SIMMER, for 12-18 minutes, until thick, stir often. Check for seasoning with a tasting spoon. If it needs it add more lime juice, hot sauce -OR- vinegar to taste. Season with the salt as needed. Use right away -OR- COOL, store in a covered container and refrigerate until ready to serve.

For best results bring the sauce to room temperature before serving.

Root beer BBQ Sauce

1 cup Your favorite Root Beer Soda Pop

3/4 cup ketchup

1/2 cup onions, finely chopped

3 tablespoons soy sauce -OR- teriyaki sauce

2-3 tablespoons fresh lime juice - to taste

1-2 tablespoons freshly grated lime zest

2 tablespoons Steak Sauce (aka: A1 Steak Sauce)

2 garlic cloves, crushed in a garlic press

1 tablespoon hot red pepper sauce - to taste

1 tablespoon apple cider vinegar

1 teaspoon liquid smoke

1/2 teaspoon ground black pepper

kosher salt -OR- sea salt - to taste

The King of Soda Pop BBQ Sauce, Great on Anything.

In a saucepan, combine the root beer, ketchup, onion, soy sauce -OR- teriyaki sauce, lime juice, lime zest, Steak Sauce, garlic, hot sauce, vinegar, liquid smoke and black pepper, mix well.

Slowly bring to a boil over medium heat, cover the pan. Reduce the heat to low, it should be a gentle SIMMER. SIMMER for 15-20 minutes, COOK until thick and rich in flavor, stir often.

Taste using a tasting spoon, add more lime juice, hot sauce -OR- vinegar as needed. Use right away -OR- COOL, strain the sauce if you like. Store in covered containers in the refrigerator, the sauce will keep for several months.

Bring the sauce back up to room temperature before serving.

Apple Butter BBQ Sauce

8 ounces store bought barbecue sauce

1/2 cup Apple Butter

1 tablespoon Worcestershire sauce -OR- soy sauce

Great BBQ Sauce on Burgers !!!

In a heavy saucepan, combine all of the ingredients together, mix well. Slowly bring to a boil over medium heat. Reduce the heat to low. Simmer on low heat for 3-4 minutes, stir often.

Divide the sauce use 1/2 to brush on the meat, while on the grill and use the other 1/2 to serve on the side. Use right away.

Brush the sauce on the burgers during the final 5 minutes of grilling and serve the extra sauce on the side.

Apple & Maple BBQ Sauce/Glaze

1 1/3 cups chicken broth

2/3 cup applesauce

5 tablespoons maple syrup

4 tablespoons apple cider vinegar

2 tablespoons cornstarch

4 teaspoons soy sauce

1/2 teaspoon ground ginger

Good Sauce/Glaze for Pork -Or- Poultry.

In a saucepan, combine all of the ingredients together, mix well. Slowly bring to a boil over medium heat, while you stir with a whisk. Reduce the heat to low, SIMMER on low for 10-12 minutes, stir often. Remove from the heat, Use right away -OR- COOL and store in a covered container in the refrigerator for up to 2 weeks.

Apple BBQ Sauce

2 cups ketchup (I like Heinz Tomato Ketchup)

1 1/3 cups seasoned rice vinegar

1 cup brown sugar

1 cup apple juice

2/3 cup bacon bits (ground in a spice grinder -OR- coffee grinder used only for spices)

1/2 cup soy sauce

1/2 cup apple cider vinegar

4 teaspoons prepared mustard

1 1/2 teaspoons garlic powder

1/2 teaspoon ground black pepper - to taste

1/2 teaspoon hot red (cayenne) pepper

2/3 cup peeled & grated apple

2/3 cup grated onion

4 teaspoons grated green bell pepper

Best sauce for ribs, pulled pork, beef brisket, chicken -OR- on any grilled foods.

In a big saucepan -OR- small pot, combine the ketchup, rice vinegar, brown sugar, apple juice, bacon bits, soy sauce, vinegar, mustard, garlic powder, black pepper & red pepper. Bring to a boil over medium-high heat, stir often. Stir in the apples, onion and green peppers. Reduce the heat to low and SIMMER, uncovered for 11-16 minutes -OR- until it starts to thicken, stir often. COOL, store in clean covered containers in the refrigerator for up to 2 weeks.

*Tip: Always warm sauce back up to room temperature before using.

Brush BBQ Sauce on the meat during the last 10-15 minutes of grilling.

Maple BBQ Sauce

3/4 cup maple syrup

2 tablespoons chili powder

2 tablespoons cider vinegar

2 tablespoons onions, finely chopped

1 tablespoon Worcestershire sauce -OR- soy sauce

1 teaspoon salt - to taste

1/2 teaspoon prepared mustard

1/2 teaspoon black pepper

Great BBQ sauce for beef, pork, game -OR- poultry !

In a bowl, whisk all of the ingredients together, mix well. You can brush sauce on both sides of 1 1/2 pounds of beef, pork, game -OR- poultry.

In a Flash Maple BBQ Sauce

1 1/2 cups store bought barbecue sauce

2/3 cup maple syrup

Good sauce for pork, ribs, beef -OR- chicken.

In a saucepan, whisk together the barbecue sauce and maple syrup, mix well. Slowly bring to a boil over medium heat, stir often. Reduce the heat to low, SIMMER for 5-6 minutes, stir often, don't burn. Use right away -OR- COOL, store in a covered container in the refrigerator for up to 2 weeks.

Always heat BBQ sauce back up to room temperature before serving.

Dude; The sauce is too thick? *Tip: Add a small amount at a time of water or apple juice this will help thin down the sauce.

*Note: Brush sauce on the meat during the final 10-15 minutes of grilling.

Ole Miss White BBQ Sauce

2 cups Mayonnaise

1 cup white vinegar

2 teaspoons onion powder

2 teaspoons salt - to taste

2 teaspoons ground black pepper - to taste

1 1/2 teaspoons garlic powder

1/2 teaspoon paprika

Great sauce for smoked turkey, chicken, pork, pulled pork -OR- burgers.

In a bowl, whisk all of the ingredients together, mix well. Cover and chill in the refrigerator for at least 4 hours -OR- overnight. Brush this BBQ sauce on at the very end of grilling -OR- smoking. It will breakdown and start to separate if it is heated too long.

BAMA White BBQ Sauce

1 cup Mayonnaise

1 cup apple cider vinegar

1 1/2 tablespoons black pepper - to taste

1 tablespoon fresh lime juice

1/2 teaspoon salt - to taste

1/4 teaspoon ground red (cayenne) pepper

Great sauce for smoked turkey, chicken, pork -OR- game.

In a bowl, whisk together all of the ingredients, mix well. Cover and refrigerate for at least 6-12 hours before using. Brush onto the meat during the last few minutes of grilling time. It will start to breakdown and separate if it is heated too long.

This sauce is a great condiment, you can also serve it as a dipping sauce.

*Tip: This recipe is easy to increase -OR- decrease!

SPICY Tar Heel BBQ Sauce

1 large bottle (46 fluid ounces) store bought ketchup

2 cups apple cider vinegar

1 cup granulated white sugar

1/2 cup butter

1/4 cup hot red pepper sauce (Texas Style) - to taste

1 tablespoon crushed red pepper flakes - to taste

Best for pulled pork, ribs, chicken -OR- anything grilled.

In a big saucepan -OR- small pot, combine and stir together the ketchup, vinegar, sugar, butter, hot sauce and red pepper flakes. COOK, over medium heat, until the butter has melted and the sauce is hot. Use right away -OR- COOL, place in a covered container. Store in the refrigerator for up to 4 weeks.

I-95 NC BBQ Sauce

1 cup ketchup

1 cup water

1/2 cup cider vinegar

6 tablespoons granulated white sugar

3 teaspoons chili powder

2 teaspoons salt- to taste

Great sauce for pork shoulder, ribs, chicken -OR- anything else grilled.

In a bowl, whisk all of the ingredients together, mix well. Place in a covered container and store in the refrigerator for at least 6 hours to let the flavors blend.

This is a easy recipe to increase -OR- decrease.

NC BBQ Basting Sauce

2-3 tablespoons canola oil -OR- olive oil

1 small sweet onion

2 garlic cloves, crushed in a garlic press

2 cups ketchup

1 1/2 cups water

2 tablespoons apple cider vinegar

2 tablespoons soy sauce

2 tablespoons teriyaki marinade and/or sauce

2 tablespoons molasses

2 teaspoons brown sugar

2 teaspoons honey

2 teaspoons prepared yellow mustard

Great BBQ basting sauce for pork, ribs, beef -OR- burgers.

In a saucepan -OR- small pot, Heat the oil over medium-high heat, sauté onions and garlic for 3-4 minutes -OR- until tender, don't burn. Add all of the remaining ingredients and bring to a boil over medium-high heat, stir often. Reduce the heat to low. SIMMER for 10 minutes, stir often. Use right away -OR- COOL, place in a covered container and store in the refrigerator for up to 1 month.

NC Mop/Basting Sauce

2 cups apple juice

2 cups apple cider vinegar

1/2 cup canola oil -OR- vegetable oil

1/2 cup Soy Sauce -OR- Teriyaki Marinade and/or Sauce

1/4 -1/2 cup salt - to taste

1/4 cup garlic powder

1/4 cup onion powder

1/2 tablespoon ground thyme

1/2 teaspoon ground black pepper

1/2 teaspoon prepared yellow mustard

Great Mop/Basting Sauce for pork, ribs -OR- poultry.

In a big saucepan -OR- small pot, combine all of the ingredient together, mix well. Bring to a boil over medium-high heat, reduce the heat to low. SIMMER for 5-7 minutes, stir often, don't burn. Use right away -OR- COOL, place in covered containers in the refrigerator for up to 3 weeks.

Big Bob's Top 45 Greatest Baseball Players All Time

YOUR TOP 45 LIST:

#1. Babe Ruth

#2. Willie Mays

#3. Walter Johnson

#4. Ty Cobb

#5. Joe Di Maggio

#6. Ted Williams

#7. Mickey Mantle

#8. Stan Musial

#9. Lou Gerhig

#10. Honus Wagner

#11. Jackie Robinson

#12. Barry Bonds

#13. Nolan Ryan

#14. Reggie Jackson

#15. Roger Clemens

#16. Hank Aaron

#17. Roger Hornby

#18. Carl Yastezemski

#19. Cal Ripken Jr.

#20. Pete Rose

#21. Hank Greenburg

#22. Jimmy Foxx

#23. Shoeless Joe Jackson

#24. George Brett

#25. Mike Schmidt

#26. Mark McGwire

#27. Yogi Berra

#28. Christy Mathewson

#29. Johnny Bench

#30. Sandy Koufax

#31. Cy Young

#32. Joe Morgan

#33. Bob Feller

#34. Warren Spahn

#35. Bob Gibson

#36. Frank Robinson

#37. Tom Seaver

#38. Steve Carlton

#39. Brooks Robinson

#40. Grover Alexander

#41. Dizzy Dean

#42. Whitey Ford

#43. Jim Palmer

#44. Tom Glavine

#45. Greg Maddux

This was a tough list to make, their have been so many great baseball players!

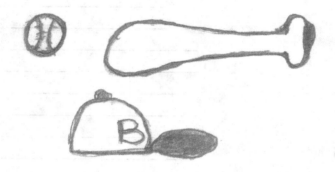

Baseball, Bat and Hat

by: Elizabeth
age 8

Big Bob's Top 20 Greatest Baseball Pitchers

Your Top 20 List:

#1. Walter Johnson

#2. Christy Mathewson

#3. Nolan Ryan

#4. Lefty Grove

#5. Roger Clemens

#6. Sandy Koufax

#7. Cy Young

#8. Bob Feller

#9. Warren Spahn

#10. Bob Gibson

#11. Tom Seaver

#12. Steve Carlton

#13. Grover Alexander

#14. Satchell Page

#15. Dizzy Dean

#16. Jim Palmer

#17. Whitey Ford

#18. Tom Glavine

#19. Greg Maddux

TIE #20. Jim "Catfish" Hunter

TIE #20 Randy "Big Unit" Johnson

So tough again we have a lot of great pitchers to pick from!

BBQ Sauce

Big Bob's Top 10 Greatest Baseball Managers All Time

Your Top 10 List:

#1. Sparky Anderson

#2. Joe Torre

#3. Connie Mack

#4. Casey Stengel

TIE #5. Tony La Russa

TIE #5. Walter Alston

#6. Bobby Cox

#7. John McGraw

TIE #8. Billy Martin

TIE #8. Tommy Lasorda

#9. Jim Leyland

TIE #10. Gene Mauch

TIE #10. Dusty Baker

Big Bob's Top 15 Greatest Baseball Radio Announcers All Time

Your Top 15 List:

#1. Ernie Harwell

#2. Vin Scully

#3. Harry Caray

#4. Mel Allen

TIE #5. Bob Uecher

TIE #5. Phil Rizzuto

#6. Jack Buck

TIE #7. Joe Garagiola

TIE #7. Red Barber

#8. Bob Murphy

#9. Al Michaels

TIE #10. Curt Gowdy

TIE #10. Dizzy Dean

#11. Lindey Nelson

TIE #12. Jack Brickhouse

TIE #12. Chuck Thompson

#13. Russ Hodges

#14. Harry Kalas

TIE #15. Rafael "Felo" Ramirez

TIE #15. Milo Hamiliton

I still remember sitting as a child in my Grandparents living room. My Granddad and I would always listen to the Reds games on the Radio. Sometimes it seems, like yesterday and it takes me back to Newark, Ohio. As a young man I had a job in our Family Business, with a lot of travel by car back then. I would travel around Michigan and listen to Ernie Harwell on the car Radio. He made you a Tiger Fan and a Ernie Harwell Fan, he was just so great at it.

Big Bob's Top 10 Best Baseball Movies All Time

Your Top 10 List:

#1. Bull Durham (1988)

#2. Field of Dreams (1989)

#3. The Natural (1984)

#4. Bang the Drum Slowly (1973)

#5. Eight Men Out (1988)

#6. The Bad News Bears (1976)

#7. A League of Their Own (1992)

#8. Pride of the Yankees (1942)

#9. 61 (2001)

TIE #10. Major League (1989)

TIE #10. The Sandlot (1993)

Notes

Notes

CHAPTER #6
Salsa, Dips
and
Chips
PRO BASKETBALL

Big Game Salsa

1 1/2 pounds ripe plum (ROMA) tomatoes, seeded and chopped

1/2 cup red onion, finely chopped

2 tablespoons fresh cilantro, chopped

2 tablespoons lime juice

1 teaspoon fresh jalapeno pepper, seeded, ribbed and finely chopped

2 cloves fresh garlic cloves, crushed in a garlic press

salt - to taste

Best for chip dunk -OR- dip, steaks, burgers, pork chops -OR- fish!

Cut the tomatoes in half from top to bottom. Use your fingers to poke out the seeds. With a sharp knife cut the tomatoes into 1/2" inch chunks. In a bowl, combine the tomatoes, onions, cilantro, lime juice, jalapeno pepper and garlic. Season to taste with the salt. Cover and let stand at room temperature for 1 hour to let the flavors blend well. Best results; Use right away or cover and refrigerate.

Grilled Tomato Salsa

1 medium sweet onion, unpeeled, cut in half crosswise

2 teaspoons -OR- more of olive oil -OR- canola oil

3-4 ripe tomatoes (1 1/2 pounds)

2 tablespoons fresh lime juice

2 tablespoons fresh cilantro, chopped

2 teaspoons canned chipotle chilies in adobo sauce, finely chopped

2 garlic cloves, crushed in a garlic press

salt - to taste

Preheat a gas -OR- charcoal grill for direct high heat

Preheat a gas grill on high heat for 10 minutes

OR

Build a charcoal fire in a outdoor grill and let it burn down, until the coals are covered in white ash.

Brush oil lightly on the grilling rack. Brush the cut sides of the onion with oil. Place the onion on the grill rack with the cut side down and put the whole tomatoes on the oiled grill rack with the onions and close the lid.

Grill the onions until they begin to soften, 3-4 minutes, then transfer to a serving plate. Grill the tomatoes, turning often, until the skins are cracked and peeling, 5-6 minutes, then transfer to the serving plate. COOL the tomatoes & onions until they are easy to handle. Cut the tomatoes with a sharp knife in half from the top to the bottom and poke out the seeds with your finger. Chop the tomatoes into 1/2" inch chunks and put in a bowl. Peel and finely chop the onion and add to the tomatoes. Mix in the lime juice, cilantro, chipotles and garlic.

Season to taste with the salt.

Cover and let stand at room temperature for 1 hour in a cool place. This will allow the flavors of the salsa to blend together. For best results; Use right away -OR- Store in a covered container in the refrigerator until ready to serve.

*Tip: When handling chilies, such as chipotles, use plastic gloves they can help you from burning your hands!

Easy Goer Tomato Salsa

1 (1 pound can) whole tomatoes, drained

1 cup store bought mild -OR- hot red salsa, containing onion, green chilies & tomatoes (however little -OR- no vinegar.)

1 small handful of fresh cilantro - to taste

1/2 - 1 tablespoon fresh lime juice - to taste

salt - to taste

ground black pepper - to taste

Great for a quick & easy dunk -OR- dip for chips.

On a cutting board, with a sharp knife chop the tomatoes into small pieces. In a bowl, combine the chopped tomatoes with the salsa, cilantro, lime juice, salt and pepper, mix lightly.

Serve right away -OR- place in a covered container in the refrigerator before serving!

Mango Salsa

1 medium ripe mango, cut lengthwise in half, take out pit, chopped (1 cup)

1/4 cup fresh red onion, finely chopped

1 tablespoon fresh mint leaves, finely chopped

1 small fresh jalapeno pepper, seeded, ribbed, finely chopped (2 teaspoons)

2 tablespoons fresh lime juice

1/8 teaspoon salt - to taste

Great with spicy dishes, such as Jamaican Jerk chicken -OR- pork.

In a plastic or glass bowl, combine all of the ingredients together, mix lightly. Cover and refrigerate for at least 1-2 hour before serving.

Mango-Peach Salsa

1/4 cup fresh lime juice

1-2 tablespoons honey - to taste

1/4 teaspoon salt

1-2 fresh ripe mangos, cut in half lengthwise, pitted, and finely chopped (1 cup)

2 cups fresh peaches, peeled, pitted and chopped

1/4 cup fresh cilantro, chopped

1-2 tablespoons green -OR- red bell pepper, finely chopped

Great for fish, planked salmon, shrimp, pork -OR- chicken on the bone.

In a plastic -OR- glass bowl, combine the lime juice, honey and salt. Add the remaining ingredients, mix well. Cover and refrigerate for at least 1-2 hours before serving.

*Tip: the best way to peel, pit and finely chop a mango is to; Score the skin lengthwise into fourths with a sharp knife and peel it like you would a banana. Cut the peeled mango lengthwise very close on both sides to the pit, then you can chop it.

Mango & Honey I shrunk the Kids Salsa

3 tablespoons fresh lime juice

1-2 tablespoons honey - to taste

1-2 teaspoons freshly grated lime zest

dash of hot red pepper sauce - to taste

1-2 mangos, cut in half lengthwise, pitted and finely chopped (1 cup)

2-3 tablespoons fresh mint leaves, finely chopped - to taste

2 tablespoons red onion, finely chopped

Best for Grilled fresh tuna, salmon, shrimp, lamb, pork -OR- chicken on the bone.

In a plastic -OR- glass bowl, combine the lime juice, honey, lime zest and red pepper sauce, mix lightly. Add ripe mango, fresh mint and red onion, mix well. Cover and refrigerate for at least 1 hour before serving.

Mango-Jalapeno Salsa

1-2 ripe mangos, peeled, pitted and cut into 1/4" inch dice (1 cup)

3 tablespoons fresh cilantro, chopped

2 tablespoons red onion, chopped

2 tablespoons fresh lime juice

1-2 teaspoons jalapeno pepper, seeded, ribbed, finely chopped

1 teaspoon garlic cloves, crushed in a garlic press

1/8 teaspoon kosher salt -OR- sea salt

Great Sweet & Spicy Salsa for Most Grilling Leftovers.

In a bowl, combine all of the ingredients together, mix well.

*Tip: If you want more heat add more jalapeno peppers.

Texan Fiesta Party Dip

1 (16 ounces) can refried beans

1 (7 ounce) can diced green chilies

2 cups guacamole homemade -OR- store bought

1 cup shredded cheddar cheese -OR- shredded Monterey jack cheese

1 cup thick & chunky store bought red salsa

1 cup sour cream (thin with milk about 1-2 tablespoons milk)

1 (4 ounce) can sliced pitted ripe black olives

Great Party Dip with Store Bought -OR- Homemade Chips.

Spread the beans onto the bottom of a 1 1/2 qt. casserole, should be about 2" thick. In a layer put chilies, salsa, guacamole, cheese and sour cream. Scatter the olives on top. Serve with tortilla chips for great dipping.

*Tip: If the beans are hard to spread, heat in the microwave -OR- stove top, this will make the beans easier to work with.

Knock-Down Chip Dip

1 (10 ounces) can store bought bean dip

1 (10 ounce) jar store bought picante sauce

3 cups homemade -OR- store bought guacamole

1 cup sour cream

1/2 cup mayonnaise

1 (2 ounce) package taco seasoning mix

4 each green onions (scallions), chopped

3 medium ripe tomatoes, finely chopped

1 (4 ounce) can sliced ripe black olives

8 ounces (2 cups) shredded cheddar cheese -OR- Monterey jack cheese

Best dip to serve with Tortilla Chips.

In a bowl, combine bean dip and picante sauce, mix well. Spread onto the bottom of a 8" X 11" inch glass dish. Carefully spread guacamole over bean mixture. In a bowl, combine sour cream, mayo, and taco seasoning mix, mix well. Spread over the top of guacamole. In another bowl, mix green onions, tomatoes and black olives. Carefully spread over sour cream mixture. Top with the shredded cheese. Serve with tortilla chips.

On the Rail Guacamole

4 avocados, halved, scoop out the flesh with a spoon.

6 tablespoons fresh lime juice

2 tablespoons olive oil -OR- canola oil

2 large garlic cloves, mashed

1/2 teaspoon hot red (cayenne) pepper

2 each green onions (scallions), chopped, 1/4"-1/2" inch lengths

1-2 jalapeno peppers, cut in half, seeded, ribbed for heat

salt - to taste

pepper - to taste

Great for a Dunk -OR- Dip w/Chips!

In a blender -OR- food processor, combine all of the ingredients together, except the salt & pepper. Using repeated pulses, blend until you reach a textured puree around 8-10 pulses.

You want to have some unpureed bits left in the Guacamole. Pour into a bowl and season with salt & pepper to your taste.

Home-Run Guacamole

3 very ripe avocados, pitted , peeled

1 fresh ripe tomato, seeded and cut into chunks

1/4 small red onion, cut into chunks

2 medium garlic cloves, mashed, chopped

1 tablespoon olive oil

3 tablespoons fresh lime juice

1 jalapeno pepper, seeded, ribbed & chopped

salt - to taste

pepper - to taste

Best for a dip, chips, grilled meat -OR- fish.

On a cutting board, with a sharp knife cut the avocado, tomato and red onion into rough 1/2" inch chunks. In a bowl mash them together with a strong sturdy fork. Then add the mashed chopped garlic, olive oil, lime juice, jalapeno, salt and pepper to taste. Finish mixing lightly with a fork. Use right away, if the guacamole must stand, put in a COOL place., do not refrigerate, cover with plastic wrap pressed down onto the surface to prevent discoloring.

My Wife's Humus Dip
My wife Cynthia is the best Chef that I have ever known.

1/2 cup canned Garbanzo Beans (aka: Chick Peas)

1/4 cup store bought Tahini Paste

2 tablespoons oil

2 tablespoons lemon juice

1 teaspoon salt - to taste

1 teaspoon sugar

1/4 teaspoon garlic powder

Best served with pita wedges!

In a bowl, Mash 1/2 cup canned beans. Mix beans with the remaining ingredients, mix well.

Use right away -OR- cover and refrigerate before serving.

Crabby Spread

1 (8 ounce) package cream cheese, softened

1/4 cup store bought bottled chili sauce

1 tablespoon soy sauce

1 teaspoon fresh lime juice

1/2 teaspoon garlic powder

1/2 teaspoon onion powder

1/2 teaspoon hot red pepper sauce

1 (6 ounce) can crabmeat, drained

Great Spread on Crackers, Bagel Chips -OR- Pita Wedges.

In a bowl, combine the softened cream cheese, chili sauce, soy sauce, lime juice, garlic powder, onion powder and hot sauce; stir in the canned crabmeat, mix lightly. Use right away or cover and refrigerate before serving.

Lizzies Tortilla Chips

12 each Corn Tortillas

1 cup canola oil -OR- peanut oil

sea salt -OR- kosher salt - to taste - (light on the salt)

Kids of all ages love freshly made warm corn tortilla chips.

Stack 2-3 tortillas on a clean cutting board, cut with a sharp knife into quarters. Repeat until all are quartered.

In a heavy fry pan, heat the oil over medium-high heat 350 degrees F, until you hear a tortilla wedge sizzle when dipped in the oil. Fry tortilla wedges in batches around 1 1/2 - 2 minutes, -OR- until crisp and light in color. Remove with a slotted spoon and drain on paper towels.

Sprinkle each batch lightly with the salt. As soon as they are removed from the oil. Serve right away while still warm -OR- store in a airtight container if you make them ahead of time.

MoJo Oven Baked Corn Tortilla Chips

12 corn tortillas

1 1/2 - 2 teaspoons canola oil -OR- vegetable oil

sea salt -OR- kosher salt - to taste - light on the salt

MoJo Chips are Great W/ Dips & Salsa

Preheat oven to 325 degrees F

Place a tortilla on a cutting board. Brush 1 side with 1/8 teaspoon of oil. Repeat with the remaining tortillas and oil. With a sharp knife, cut tortillas into quarters, sixths -OR- eights, depending on which size of chips you like. Arrange as many wedges in a single layer as will fit on a baking sheet. Bake in the middle of the oven 7-10 minutes -OR- until chips are crisp and lightly brown. Keep watch the last 2 minutes or so to avoid burning, this can happen very fast.

Remove the chips from the oven and COOL, on paper towels. Sprinkle lightly with salt to taste while still hot. Repeat baking in batches until all chips are toasted. Serve right away hot -OR- warm. You can store chips in a airtight container if you make them ahead of time.

Grilled Party Nachos

10 cups Store Bought Restaurant Style Tortilla Chips

2 (15 ounce) cans black beans, rinsed, drained & mashed

1 - 2 (4.5 ounce) cans chopped green chilies, drained

1 (1.25 ounce packet) taco seasoning mix

4 fresh ripe plum (ROMA) tomatoes, chopped

4 each green onions (scallions) sliced (4 tablespoons)

4 cups (16 ounces -OR- 1 pound) shredded Monterey Jack cheese -OR- Cheddar cheese

Serve with the following:

1 small bowl - sour cream

1 small bowl - guacamole

1 small bowl - chunky red salsa

Your Whole Gang Will Love These Nachos!

Preheat a gas grill -OR- heat coals for direct medium heat

Preheat a gas grill on high heat for 10 minutes, then turn down to medium heat

Cut 2 each - 30" X 18" inch pieces of heavy-duty foil; - spray cooking oil spray (aka: PAM)

Spread tortilla chips evenly onto both sheets of foil. In a bowl, combine the beans, chilies, and taco seasoning mix, mix lightly; spoon evenly over tortilla chips. Top each with tomatoes and green onions. Sprinkle both with cheese. Wrap the foil tightly around nachos. However not to tight, the foil shouldn't touch the top of the cheese.

Place the 2 foil packets on the grill rack seam side up; close the grill lid: grill over direct medium heat for 7-9 minutes -OR- until the cheese melts, don't burn. Serve right away with the sour cream, guacamole and chunky red salsa on the side.

Super Bowl of Nachos

50-60 each corn tortilla chips, store bought & any shape

1 (16 ounce) can refried beans

1/2 cup shredded Monterey Jack cheese

1/2 cup shredded Cheddar cheese

4 each green onions (scallions), finely chopped

Toppings:

1 large avocado, peeled & cut into 1/4" inch dice

4-6 pickled -OR- fresh, seeded jalapeno peppers, cut into strips

1 cup sour cream

1/2 - 3/4 cup store bought (aka: jar) mild -OR- hot red salsa

Preheat your oven broiler

On a baking sheet, arrange tortilla chips in a single layer. Top each chip with 1 teaspoon of refried beans. Push the chips together into a large round; overlapping, its OK. Scatter cheese and green onions over the entire surface of chips. Broil 4" inches from the heat source for 2-3 minutes -Or- until the cheese bubbles. Remove the pan from the oven. Slide the nachos onto a large serving platter. top with the avocado & jalapeno strips. Dollop with sour cream & red salsa. Serve right away.

Pickled Red Onions

2 tablespoons canola oil -OR- olive oil

2 medium onions, cut in half & thinly sliced

1 tablespoon red wine vinegar

1 teaspoon fresh oregano

1/2 teaspoon sugar

1/2 teaspoon fresh basil, chopped

1/4 teaspoon kosher salt -OR- sea salt, to taste

1/8 teaspoon pepper

Best for grilled game birds -OR- grilled poultry !

In a fry pan, heat the oil over medium-high heat. Add red onions and cook, stirring often, until soft, around 2 minutes, Add vinegar, oregano, sugar, basil , salt and pepper. COOK, stirring, until tender and limp 2-4 minutes. Serve right away, while still hot.

Pickled Jalapeno Peppers

Makes: 4 pints

2 quarts fresh jalapeno peppers

2 cups white wine vinegar

2 cups water

1/2 teaspoon pickling spices -OR- pickling salt

8 fresh garlic cloves

Buy store bought pickled jalapeno peppers -OR- make your own !

Big Bob's Top 8 Steps to Making Pickled Jalapeno Peppers

#1. Slice jalapeno peppers -OR- leave them whole.

#2. To prevent bursting, cut 2 small slits in each whole pepper.

#3. Pack peppers tightly into clean, hot jars.

#4. Combine the white wine vinegar and water; heat to a SIMMER.

#5. Do not boil!

#6. Pour hot vinegar over peppers, leaving 1/2" inch headspace in the jar.

#7. Add pickling spices -OR- pickling salt & add 2 garlic cloves to each jar then seal.

#8. Process in a Boiling Water Bath for 10 mintues.

Makes: 4 pint jars of pickle jalapeno peppers

*Tip: When canning foods be very careful, learn as much as you can about the canning process.

Please read all the directions on the canning jar box and the inside direction sheets. Carefully follow the recipe steps in this book.

Salsa, Dips and Chips

Big Bob's Top 25 Greatest NBA Players All Time

Your Top 25 List:

#1. Michael Jordan
#2. Bill Russell
#3. Magic Johnson
#4. Kareem Adbul Jabbar
#5. Wilt Chamberlain
#6. Oscar Robertson
#7. Dr. J (Julius Erving)
#8. Jerry West
#9. Bob Cousy
#10. Larry Bird
#11. Elgin Baylor
#12. Shaquille O'Neal
#13. George Mikan
#14. John Havlicek
#15. John Stockton
#16. Willis Reed
#17. Moses Malone
TIE #18. Isiah "ZEKE" Thomas
TI# #18. Karl "THE Mailman" Malone
#19 Walt Frazier
TIE #20. Dominique Wilkins
TIE #20. Kobe Bryant
#21. John "Jack" Twyman
#22. Dave Bing
TIE #24. Alex English
TIE #24. Charles Barkley
TIE #25. Tim Duncan
TIE #25. Reggie Miller

Big Bob's Top 35 Favorite NBA Players All Time

Your Top 35 List:

#1. Jerry West

#2. Rick Barry

#3. Magic Johnson

#4. Gail Goodrich

#5. John Havlicek

#6. Jabbar

#7. Bob McAdoo

#8. Pistol Pete Maravich

#9. Earl "The Pearl" Monroe

#10. Dr. J

#11. Walt "Clyde" Frazier

#12. Bill Russell

#13. Bob Cousy

#14. Dave Bing

#15. SHAQ

#16. George "the Iceman" Gervin

#17. Isiah Thomas

#18. Moses Malone

#19. Sir Charles Barkley

#20. MJ

#21. Wilt

#22. "Larry"

#23. Patrick Ewing

#24. Hakeem "the Dream" Olajuwon

#25. Dominique Wilkins

#26. Willis Reed

#27. Arvydas Sabonis

#28. David Robinson

#29. Kobe

#30. Dan Issel

#31. Manute Bol

#32. Tiny Archibald

#33. Dennis Rodman

#34. Vinnie "the Microwave" Johnson

TIE #35. Kent Benson

TIE #35. Vince Carter

Big Bob's Top 10 Best NBA Coaches All Time

Your Top 10 List:

#1. Red Auerbach

#2. Phil Jackson

#3. Pat Riley

#4. Chuck Daly

#5. Don Nelson

#6. John Kundla

#7. Lenny Wilkens

#8. Red Holzman

#9. Jack Ramsay

#10. Bill Fitch

_____

_____

_____

_____

_____

_____

_____

_____

_____

_____

CHAPTER #7

Steaks

SOCCER

Peppered Knicks NY Strip Steaks

Serves:4

4 each 1" inch NY Strip Steaks

1/4 cup black peppercorns

3-4 tablespoons Lemon Pepper Seasoning

kosher salt -OR- sea salt

vegetable oil for brushing on the grill rack

Place the peppercorns in a coffee grinder -OR- food processor, until the corns are coarsely crushed and broken. If you don't have a food processor -OR- coffee grinder, use a mortor & pestle -OR- place whole peppercorns on a cutting board and crush with the bottom of a heavy frying pan. Coat one side of steaks with the crushed peppercorns and press in firmly.

Sprinkle the steaks with the lemon pepper seasoning and coarse salt. Turn the steaks over and repeat the same process. Place the steaks in the refrigerator, uncovered for 4-6 hours.

Preheat a gas -OR- charcoal grill to direct medium-high heat

Brush the grill rack with vegetable oil

Place the steaks on the grill rack over hot coals, COOK for 6-8 minutes, turning 1 time. Grill to the desired doneness, always COOK steaks until they are done to your liking. Take steaks off the grill when done and let rest for at least 5 minutes. Serve right away with your favorite Steak Sauce. I like Peter Luger, A1 Steak Sauce and Homemade Steak Sauce.

Quick Step Steak Sauce

3/4 cup ketchup

3/4 cup Worcestershire Sauce

dash onion powder - to taste

dash garlic powder - to taste

This is an easy steak sauce to make, just add equal parts of Ketchup & Worcestershire sauce, then a dash of onion powder & garlic powder to taste.

In a bowl, whisk together all of the ingredients, mix well. Cover and refrigerate until ready to serve with steak.

Big Bob's B1 Steak Sauce

1/2 cup dark raisins, chopped

1/2 cup orange juice

1/4 cup Worcestershire Sauce

1/4 cup white vinegar

2 tablespoons prepared mustard

2 tablespoons ketchup

2 tablespoons bottled chili sauce

1 tablespoon grated fresh orange zest

In a saucepan, combine all of the ingredients and bring to a boil. Boil for 2 minutes, stirring constantly and remove from the heat. Allow to COOL until lukewarm. Pour mixture into a blender until it is pureed (smooth). Place in clean covered containers, tightly sealed. Place in the refrigerator for no more than 3 months -OR- use right away.

Big Bob's B2 Steak Sauce

2 cups ketchup

2/3 cup onion, chopped

1/2 cup fresh orange juice

1/2 cup Worcestershire Sauce

1/2 cup water

1/2 cup white vinegar

1/4 cup soy sauce

1/4 cup packed dark brown sugar

2 each large garlic cloves, crushed in a garlic press

2 tablespoons prepared mustard

Steaks

1 tablespoon freshly grated orange zest

In a big saucepan, combine all of the ingredients, mix well. Bring to a boil over medium heat, reduce the heat to low. SIMMER for 25-30 minutes, stir often. Take the pan off the heat, COOL until lukewarm. Pour the mixture into a blender and puree until smooth. Cover and refrigerate until ready to use.

Grilled Marinated Organic Strip Steaks

Serves: 4

Steak Marinade:

2 tablespoons organic olive oil

1 1/2 tablespoons organic balsamic vinegar

4 garlic cloves, crushed in garlic press

salt, to taste

freshly ground black pepper, to taste

4 each Organic Strip steaks, 8 ounces each

1 - 1/2 tablespoons organic olive oil

salt - to taste

freshly ground black pepper - to taste

16 ounces mushrooms, sliced

4 ounces Blue Cheese, Crumbled

In a bowl, combine all of the Steak Marinade ingredients together, mix well. Place the steaks in a extra large resealable plastic bag. Pour the steak marinade over the steaks and turn the bag to coat the steaks. Seal the bag tightly and place in the refrigerator to marinate for 2-3 hours.

Preheat a gas -OR- charcoal grill to direct medium-high heat

Lightly brush the grill rack with olive oil

Place the steaks on the grill and COOK, for 5 minutes per side, until grilled to the desired doneness is reached. While steaks are grilling, in a saucepan sauté the mushrooms in the olive oil, with a pinch of salt. COOK for 5 minutes over medium heat, stirring constantly, or until the mushrooms have given up most of their liquid. Season the mushrooms with freshly ground black pepper. Add the blue cheese and stir in to blend. Take the steaks off the grill, let them rest 5 minutes. Then smother with the mushrooms and blue cheese mixture.

Serve right away!

Wild Bill's Grilled Buffalo Steaks

Serves: 4

4 each Buffalo Steaks

3/4 cup good quality red wine

1/2 cup olive oil

5 garlic cloves, crushed in a garlic press

1 teaspoon onion powder

1/2 teaspoon salt - to taste

1/4 teaspoon ground black pepper

In a bowl, combine the red wine, oil, garlic, onion powder, salt and pepper, mix well. Place the steaks in resealable extra large plastic bag. Pour the red wine mixture over the steaks in the bag. Seal the bag and marinate in the refrigerator for 6 hours or over night.

Preheat a gas -OR- charcoal grill to direct medium heat

Lightly brush vegetable oil onto the grill rack.

Remove the steaks from the bag and throw out the marinade. Place the steaks on the grill rack over medium heat and COOK for 5-6 minutes per side. Grill to the desired doneness and take the steaks off the grill. Let the steaks rest for 5 minutes and serve right away.

Blues T-Bone Steak

Serves: 4

4 each T-bone steaks, 1" inch thick

kosher salt -OR- sea salt - to taste

2 large Vidalia -OR- Sweet Onions, chopped

1/2 cup unsalted butter

3 tablespoons good quality red wine

2 tablespoons canola oil -OR- vegetable oil

4 ounces blue cheese

Vegetable oil to brush on the grill rack

Sprinkle salt on the steaks and let stand at room temperature for 30-45 minutes. In a saucepan sauté the onions in butter and oil over medium heat, until they are soft and starting to brown.

Turn up the heat to medium-high and add red wine. Cook until most of the liquid has been cooked off. Remove the pan from the heat and set aside.

Preheat a gas -OR- charcoal grill to direct medium-high heat.

Lightly brush vegetable oil onto the grill rack.

Place the steaks on the grill rack, grill for 5-6 minutes per side or until they reach the desired doneness. Take the steaks off the grill, place on a platter. Let the steaks rest for 5 minutes.

Top with blue cheese and onions. Serve right away !

Grilled Porterhouse Steak W/ Horseradish Sauce

Serves: 4-6

2 each (1 1/4" inch thick) Porterhouse Steaks

1 teaspoon salt - to taste

1 teaspoon freshly ground black pepper - to taste

Pat steaks dry and season both sides of the steaks with salt and pepper. Let the steaks stand at room temperature for 30 minutes.

Preheat a gas -OR- charcoal grill to direct medium-high heat.

Lightly brush vegetable oil -OR- olive oil onto the grill rack

Place the steaks on the grill rack over medium-hot coals. COOK for 9-13 minutes, for rare an instant-read thermometer inserted into the meat should read 120 degrees F. When the steaks are cooked to the desired doneness, take them off the grill. Let the steaks rest on a cutting board for 10 minutes at room temperature. Slice the meat thinly and serve with the horseradish sauce.

Horseradish Sauce

Makes 1 1/2 cups

3/4 cup sour cream

3/4 cup mayonnaise

3 tablespoons grated fresh horseradish

2 tablespoons fresh lemon juice

1 tablespoon Dijon mustard

1/2 teaspoon sugar

1/2 teaspoon ground red pepper

Horseradish Sauce & Beef are a match made in Heaven !!!

In a bowl, whisk all of the ingredients together, mix well. Cover and refrigerate before serving.

Grilled Big Easy Bourbon Street Ribeye Steak

Serves: 4

Big Easy Marinade:

1 cup good quality Bourbon

1 cup brown sugar

1 cup canola oil -OR- vegetable oil

1 cup prepared mustard

1/2 cup Worcestershire Sauce

1/2 cup soy sauce

4 each Ribeye Steaks (12 ounces each)

In a bowl, whisk all the Big Easy Marinade ingredients together, mix well. Marinate the 4 steaks in Big Easy Marinade in the refrigerator for 6-8 hours, don't go over 8 hours.

Preheat a gas -OR- charcoal grill to direct high heat (Grill it hot & fast)

Lightly brush vegetable oil onto the grill rack

Take the steaks out of the marinade and throw-out the marinade. Place the steaks on the grill rack over high heat. Grill to the desired doneness. Take the steaks off the grill, place on a platter. Let steaks rest for 5 minutes and serve right away.

Ribeye Steaks W/ Grilled Corn Salsa

Serves: 4

4 (10 ounces) ribeye steaks. 1 1/2 inches thick

2 tablespoons olive oil -OR- canola oil

2 teaspoons kosher salt

1/2 teaspoon freshly ground black pepper

Grilled Corn Salsa

Brush both sides of the steaks with olive oil -OR- canola oil. Sprinkle both sides of the steaks with kosher salt and black pepper. Let the steaks stand at room temperature for 20-25 minutes.

Preheat a gas -OR- charcoal grill to direct medium-high heat

Place the steaks on the grill rack, close the grill lid. Grill the steaks over direct medium-high heat for 9-11 minutes (medium-rare to medium), turning only once. COOK to the desired doneness. Take the steak off the grill and place on a platter. Let the steaks rest at room temperature for 5-7 minutes. Serve right away.

Grilled Corn Salsa

Vinaigrette for Grilled Corn Salsa:

2 tablespoons olive oil -OR- canola oil

2 1/2 teaspoons balsamic vinegar

1/4 teaspoon kosher salt - to taste

1/8 teaspoon ground black pepper

2 ears fresh corn on the cob

2 teaspoons olive oil -OR- canola oil

1/2 cup ripe tomatoes, finely chopped

1/4 cup red onion, finely chopped

1/4 cup cucumbers, finely chopped

1/4 cup fresh basil, thinly sliced

In a bowl, whisk together 2 tablespoons olive oil, balsamic vinegar, salt and pepper, set aside.

Lightly brush 2 teaspoons of oil onto the corn on the cob.

Preheat a gas -OR- charcoal grill for direct medium heat

Place the corn on the grill rack, close the lid. Grill the corn over direct medium heat until tender and lightly charred, turning often. Set aside and let COOL.

With a sharp knife cut the kernels from corn into a bowl. Stir in the tomatoes, onions, cucumbers, fresh basil and the vinaigrette. Serve right away with the Ribeye Steaks.

Airplane Hanger Steaks

Serves: 4

4 (8 ounces each) hanger steaks

Airplane Marinade:

2 1/2 cups balsamic vinegar

1 1/3 cups brown sugar

1/2 cup Worcestershire Sauce

1 tablespoons kosher salt

In a bowl, whisk together 2 cups balsamic vinegar, brown sugar, Worcestershire sauce and 1 tablespoon of kosher salt. Mix well until the brown sugar has dissolved. Place the hanger steaks in a resealable large plastic freezer bag. Pour the Airplane Marinade over the steaks, seal bag and turn bag to coat the steaks. Marinate the hanger steaks in the refrigerator 4 hours -OR- overnight. In a saucepan heat 1/2 cup balsamic vinegar. Bring to a boil and then reduce by half. Set aside and allow to COOL. The vinegar will begin to thicken as it COOLS.

Preheat a gas -OR- charcoal grill to direct high heat.

Remove the steaks from the marinade. Place the steaks on a hot grill rack over high heat.

COOK steaks for around 3-4 minutes per side basting often with thickened balsamic vinegar. Grill until done (rare to medium rare), remove steaks from the grill and let rest for 5 minutes.

Serve Right Away.

Spicy Lime Pesto Flat Iron Steaks

Serves: 4

Spicy Lime Pesto:

1/3 cup store bought prepared basil pesto sauce

1 tablespoon fresh lime juice

2 teaspoons freshly grated lime zest

1/4 - 1/2 teaspoon crushed hot red pepper flakes

4 beef shoulder top blade (flat iron) steaks (8 ounces each)

4 garlic cloves, crushed in a garlic press

kosher salt -OR- sea salt

In a bowl, combine the pesto sauce, lime juice, lime zest, and crushed red pepper flakes. Set aside. Press garlic evenly on both sides of each flat iron steak.

Preheat a gas -OR- charcoal grill for direct medium-high heat.

Place the steaks on the grill rack over medium-high heat, close grill lid. Grill for 9-14 minutes for medium rare, don't COOK over medium doneness, turning only once. Season with salt to taste. Let steaks rest for 5-6 minutes, then top steaks with lime pesto. Serve right away.

*Tip: The flat iron -OR- blade steak is the best cut of the chuck cuts of beef. This type of steak, must be grilled fast to keep it tender. Buy Certified Angus Beef -OR- Choice -OR- Prime Beef.

LT's Grilled Flank Steak

Serves: 4-6

1 (1 1/2 - 2 pounds) Flank Steak garlic powder, to taste kosher salt, to taste freshly ground black pepper, to taste

1/3 cup soy sauce -OR- teriyaki sauce

1/3 cup fresh orange juice

3 tablespoons olive oil -OR- canola oil

Place the flank steak on a flat surface and prick both sides all over with a fork. Sprinkle both sides lightly with the garlic powder, season both sides with salt and pepper, set aside.

In a bowl, combine the soy sauce -OR- teriyaki sauce, orange juice and oil, mix well. Place the steak in a resealable large plastic freezer bag. Pour the marinade over the steaks, seal bag, turn the bag to coat the steak with marinade. Marinate overnight in the refrigerator.

Preheat a gas -OR- charcoal grill for direct medium-high heat.

Remove the steaks from marinade, place the steak on the grill over medium-hot coals. Grill for around 7-9 minutes for medium-rare, turning only once.

Take the steak off the grill, let rest for 5-6 minutes on a cutting board. With a sharp knife slice thinly across the grain, serve right away!

Go Long Flank Steak W/ Grilled Onions

Serves: 4 hungry people

1 (1-1/4 to 1-1/2 pounds) Flank Steak

8 slices red onion, 1/2" inch thick each

kosher salt - to taste

freshly ground black pepper - to taste

Vegetable oil for brushing on the grill rack

Preheat a gas -OR- charcoal grill for direct high heat

Brush the grill rack with vegetable oil

To season, sprinkle the salt and pepper on both sides of the flank steak and onion slices. Place steak and onion slices on the grill rack, over direct high heat. COOK the onions for around 6 minutes or until tender, turning only once. COOK the flank steak for 9-12 minutes for medium rare or desired doneness, turning only once. Take steak and onion slices off of the grill. Let the steak rest on a cutting board for 5-7 minutes. With a sharp knife slice the steak at an angle (on the bias) very thin slices, serve steak with the grilled onions and your favorite steak sauce.

Also serve with grilled potatoes, tossed salad and freshly baked bread.

*Tip: But good quality flank steak, use Choice -OR- Prime and if you can buy Certified Angus Beef !

Grilled Skirt Steak Fajitas

Serves: 6 (2 fajitas per person)

5 garlic cloves, finely chopped & mashed to a paste W/ kosher salt

1/4 cup fresh lime juice

1 1/2 teaspoons ground cumin

2 tablespoons olive oil -OR- canola oil

2 pounds trimmed skirt steak & cut into large pieces to fit your grill

3 green & red bell peppers, sliced thin

1 large red onion, sliced thin

1/4 cup fresh cilantro sprigs

12 each (7" -OR- 8") flour tortillas, warmed

Sides:

Tomato Salsa

Guacamole

Sour Cream

Fresh Lime Wedges

Combine the garlic, lime juice, cumin and oil in a resealable large plastic freezer bag. Seal the bag and shake to mix well. Place the skirt steak, peppers, onion and cilantro sprigs into the bag, squeeze all the air out of the bag. Seal bag, turn the bag to coat the steak and the vegetables evenly. Refrigerate the steak & vegetables overnight to allow it to marinate.

Preheat a gas -OR- charcoal grill for direct high heat

Remove the skirt steak from the marinade and place on a platter, reserve the marinade and vegetables, set aside.

Preheat a heavy skillet to the smoking point. Drain peppers, onion & cilantro, and quickly stir-fry over high heat until almost charred and soft, but not mushy. Set aside and keep warm.

Place the skirt steak on the grill rack over high heat until medium rare, around 2-3 minutes per side. Take steak off of the grill, let rest on a cutting board for 5 minutes. With a sharp knife slice the meat against the grain into thin strips and serve right away with warm tortillas, stir-fry pepper mixture, salsa, guacamole, sour cream and lime wedges.

Southwest Steak W/ Black Beans

Makes: 4 Servings

SW Steak Rub:

2 teaspoons garlic salt

2 teaspoons chili powder

1/4 teaspoon ground hot red (cayenne) pepper - to taste

1 (1-1/2 pounds) boneless sirloin steak, trimmed (1" inch thick)

Vegetable oil for brushing on grill rack.

1 teaspoon olive oil -OR- canola oil

1 cup fresh red -OR- green bell peppers, finely chopped

2-3 garlic cloves, crushed in a garlic press

1 fresh jalapeno pepper, seeded, ribbed, finely chopped

1/2 cup store bought jar -OR- bottled chunky red salsa

1 (15 ounce) can black beans, rinsed & drained

1/4 cup fresh cilantro, finely chopped

In a bowl, combine the garlic salt, chili powder and red pepper. Remove 1 teaspoon of the SW steak rub and set aside. Sprinkle remaining SW steak rub evenly over steaks, pressing (rubbing) the SW steak rub into the steak. Let the steak stand at room temperature for 30 minutes before grilling.

Preheat a gas -OR- charcoal grill for direct high heat.

Brush vegetable oil onto the grill rack.

Place the steak on the grill rack over direct high heat, close grill lid, COOK for 6-8 minutes for medium rare -OR- cooked to desired doneness, turning only once. Take steak off the grill, let rest on a cutting board for 5-6 minutes, cut into very thin slices. Serve with black beans and freshly baked cornbread.

In a saucepan, add the oil, over medium-high heat, until the oil is hot. Add the bell peppers and crushed garlic and sauté around 4 minutes. Add the reserved SW steak rub mixture, jalapeno pepper, salsa and black beans. COOK for 1-2 minutes or until hot, stirring constantly.

To Serve: on each of 4 plates, place 1/2 cup bean mixture, place very thin slices of beef over bean mixture.

Top each serving with about 1 tablespoon of fresh cilantro.

*Tip: Always use quality ingredients for best results. I'm a huge fan of Certified Angus Beef, always use Choice -OR- Prime Beef when grilling!

Sirloin Steak W/ Grilled Tomato Salsa

Serves: 4

1 (1-1/2 pounds) boneless sirloin steak, 1-1/2" inches thick

1/2 teaspoon salt - to taste

1/8 teaspoon ground black pepper

Grilled Tomato Salsa:

2 large ripe tomatoes (1 pound), cored, cut in half horizontally & seeded.

Vegetable Oil for brushing on the grill rack.

1/2 cup red onions, thinly sliced

1-1/2 tablespoons red wine vinegar

1-1/2 tablespoons olive oil

1/4 teaspoon salt - to taste

1/8 teaspoon freshly ground black pepper - to taste

8 basil leaves, thinly sliced

Sprinkle salt and pepper on both sides of the steak. With a sharp knife cut the ripe tomatoes, place the tomato halves, cut sides down, on paper towels. Let the steak and tomatoes stand at room temperature for 30-45 minutes before grilling.

Preheat a gas -OR- charcoal grill for direct high heat.

Brush the grill rack with vegetable oil

Place the tomatoes on the grill rack, cut sides down, over direct high heat for 3-5 minutes. Turn the tomato halves over and grill for around 1 more minute. Remove from grill and COOL for 5-7 minutes. Cut the tomato halves into 1" inch pieces. In a bowl, combine tomato pieces, onion, vinegar, oil, salt, pepper and basil. Place the steak on the grill rack over direct high heat, close the grill lid. Grill until cooked 9-11 minutes for medium-rare or desired doneness. Take the steak off the grill let rest for 5-6 minutes on a cutting board. With a sharp knife cut the steak into very thin slices. Toss the grilled salsa and serve with the steak right away.

South of the Border Tri-Tip Steak

Serves: 6-8

3-4 pounds Beef Tri-Tip with most of the fat trimmed off

Tequila Marinade:

1/3 cup good quality Tequila

3 tablespoons sesame oil

2 tablespoons spicy brown mustard

1 1/2 tablespoons balsamic vinegar

3 garlic cloves, crushed in a garlic press

1 1/2 tablespoons fresh lime juice

1 teaspoon kosher salt - to taste

1 teaspoon freshly ground black pepper

Place the tri-tip steak on a cutting board prick both sides all over with a fork, set aside. In a bowl, whisk together the tequila, sesame oil, mustard, vinegar, garlic, lime juice, salt and pepper, set aside. Place the tri-tip steak in a resealable large plastic bag, pour the tequila marinade over the steak in the bag. Seal bag and refrigerate overnight and turn the bag often.

Preheat a gas -OR- charcoal grill for direct high heat.

Place the steak top-side down on the grill rack over high heat 3-5 minutes for good grill marks. Reduce the heat to medium heat (or move to a cooler place on the grill rack), turn the meat over and close the grill lid. Grill for 20-25 minutes or until a meat thermometer inserted in the center reads 135-140 degrees F for medium, don't over cook. Let rest on a platter for 5 minutes.

Slice very thinly and serve right away.

Teriyaki Lamb Steaks

Serves: 4

4 each Lamb round steaks, around 6 ounces each

Teriyaki Marinade:

1 cup teriyaki sauce

1/4 cup fresh orange juice

2 tablespoons brown sugar

1/2 teaspoon ground ginger

1/2 teaspoon nutmeg

In a bowl, combine the teriyaki sauce, orange juice, brown sugar, ginger and nutmeg, mix well.

Place the lamb steaks in a resealable large plastic bag and pour the teriyaki marinade over the lamb steaks. Seal the bag and marinate in the refrigerator for at least 4 hours -OR- overnight.

Preheat a gas -OR- charcoal grill for direct medium-high heat.

Lightly brush vegetable oil onto the grill rack.

Place the lamb steaks on the grill rack over medium-high heat and grill for 4-6 minutes per side.

Baste the lamb often with the marinade. COOK, until the lamb reaches the desired doneness.

Take the lamb steaks off the grill and let them rest for 5 minutes. Serve right away!

Big Bob's Top 30 Greatest Soccer Players All Time

Your Top 30 List:

#1.Pele

#2. Maradona

#3. Lev Yashin

#4. Lothar Matthaus

#5. Ferenc Puskas

#6. Franz "The Kaiser" Beckenbauer

#7. Johan Cruyff

#8. Eusebio de Silva Ferreira

#9. Bobby Charlton

#10. Stanley Matthews

#11. Alfredo Di Stefano

#12. Ronaldo

#13. Roberto Baggio

#14. Marco van Basten

#15. Michel Platini

#16. Ruud Gullit

#17. Peter Schmeichel

#18. Gabriel "OMAR" Batistuta

#19. ZICO (Artur Antunes Coimbra)

#20. Zbigniew Boniek

#21. George Best

#22. Gordon Banks

#23. Eric Cantona

#24. Teofilo Cubillas

TIE #25. Geoff Hurst

TIE #25. Kenny Dalglish

#26. Robbie Fowler

#27. Zinedine Zidane

#28. Zagallo

TIE #29. Johan Nieskens

TIE #29. Ian Rush

TIE #30. Carlos Valderama

TIE #30. Rivelino

Big Bob's Top 9 Best World Cup Teams All Time

Your Top 9 List:

#1. Brazil 1970

#2. Brazil 1958

#3. Italy 1982

#4. Argentina 1986

#5. West Germany 1974

#6. Hungary 1954

#7. England 1966

#8. Italy 1938

#9. The Netherlands 1974

_____

_____

_____

_____

_____

_____

_____

_____

_____

Big Bob's Top 10 World Cup Players Performances All Time

Your Top 10 List:

#1. Pele 1958

#2. Maradona 1986

#3. Eusebio 1966

#4. Gerd Muller 1970

#5. Zindine Zidane 1998

#6. Paolo Rossi 1982

#7. Just Fontaine 1958

#8. Garrincha 1962

#9. Sandor Kocsis 1954

#10. Giuseppe Meazza 1934

_____

_____

_____

_____

_____

_____

_____

_____

_____

_____

Big Bob's Top 10 Greatest Women's Soccer Players All Time

#1. Mia Hamm

#2. Rosely

#3. Kristine Lilly

#4. Julie Foudy

TIE #5. Michelle Akers

TIE #5. Shannon MacMillan

#6. Tiffeny Milbrett

#7. Debbie Keller

#8. Joy Fawcett

#9. Brandi Chastain

TIE #10. Carla Overbeck

TIE #10. Tisha Venturini

Your Top 10 List:

_____

_____

_____

_____

_____

_____

_____

_____

_____

_____

_____

Soccer Ball

by: Elizabeth
age 8

Notes

CHAPTER #8

Burgers

and

Dogs

COLLEGE BASKETBALL

GRILL

MASTER

AT

WORK

Greek Certified Angus Beef Burger

Serves: 6

2 pounds Certified Angus Beef ground chuck

kosher salt - to taste

ground black pepper - to taste

6 each Kaiser Rolls

1/2 stick (2 ounce) melted butter

6 slices red onion

6 slices beefsteak tomato

1 cup crumbled feta cheese

1/2 cup store bought prepared olive tapenade

In a bowl, season the beef with salt and pepper, lightly mix.

Shape the meat into 6 round equal portion patties.

Preheat a gas -OR- charcoal grill for direct medium-high heat.

Lightly brush the grill rack with vegetable oil.

Place the patties on the grill rack over medium-high heat. Grill the burgers to the desired doneness. Brush the Kaiser rolls with butter and toast on the outer edges of the grill rack. Take the burgers and rolls off the grill when done.

To Assemble: Place down a toasted roll bottom, add a onion and tomato slice onto each roll. Add a burger and top with the feta cheese and the olive tapenade. If you want, you can add a lettuce leaf or 2.

Serve right away !!!

Grilled Buffalo Bills Burgers

Makes: 8 Buffalo Bills Burgers

2 pounds ground buffalo meat

2 cups store bought barbecue sauce (your favorite)

1-2 teaspoons kosher salt - to taste

1/2 teaspoon ground black pepper - to taste

1/2 teaspoon garlic powder

8 each hamburger buns

8 romaine lettuce leaves

8 slices red onion

8 large slices ripe tomato, mayo & vegetable oil for brushing on the grill

Preheat a gas -OR- charcoal grill for direct medium-high heat

Lightly brush vegetable oil onto the grill rack

Shape the Buffalo meat into 8 equal 1 1/2" thick patties. Season each patty with salt, pepper and garlic powder and place the patties on the grill rack. Brush the top of patty with your favorite barbecue sauce and Cook for around 4 minutes. Turn the burger over, brush the burgers with barbecue sauce again and COOK for 3-5 minutes more. Grill to the desired doneness, take the burgers off the grill when done.

To Assemble: Place down a bun bottom, add a lettuce leaf and a burger, add a onion and a tomato slice. Spread mayo on the cut side of the top bun and place the bun top on the tomato slice.

Serve right away!

Curried Lamb Burgers W/ Cucumber Mint Yogurt Sauce

Makes: 8 Curried Lamb Burgers

2 pounds ground lamb

onion salt- to taste

garlic salt - to taste

1/2 cup softened unsalted butter

1 1/2 teaspoons curry powder

8 hamburger buns

Cucumber Mint Yogurt Sauce

8 large sweet onion slices

8 large ripe tomato slices

8 romaine lettuce leaves

Shape the lamb into 8 equal patties. Season both sides of the lamb patties with onion and garlic salt. Let the patties stand at room temperature for 15-30 minutes before grilling time.

Preheat a gas -OR- charcoal grill for direct medium-high heat

Lightly brush the grill rack with vegetable oil.

Place the lamb patties on the grill rack over medium-high heat and COOK for 14-18 minutes.

Grill the lamb burgers to the desired doneness, turning only once. Take the burgers off the grill when done and place on a platter. In a bowl, combine the softened unsalted butter and curry powder, mix well. Brush the curry butter on both sides of the hot lamb burgers. Serve burgers with mint yogurt sauce, onion, tomato, lettuce on a hamburger bun.

Cucumber Mint Yogurt Sauce

Makes: 2 1/4 cups

2 each (8-ounce) containers plain yogurt

2 medium cucumbers, peeled, seeded, finely chopped

3 tablespoon fresh mint, chopped

4 teaspoon white wine vinegar

2 garlic cloves, crushed in a garlic press, dash white pepper - to taste and dash salt - to taste

In a bowl, combine all of the ingredients together, mix well. Cover and refrigerate - before serving.

Spicy Southwest Turkey Burger

Serves: 4

Chipotle Ketchup:

1/2 cup ketchup

1 (7ounce) can chipotle peppers in adobo sauce

Turkey Burgers:

1 pound ground turkey

1/3 cup bread crumbs

1/4 cup fresh cilantro, finely chopped

1/4 cup shredded Parmesan Cheese

1/4 teaspoon salt - to taste

1/4 teaspoon black pepper - to taste

Vegetable oil to brush on the grill rack

4 hamburger buns

4 romaine lettuce leaves

4 large slices ripe beefsteak tomato mayo - to taste

Remove 2 chilies & 2 teaspoons adobo sauce from the can. Set aside and store for another day the remaining peppers and sauce. Finely chop the peppers. In a bowl, combine the finely chopped peppers, adobo sauce and ketchup, mix well. Set aside.

In a bowl, combine the turkey, bread crumbs, fresh cilantro, cheese, salt and pepper. Mix lightly with your hands, do not overwork the meat mixture. Shape meat into 4 patties, around 1" inch thick.

Preheat a gas -OR- charcoal grill for direct medium heat. Lightly brush the grill rack with vegetable oil.

Place turkey burgers on the grill rack over medium heat and close grill lid. Grill the turkey burgers for 9-14 minutes, turning only once. COOK, turkey burgers until fully cooked, but not dried out. Take burgers off the grill when done, place on buns and top to your liking. Serve Right Away !!!

Spicy Burgers W/ Tomato-Avocado Salsa

Serves: 6

2 pounds ground chuck

2 teaspoons chipotle Chile powder

1-2 teaspoons kosher salt - to taste

Vegetable oil to brush on the grill rack

6 toasted English muffins

Tomato-Avocado Salsa

mayo

6 romaine lettuce leaves

In a bowl, combine beef, Chile powder and salt, mix lightly. Divide meat mixture into 6 patties, do not over work the meat mixture. Cover and refrigerate for at least 1 hour or more.

Preheat a gas -OR- charcoal grill for direct medium heat

Brush vegetable oil onto the grill rack.

Place the patties on the grill rack over medium heat, close the grill lid. Grill for 8-11 minutes for medium doneness, turning only once. Place English muffins cut side down on the edges of the grill rack, grill 1 minute -OR- until toasted. Take burgers off the grill, place 1 patty on the bottom half of each muffin; top each burger with Tomato-Avocado Salsa, lettuce and mayo. Top with muffin half and serve right away.

Tomato-Avocado Salsa

2 cups peeled, ripe tomatoes, chopped

1 cup onion, chopped

1/2 cup fresh cilantro, chopped

1/2 cup ripe avocado, peeled, chopped

2-3 tablespoons fresh lime juice

1/2 teaspoon kosher salt

2 fresh garlic cloves, crushed in a garlic press

Great Salsa to serve with Burgers & Chips!

In a bowl, combine all of the ingredients together, mix gently. Serve right away.

Pizza Burgers

Makes: 8 burgers

2 pounds ground beef 80% - 85% lean

1/3 cup grated Parmesan cheese

1/4 cup onion, finely chopped

1/4 cup canned pitted ripe olives, chopped

2 fresh garlic cloves, crushed in a garlic press

1 teaspoon kosher salt - to taste

dash pepper - to taste

1 teaspoon dried oregano, crushed

1 teaspoon dried basil, crushed

1 (6 ounce) can tomato paste

8 slices mozzarella cheese

8-16 slices fresh plum (ROMA) tomato

16 slices toasted Italian Bread

Great Burgers for Summer Friday Nights!

In a bowl, combine the beef, cheese, onion, olives, garlic, salt, pepper, oregano, basil and tomato paste, mix lightly. Shape into 8 oval patties to fit Italian bread slices. Let patties stand at room temperature for 15-30 minutes before grilling time.

Preheat a gas -OR- charcoal grill for direct medium heat lightly brush vegetable oil onto the grill rack.

Place burgers on the grill rack over medium heat, COOK for 5-7 minutes. Turn over burgers; top each burger with cheese and tomato. Grill for 5 minutes more -OR- to desired doneness.

Toast 16 slices of Italian bread that where sliced at a angle, grill on the outer edges of the grill rack until toasted.

Serve burgers on toasted Italian bread, right away.

Knock-Out Burgers

Makes: 4 burgers

1 pound ground beef 80%-85% lean

1/4 cup Worcestershire sauce

1/4 cup onion, finely chopped

2 tablespoons fresh cilantro leaves, chopped

1/4 teaspoon kosher salt - to taste

1/8 teaspoon freshly ground black pepper

4 toasted hamburger rolls -OR- toasted English muffins

4 onion slices

4 tomato slices

4 lettuce leaves

Ketchup - to taste

Mayo - to taste

Great Burger for All Types of Sporting Events!

In a bowl, lightly mix the beef, Worcestershire sauce, onion, cilantro, salt and pepper, mix together. Shape into 4 patties and let stand at room temperature for 15-30 minutes before grilling time.

Preheat a gas -OR- charcoal grill for direct medium heat.

Lightly brush vegetable oil onto the grill rack.

Place burgers on the grill rack over medium heat. Grill until burgers reach the desired doneness.

When burgers are done cooking, take them off the grill. Toast the buns on the outer edges of the grill rack. Serve the burgers right away on toasted buns with onion, tomato, lettuce, ketchup and mayo.

Blue Blitz Burgers

Makes: 8 burgers

2 pounds ground beef

1/3 cup onions, finely chopped

1/3 cup blue cheese, crumbled

2 teaspoons kosher salt - to taste

1 tablespoon Worcestershire Sauce

vegetable oil to brush on the grill rack

8 toasted English muffins -OR- hamburger buns

8 red onion slices

8 ripe tomato slices

8 lettuce leaves

Ketchup - to taste

Mayo - to taste

In a bowl, combine the beef, onion, blue cheese, salt and Worcestershire sauce, mix lightly.

Shape the beef into 8 patties. Let patties stand at room temperature for 15-30 minutes before grilling time.

Preheat a gas -Or- charcoal grill for direct medium heat.

Lightly brush the grill rack with vegetable oil.

Grill burgers over medium-hot coals 5 minutes, turn over and grill 5 more minutes -OR- to desired doneness. Toast muffin -OR- buns on the outer edge of the grill rack, cut side down.

Grill until toasted around 1 minute -OR- until done toasting. Take burgers off the grill, place on toasted muffins -OR- buns. Serve the burgers with onion, tomato, lettuce, ketchup and mayo.

Sloppy Joes

Makes: 10 Sloppy Joes

2 pounds ground beef

2 each onions, chopped (1 cup)

1 cup ketchup

2/3 cup green bell peppers, chopped

2/3 cup celery, chopped

1/2 cup water

2 tablespoons Worcestershire Sauce

2 teaspoons kosher salt - to taste

1/4 teaspoon hot red pepper sauce - to taste

10 each toasted buns

Will help feed your whole gang!

Cook, stir beef & onion in a skillet until ground beef is light brown; drain. Stir in ketchup, celery, green bell peppers, water, Worcestershire sauce, salt and hot sauce, mix well. Cover and COOK, over low heat until vegetables are tender, around 10-15 minutes, stir often. Fill toasted buns with hot sloppy Joe mixture.

NY Coney Island Hot Dog Sauce

1 1/2 pounds Ground Beef

1 large onion, finely chopped

32 ounces tomato puree

1 cup light brown sugar

2 tablespoons apple cider vinegar

2 teaspoon prepared yellow mustard (I like French's)

2 teaspoons salt

1 1/2 teaspoons chili powder

1 teaspoon celery seed

Best Coney Sauce on Dogs; Add Fresh Chopped Onions & Yellow Mustard on Top!

In a big skillet, add beef and onions, cook until very lightly brown. Make sure to break up the ground beef as fine as possible. Drain all the fat off and set skillet to the side. In a big saucepan, combine all of the remaining ingredients and COOK, over medium heat for 11-16 minutes, stir often. Add the browned beef and onions. Stir, mix well, lower heat to low, SIMMER for 2-2 1/2 hours, stir often. Use right away or COOL, store in the refrigerator 1-2 weeks -OR- freeze for 1-2 month's.

Easy Coney Sauce for Frankfurters

Makes: Sauce for 8 or more franks

1/2 pound ground beef

1/4 cup onions - finely chopped

1/4 cup water

1 garlic clove, crushed with a garlic press

1 (8 ounce) can tomato sauce

1/2 teaspoon chili powder

1/2 teaspoon salt

8 each frankfurters (W/ natural casing, I like Nathan's Famous)

8 each toasted hot dog buns, fresh raw onions, chopped, ballpark prepared mustard, Coney Sauce above

In a skillet brown beef slowly over medium-low heat, break up beef with a fork until fine. Add onion, water, garlic, tomato sauce, chili powder and salt. Lower heat to low, SIMMER, uncovered 10-12 minutes, stir often, Make sure the sauce is heated through. Use right away!

Grill the franks over medium-high heat until done. Serve on a toasted bun, top with mustard, Coney sauce and raw chopped fresh onions.

Chili & Cheese Dogs

Makes: Coney Sauce for 8 or more Dogs

2 tablespoons canola oil -OR- olive oil

1 medium onion - finely chopped

1 pound ground beef

1 cup ketchup

1 tablespoon prepared yellow mustard

1 teaspoon chili powder, kosher salt - to taste, ground black pepper - to taste

8 (2 ounce size) all beef hot dogs

8 toasted hot dog buns yellow mustard - to taste (I like French's) chili sauce - above

1 cup shredded cheddar cheese

fresh raw onions, chopped

Great Chili & Cheese Dogs, Serve W/ Root beer Floats & enjoy.

Chili: In a skillet heat the oil over medium heat. When the oil has a haze, add the onion and COOK. Stir the onions until they are soft and translucent, around 5-6 minutes. Add the ground beef break it up with a fork, until fine and COOK until light browned, around 10-12 minutes, stir often. Stir in the ketchup, mustard and chili powder; lower the heat to low, SIMMER for 14-16 minutes, until thick, stir often. Season the chili with salt and pepper to taste. Use Right Away!

Grilled Hot Dogs: While the chili is cooking, the chili is a good item to place on the side burner of a gas grill. Grill the hot dogs on the grill rack over medium-high heat, COOK until done, don't burn the dogs. Toast hot dog buns on the outer edges of the grill rack.

To Serve: Place a grilled hot dog on a toasted bun, put yellow mustard, chili, some cheddar cheese and top with chopped raw fresh onion.

Nothing is Better than a Great Grilled Hot Dog.

Hot Dog Beer Chili Sauce

Weekend Big Game Slow Cooker Recipe:

2 pounds ground beef

2 cups chopped onion

3-4 tablespoons chili powder

2 cups ketchup

1 (15 ounce) can tomato sauce

1 (12 ounce) can beer (1 1/2 cups)

4-5 tablespoons prepared yellow mustard

In a big skillet brown beef and onions over medium heat, until the meat is no longer pink. Stir the meat to separate, drain fat, stir in the chili powder and put the meat mixture into a 5-quart slow cooker. Add the ketchup, tomato sauce, beer and mustard, mix well. COVER, COOK, on LOW for 3 hours.

Serve on top of hot dogs and top with mustard, chopped fresh raw onions and shredded Cheddar Cheese.

BIG GAME CORN DOGS

Serves: 8 hungry sports fans

2 pounds Hot Dogs

vegetable oil

2 cups All-Purpose Flour

4 tablespoons yellow cornmeal

3 teaspoons baking soda

1 teaspoon salt

6 tablespoons shortening

1 1/2 cups milk

2 eggs, beaten

Using paper towels pat dry the hot dogs.

Heat the vegetable oil (3 inches thick) to 360 degrees F.

In a bowl, mix flour, cornmeal, baking soda and salt. Cut in the shortening. Stir in milk and eggs.

Dip hot dogs into batter, allow excess batter to drip off into a bowl. FRY, turning once, until brown, around 5-6 minutes, take out and drain on paper towels. Insert a wooden skewer into the end of each corn dog. Serve right away with mustard and ketchup.

I like just mustard on my corn dog!

Big Bob's Top 10 Best NCAA College Basketball Programs All Time

Your Top 10 List:

#1. UCLA Bruins

#2. DUKE Blue Devils

#3. UNC Tar heels

#4. KENTUCKY Wildcats

#5. KANSAS Jayhawks

#6. INDIANA Hoosiers

#7. UCONN Huskies

#8. GEORGETOWN Hoyas

#9. MSU Spartans

#10. MARYLAND Terrapins

Basketball and Hoop

by: Elizabeth
age 9

Big Bob's Top 30 Greatest College Basketball Players All Time

Your Top 30 List:

#1. Lew Alcindor

#2. Pistol Pete

#3. Wilt

#4. Bill Walton

#5. Magic Johnson

#6. Christian Laettner

#7. Larry Bird

#8. Patrick Ewing

#9. David Thompson

TIE#10. Jerry West

TIE #10. Jerry Lucas

#11. Oscar Robertson

#12. Danny Manning

#13. Isiah Thomas

#14. Michael Jordan

#15. Bill Russell

#16. George Mikan

#17. David Robinson

#18. Elvin Hayes

#19. Grant Hill

#20. Tim Duncan

#21. James Worthy

#22. Elgin Baylor

#23. John Havlicek

#24. Ralph Sampson

#25. Bill Bradley

#26. Phil Ford

#27. Chris Mullen

#28. Bobby Hurley

#29. Sam Perkins

TIE #30. Danny Ferry

TIE #30. Scott May

Big Bob's Top 45 Greatest NCAA College Basketball Coaches All Time

Coach :	Notable School:	Your Top 45 List:
#1. John Wooden	UCLA	_____
#2. Dean Smith	UNC	_____
#3. Mike Krzyzewski	Duke	_____
#4. Adolph Rupp	Kentucky	_____
#5. Everett Dean	Stanford	_____
#6. Ed Jucker	Cincinnati	_____
#7. Kenneth Loeffler	La Salle	_____
#8. Phil Woolpert	USF	_____
#9. Fred Taylor	Ohio State	_____
#10. Bobby Knight	Indiana(TIE)	_____
#10. Branch McCracken	Indiana(TIE)	_____
#11. Bud Foster	Wisconsin	_____
#12. Phog Allen	Kansas	_____
#13. Pete Newell	Cal	_____
#14. Larry Brown	Kansas	_____
#15. Rick Pitino	Louisville	_____
#16. Tom Izzo	Michigan State	_____
#17. Roy Williams	UNC(TIE)	_____
#17. Vic Bubas	Duke(TIE)	_____
#18. Steve Fisher	Michigan	_____
#19. Jim Calhoun	Connecticut	_____
#20. Tubby Smith	Kentucky(TIE)	_____
#20. Hank Iba	Oklahoma A&M(TIE)	_____
#21. George Ireland	Loyola-Chicago	_____
#22. Doggie Julian	Holy Cross	_____
#23. Harold Combes	Illinois	_____
#24. Harold Olsen	Ohio State	_____
#25. John Thompson	Georgetown	_____
#26. Joe B. Hall	Kentucky	_____
#27. Al McGuire	Marquette	_____
#28. Jerry Tarkanian	UNLV	_____
#29. Gary Williams	Maryland	_____
#30. Jimmy V.	NC State(TIE)	_____
#30. Rollie Massimino	Villanova(TIE)	_____
#31. Nat Holman	CCNY	_____

#32. Denny Crum   Louisville   _____

#33. Lute Olson   Arizona   _____

#34. Nolan Richardson   Arkansas   _____

#35. Jim Boeheim   Syracuse   _____

#36. Jud Healthcote   Michigan State   _____

#37. Harold Hobson   YALE   _____

#38. Jim Harrick   UCLA   _____

#39. Ray Meyer   DePaul   _____

#40. Don Haskins   UTEP   _____

#41. Digger Phelps   Notre Dame   _____

#42. Lou Henson   Illinois   _____

#43. Lou Carnesecca   St. Johns   _____

#44. Norm Stewart   Missouri   _____

#45. Eddie Sutton   OSU   _____

After this list you now are sure I'm crazy! No way this list is not only about overall record. I judged mostly on March Madness and how well each coach did in the Final Four. So the coaches at the top of the list do there best work in Crunch Time when it really counts!

Notes

Notes

CHAPTER #9

Poultry

HORSE RACING

Dr. Pepper BBQ Grilled Chicken

Makes: 6-8 servings

1 (12 ounce) can Dr. Pepper

1 cup ketchup

1/4 cup packed brown sugar

2 1/2 tablespoons prepared mustard

1 1/2 tablespoons soy sauce

1 tablespoon fresh lime juice

1/2 teaspoon ground black pepper - to taste

1/2 teaspoon salt - to taste

2-3 garlic cloves, crushed in a garlic press

4 pounds split chicken breast

In a bowl, combine the Dr. Pepper, ketchup, brown sugar, mustard, soy sauce, lime juice, black pepper, salt and garlic. Bring to a boil, reduce the heat and SIMMER for 30 minutes, stir often. LET COOL.

Place the chicken in a large resealable freezer bag. Pour 1/2 of the sauce over the chicken in bag, seal bag. Let the chicken stand at room temperature for 30-45 minutes to marinate turn the bag to coat the chicken often.

Preheat a gas -OR- charcoal grill for direct medium-high heat

Place the chicken on the grill rack over medium-hot coals, close the grill lid. COOK for around 35-45 minutes, until a meat thermometer inserted in the thickest part registers 175-180 degrees F, turning chicken often. In the final minutes of grilling brush the chicken with the remaining BBQ sauce. Take the chicken off the grill and serve right away.

Sun Devil "SPICY" JAVA BBQ Chicken

Serves: 4

1/3 cup brewed very strong black coffee

6 tablespoons unsalted butter

3 tablespoons teriyaki sauce

2 tablespoons ground hot chili powder

1 tablespoon ketchup

1 tablespoon packed brown sugar

1/4 teaspoon salt - to taste

4 pounds chicken, cut into serving pieces

To make the BBQ Sauce:

In a big saucepan, combine the coffee, butter, teriyaki sauce, chili powder, ketchup, brown sugar and salt. Bring to a boil, reduce the heat to medium-low heat. SIMMER uncovered for 9-16 minutes. Set aside.

To Grill the BBQ Chicken:

Preheat a gas -OR- charcoal grill to direct medium heat

Position the grill rack 5" inches above your heat source.

Place the chicken pieces on the grill rack, skin side up, over medium heat. COOK for 50-60 minutes turning only once. Brush the BBQ sauce on the chicken during the final 15 minutes of grilling. COOK the chicken to a internal temperature of 175-180 or more degrees F., don't touch the bone when using the meat thermometer. Also to test for doneness, you can insert tip of a sharp knife into the largest chicken breast. If the juices run clear and the knife tip is hot, the chicken is done. Take the chicken pieces off the grill when done and serve right away!

Big Bob's BBQ Chicken Sandwich

Makes: 8 BBQ Chicken Sandwiches

1 cup Zesty Italian Salad Dressing (I Like Kraft)

8 small boneless skinless chicken breasts halves (2 pounds)

1 cup store bought Original barbecue sauce (I like Kraft)

3 tablespoons honey

1 tablespoon prepared spicy brown mustard

8 slices, American Cheese (I like Kraft singles -OR- The cheese singles on Sale that week.)

8 hamburger buns

8-16 thin slices red onion

8 large slices ripe tomato

8 Romaine lettuce leaves

Mayo - to taste

Place the chicken in a large resealable freezer bag, pour the Italian Dressing over the chicken.

Seal the bag, turn the bag to coat the chicken with marinade. Place the bag in the refrigerator for 6-24 hours to marinate. (Don't marinate more than 24 hours.)

Preheat a gas -OR- charcoal grill to direct medium heat Lightly brush vegetable oil onto the grill rack.

In a bowl, combine the barbecue sauce, honey and mustard, mix well; set aside.

Take the chicken out of the marinade and throw out the marinade. Place the chicken on the grill rack over medium heat. Grill for 13-16 minutes -OR- until proper doneness. COOK to a internal temperature of 175-180 degrees F. During the final minutes of grilling brush BBQ sauce onto both sides of chicken. Top each chicken breast with 1 slice of American cheese and let the cheese melt. Take the chicken off the grill when done. Place chicken in buns and top with onion, tomato, lettuce and spread mayo on the cut side of the top bun.

Serve Right Away, enjoy!!!

BOB'S BEER CAN GRILLED CHICKEN

SERVES: 6-8

Beer Can Dry Rub:

1 cup kosher salt

1/4 cup ground black pepper

1/4 cup garlic powder

1/4 cup onion powder

Beer Can Chicken:

2 whole chickens, around 3 pounds each

2 (12 ounces, each) cans beer

2 sprigs fresh rosemary

In a bowl, combine the salt, pepper, garlic powder and onion powder, mix well. The dry rub will keep in a airtight container (aka: jar) in a dark pantry for up to 6 months.

Preheat a gas -OR- charcoal grill for indirect high heat

Place a drip pan under the chickens.

Wash and drain the chickens. Coat the chickens inside and out with the beer can dry rub, to taste. Open up the cans of beer and pour 1/4 cup from both. Put a sprig of fresh rosemary into both cans. Place the beer cans, keeping them upright, into the rear cavity of the chickens.

Carefully place the chickens, standing up on the beer cans, place on the cool side or unlit part of the grill, over a drip pan. Make sure not to spill any beer, the grill rack must be level.

Close the grill lid and COOK until the chickens are done. They must reach an internal temper - ature of 175-180 degrees F, using a instant read meat thermometer. Grill for around 50-60 minutes, turning the chicken very carefully, as needed. The chickens are done when the juices run clear when the meat is pierced with a sharp knife. Using heavy duty oven mitts carefully remove the beer cans from the chickens, throw out the beer cans. On a clean cutting board using a sharp knife cut the chickens into quarters, Serve right away!!!.

Lime-Thyme Grilled Organic Chicken Breast

Serves: 4-6

Juice of 4 large fresh limes

1/4 cup loosely packed fresh thyme, chopped

3 garlic cloves, crushed in a garlic press, freshly ground black pepper - to taste

3 boneless, skinless Organic Chicken Breast, trimmed and halved.

Vegetable oil for brushing on the grill rack

In bowl, combine the lime juice, fresh thyme, garlic and pepper, mix well. Place the organic chicken breasts in a resealable large plastic freezer bag. Pour the lime juice mixture over the chicken, turn the bag to coat the chicken breast. Seal the bag and marinate the chicken in the refrigerator for 3-6 hours (don't marinate for more than 6 hours).

Preheat a gas -OR- charcoal grill for direct medium-high heat

Lightly brush vegetable oil onto the grill rack.

Take the chicken out of the lime juice marinade, throw out the marinade. Place the chicken breasts on the grill rack over medium-high heat. COOK for 11-16 minutes, turning only once, COOK until done.

Serve right away!!!

Devil Rays Mahogany-Glazed Organic Chicken

Serves: 3-4

3/4 cup (6 ounces) Dark Beer

1/4 cup teriyaki marinade and/or sauce

1 small onion, thinly slice

1/2 tablespoon sea salt -OR- kosher salt

1/2 tablespoon prepared mustard

1 teaspoon sweet paprika

1 each Organic "Fryer" Chicken, 3 pounds

Vegetable oil to brush on the grill rack

1/2 tablespoon molasses

In a bowl, combine the beer, teriyaki sauce, onion, salt, mustard and paprika, mix well. Place one Organic Whole Chicken, breast side down, in a shallow pan and pour the marinade over the chicken. Cover and refrigerate for at least 6 hours -OR- overnight.

Preheat a gas -OR- charcoal grill for indirect medium-high heat. *Tip: When using a gas grill only light one side of the grill!

Always place a drip pan under the chicken!

Lightly brush the grill rack with vegetable oil.

Take the chicken out of the marinade. Put the marinade in a saucepan, set aside. Place the chicken on the cooler part of the grill, set-up for indirect heat grilling, over a drip pan. Close the grill lid and grill for 1 hour and 25 minutes -OR- until the juices run clear when you pierce the thigh meat with a fork -OR- tip of a sharp knife. Insert a instant read thermometer into the thickest part of the thigh meat should be at least 175-

185 degrees F. or higher. Don't let the thermometer touch the bone. Turn the chicken over 4-5 times during the grilling to brown the chicken evenly on all sides.

Bring the marinade in the saucepan to a boil over medium-high heat. Reduce the heat to low, SIMMER until reduced to around 1/2 cup. Stir in the molasses and COOK for 5 more minutes.

Remove 1/4 cup of the marinade and set aside the rest. During the final 5 minutes of grilling, brush the chicken with the 1/4 cup of the marinade. Keep turning the chicken to crisp the skin on all sides. Let the chicken rest for 10 minutes before serving. Serve the chicken with the remaining marinade, serve right away.

Grilled Organic Turkey

Serves: 8

10-12 pound Organic Free-Range Turkey

Vegetable oil for brushing on the grill rack

Canola Oil

Kosher Salt -OR- Sea Salt - to taste

Freshly ground black pepper

3 carrots, coarsely chopped

1 large onion, coarsely chopped

4 garlic cloves, coarsely chopped

3 tablespoons flat leaf parsley, chopped

1 tablespoon fresh sage, chopped

Preheat a gas grill to indirect medium-high heat

Lightly brush vegetable oil onto the grill rack.

Always place a drip pan under the Turkey!

Set a drip pan under the grill rack on the side of the gas grill not turned on, where the turkey will set. Fill the drip pan halfway with water. Place an oven thermometer inside the grill, close the grill lid and let the temperature reach 350 degrees F.

Rub the Organic Turkey inside and out with oil. Season the turkey inside and out with salt and pepper. Stuff the cavity of the with carrots, onion and garlic, parsley and sage.

Poultry

Place the turkey on the grill rack over a drip pan. Close the grill lid and COOK for 2 1/2 - 3 hours, maintain the internal temperature of the gas grill at 325 degrees F. The Turkey is done when a meat thermometer inserted into the thickest part of the thigh meat reaches 175-180 degrees F. and the juices run clear when the thigh meat is pierced with a fork or the tip of a sharp knife.

Big Bob's Top 15 Greatest Jockey's All Time

Your Top 15 List:

#1. Willie Shoemaker _____

#2. Laffit Pincay Jr. _____

#3. Jerry Bailey _____

#4. Eddie Arcaro _____

#5. Angel Cordero Jr. _____

#6. Pat Day _____

#7. Ron Turcotte _____

#8. Chris McCarron _____

#9. Kent Desormeaux _____

TIE #10. Steve Cauthen _____

TIE #10. Lester Piggot _____

#11. Corey Nakatani _____

#12. Julie Krone _____

#13. Pat Eddery _____

#14. Gordon Richards _____

#15. Yves Saint-Martin _____

Big Bob's Top 40 Greatest Thoroughbred Race Horses All Time

Your Top 40 List:

#1. Secretariat

#2. Man O' War

#3. John Henry

#4. Cigar

#5. Seabiscuit

#6. Seattle Slew

#7. War Admiral

#8. Citation

#9. Kelso

TIE #10. Whirlaway

TIE #10. Northern Dancer

#11. Count Fleet

#12. Sir Barton

#13. Gallant Fox

#14. Genuine Risk

#15. Bold Ruler

#16. OMAHA

#17. Bold Forbes

#18. Assault

#19. Holy Bull

#20. Native Dancer

#21. Majestic Prince

#22. Affirmed

#23. Alydar

#24. Spectacular Bid

#25. Ack Ack

#26. Easy Goer

#27. Alysheba

#28. Go for Wand

#29. Ruffian

#30. Foolish Pleasure

#31. Slew O' Gold

#32. Afleet Alex

#33. Personal Ensign

#34. Silver Charm

TIE #35. Winning Colors _____

TIE #35. Peter Pan _____

#36. Sunday Silence _____

#37. Black Gold _____

#38. Cafe Prince _____

TIE #39. UNBRIDLED _____

TIE #39. A.P. Indy _____

TIE #40. Smarty Jones _____

TIE #40. Summer Squall _____

Notes

CHAPTER #10
Grilled Seafood
ICE HOCKEY

Ozzie's Grilled Sesame Shrimp

Serves: 8

2 tablespoons sesame seeds

2 tablespoons sesame oil

5 garlic cloves, crushed in a garlic press

2 tablespoons teriyaki marinade and sauce

2 tablespoons fresh lime juice

40 raw large shrimp, peeled, deviened and tails left on.

16 each (4 lime wedges each of 4 skewers) fresh lime wedges

12-10" inch bamboo skewers, presoaked in a shallow pan of water for 1 hour.

In a bowl, whisk together the sesame seeds, sesame oil, garlic, teriyaki sauce and lime juice. Add the shrimp and toss to coat evenly. Thread 5 shrimp onto each of the 8 presoaked skewers. Cover the shrimp with plastic wrap and place in the refrigerator for 2-4 hours to marinate.

Preheat a gas -OR- charcoal grill for direct medium-high heat Lightly brush vegetable oil onto the grill rack.

Place the shrimp and the lime wedges onto the grill rack over medium-hot heat. COOK until the limes have grill marks on both sides and the shrimp shells are pink and the flesh is opaque, around 3-4 minutes on each side, turning only once. Take the shrimp off the grill and serve on a platter with grilled lime wedges.

Big Daddy's Grilled Garlic Shrimp

Serves:4

1/2 cup olive oil -OR- canola oil juice of 2 fresh limes

6 large garlic cloves, crushed in a garlic press

2 tablespoons fresh cilantro, chopped

20 raw extra large shrimp, peeled, deviened with tails left on

8 (4 lime wedges each of 4 skewers) lime wedges

6-10" bamboo skewers, presoak in a shallow pan of water for 1 hour.

In a bowl, whisk together the oil, fresh lime juice, garlic and fresh cilantro. Add the shrimp and toss to coat evenly. Cover the bowl with plastic wrap and place in the refrigerator for 2 hours to marinate. Thread 5 shrimp onto each presoaked skewer.

Preheat a gas -OR- charcoal grill to direct medium-high heat. Lightly brush vegetable oil onto the grill rack.

Place the shrimp and the limes on the grill rack over medium-hot heat, grill the limes until both sides have grill marks. Grill the shrimp until the shells are pink and the flesh is opaque.

COOK, around 3 minutes on each side. Take the shrimp off the grill and serve on a platter with the grilled lime wedges.

Grilled BBQ Shrimp

Serves: 4

24 extra large shrimp (aka: 16-20 count per pound) peeled, deviened

3/4 cup store bought barbecue sauce (Your favorite brand)

2 tablespoons fresh rosemary, chopped

1 tablespoon apple cider vinegar

6 (8" -OR- 10" inch wooden skewers) soaked at least 1 hour in water.

Put the shrimp in a large resealabe freezer bag, set aside. In a bowl, whisk together the barbecue sauce, rosemary and vinegar, mix well. Pour the barbecue sauce over the shrimp in the bag. Press the air out of the bag and seal the bag tightly. Turn the bag to coat the shrimp with the marinade and place in the refrigerator for 3 hours, turning often.

Preheat a gas -OR- charcoal grill for direct high heat

Lightly Brush vegetable oil onto the grill rack

Take the shrimp out of the marinade and throw out the marinade. Thread the shrimp onto the presoaked skewers, running the skewer through the neck and tail. Place the shrimp skewers on the grill rack over high heat and COOK for 2-4 minutes -OR- until opaque in the center of shrimp and firm to the touch.

Grilled Scallop & Tomato Kebobs

Serves: 4

20 large sea scallops, around 1 1/2 ounces each

24 each ripe grape tomatoes

8 (10" or 12" inch wooden skewers) soaked at least 1 hour in water.

3 tablespoons teriyaki sauce (I like Lawry's)

3 tablespoons olive oil -OR- canola oil

Thread scallops and grape tomatoes alternately onto skewers. In a bowl, whisk together the teriyaki sauce and oil, mix well. Brush the teriyaki mixture onto the kebobs, make sure they are well coated. Let the scallops stand at room temperature for 15 minutes before grilling time.

Preheat a gas -OR- charcoal grill to direct high heat. Lightly brush vegetable oil -Or- olive oil onto the grill rack

Place the scallops on the grill rack over high heat and close the grill lid. COOK for 3-5 minutes, or until just opaque in the center, turning only once and basting with the teriyaki mixture.

Scallops and tomatoes COOK, very quickly so keep a close watch on them. Take off the grill as soon as done.

Serve Right Away!!!

Grilled Lobster

Serves: 4-6

6 large cooked lobsters (about 1 1/2 pounds -OR- more each)

1 1/2 cups melted butter

12 each fresh lemon wedges

Preheat a gas -OR- charcoal grill for direct medium heat

Place whole lobsters on the grill rack, over medium heat and close grill lid. Grill for

10 minutes, 5 minutes per side, turning once. Take the lobsters off the grill when they are hot to the touch. When served bash open and serve warm -OR- hot with the melted butter and lemon wedges.

Serve right away!

1st. & 10 Grilled Whole Catfish

Serves: 4

4 whole catfish, cleaned, tails on (1 to 1 1/2 pounds each)

3rd. & 1 Basting Sauce:

4 ounces (1 stick) melted butter

1/3 cup fresh lime juice

1/3 cup fresh orange juice

dash hot red pepper sauce (aka: Tabasco)

2 tablespoons teriyaki sauce

1 teaspoon prepared mustard

1 teaspoon kosher salt

1 teaspoon freshly ground black pepper

1 teaspoon chili powder

vegetable oil for brushing on the grill rack

Preheat a gas -OR- charcoal grill for direct medium heat

Lightly brush the grill rack with vegetable oil

In a bowl, whisk together the 3rd. and 1 basting sauce ingredients, mix well. Place whole catfish on a well-oiled grill over medium coals. Grill, basting often for around 20 minutes, turn over and grill for around 15 minutes -OR- until fish flakes easily with a fork .

Serve right away!

Big Daddy's Lime Salmon

Serves:4

4 Salmon fillets -OR- steaks

Lime & Dill Marinade:

Juice of 3 fresh limes

3 tablespoons olive oil -OR- canola oil

1 1/2 teaspoons fresh lime zest

1 1/2 teaspoons dried dill

2 garlic cloves, crushed in a garlic press

Vegetable oil to brush on the grill rack

Preheat a gas -OR- charcoal grill for direct medium heat. Brush vegetable oil onto the grill rack!

Place the salmon in a resealable large plastic bag. In a bowl, whisk together all of the Lime & Dill Marinade ingredients, mix well. Pour marinade over the salmon, seal bag and turn bag to coat the salmon. Place the bag in the refrigerator to marinate for 2-3 hours. Place the salmon on a well-oiled grill rack over medium coals, basting with the marinade, for around 4 minutes on each side -OR- until fish flakes easily.

Serve right away!

Big Bob's Grilled Swordfish Steaks

Serves: 6

6 fresh swordfish steaks; around 1" inch thick each

1/2 cup olive oil -OR- canola oil

1/4 cup fresh lime juice

1-2 teaspoons kosher salt - to taste

1/2 teaspoon soy sauce

1/8 teaspoon ground black pepper, dash hot red pepper sauce (aka:Tabasco Sauce)

1/4 teaspoon sweet paprika

Vegetable oil for brushing on the grill rack

Preheat a gas -OR- charcoal grill for direct medium heat. Brush vegetable oil onto the grill rack

Rinse the swordfish steaks well under cold water, pat dry. In a bowl, combine the oil, lime juice, salt, soy sauce, pepper and hot sauce, mix well. Brush the fish with the lime juice mixture, then sprinkle with around half of the paprika. Set the remaining lime juice mixture and paprika aside.

Place the swordfish on a well-oiled grill rack over medium coals, grill for around 8 minutes on each side -OR- until the fish flakes easily with a fork. Baste with lime juice mixture often and sprinkle with the remaining paprika.

Serve right away!

Fishing Trip Grilled Trout

Serves: 4

4 whole trout, cleaned

4 strips of smoked bacon

4 sprigs of fresh thyme

1 large fresh lime

salt - to taste

ground black pepper - to taste

Brush vegetable oil onto the grill rack!

preheat a gas -OR- charcoal grill for direct medium-high heat

In a frying pan, slightly cook the bacon, so that it's started to be cooked but is still pliable.

Rinse the trout under cold water and pat dry. Place a sprig of thyme inside of each trout. Wrap each trout with a strip of bacon and secure with a toothpick. Place trout on the well-oiled grill rack over medium-high heat, COOK for 4-7 minutes per side. Grilling time is based on the size of the trout. When the fish turns opaque in the center and easily flakes then the trout is done.

Throw out the bacon and squeeze fresh lime juice over each trout. Serve right away!

This is a great recipe even, if you catch the trout -OR- buy it!

Grilled Fresh Bluefish W/ Eggplant

Serves: 4

4 Bluefish Fillets (6 ounces each)

1 large green -OR- red bell pepper, cored, seeded & quartered

1 eggplant, trimmed and cut into 1/2" inch slices

3/4 cup store bought Italian salad dressing

1/4 cup olive oil -OR- canola oil

3 garlic cloves, crushed in a garlic press

1/4 cup fresh basil, finely chopped

kosher salt -OR- sea salt - to taste

freshly ground black pepper - to taste

Serve fresh lemon wedges with the fish

Brush the grill rack with vegetable oil

Preheat a gas -OR- charcoal grill for direct medium-high heat

In a bowl, combine the Italian dressing, oil, garlic, basil, salt and pepper, mix well; brush onto the eggplant slices and bell peppers, grill until tender (5-8 minutes), turning often. Take the veggies off the grill and place on a platter to cool. Brush the Italian Dressing mixture over both sides of the bluefish fillets and grill until opaque through (8-11 minutes), turning fish only once.

Baste the fish and veggies with Italian Dressing Mixture during the grilling. Take the fish off the grill and serve with grilled veggies. Serve the fish with the lemon wedges.

Smoked Halibut Steak W/ Lemons

Serves: 6

6 Halibuts Steaks

3 each extra large fresh lemons, olive oil -OR- canola oil, freshly ground black pepper

2-3 cups wood chips, soak wood chips for at least 30 minutes in water.

Soak the wood chips in water for at least 30 minutes. Place soaked wood chips in a smoker box -Or- wrap soaked wood chips in aluminum foil to form a pocket, punch holes into the top of the foil.

Brush the grill rack with vegetable oil !

Preheat a gas -OR- charcoal grill for direct high heat.

Place the smoker box -OR- smoker pocket on the grill, when it smokes it is time to put the fish on the grill rack.

Gently rinse the Halibut Steaks under cold water and pat dry. Brush the fish with oil, sprinkle with pepper and cut the lemons into slices. when the grill is good and hot, place the Halibut on the grill rack. Place the lemon slices on top of the steaks to cover, use around 1/2 of a lemon on each steak. Reduce the heat to medium -OR- move fish to a cooler spot on the grill. Turn steaks over after around 4-6 minutes, cooking time depends on the thickest of the Halibut Steaks. COOK the steaks until done. Take Halibut off the grill and serve right away.

Cedar Rapids Plank Halibut

Serves: 4

4 Halibut Fillets (8ounces each)

2 tablespoons olive oil

1 teaspoon kosher salt -OR- sea salt - to taste

1 teaspoon freshly ground black pepper

1 cedar plank, soaked in water -OR- apple juice for at least 1 hour

Serve with fresh lime and lemon wedges

Preheat a gas -OR- charcoal grill for direct medium heat

Brush the halibut fillets with olive oil. Rub salt and black pepper onto the halibut fillets. Place the fish on a pre-soaked cedar plank and place on the grill rack . Allow the fish to COOK for 10-15 minutes. Remove the fish from the grill when done and serve with the lime & lemon wedges.

R.P.S. Cedar Plank Trout

Serves: 4

4 whole trout, cleaned, (12 ounces each)

1 cup fresh dill, chopped

6 tablespoons olive oil -OR- canola oil

2 large fresh limes, thinly sliced

2 teaspoons kosher salt -OR- sea salt

1 teaspoon ground black pepper

2 ea., untreated, thin, clean Cedar Planks large enough to fit the fish

Soak the cedar planks submerged in water for 1 hour.

Preheat a gas -OR- charcoal grill for direct medium heat

Lightly coat the inside and outside of fish with oil. Season the fish inside and outside with salt, pepper, stuff with lime slices and fresh dill.

Place presoaked cedar planks on the grill rack over direct medium heat. When the cedar planks start to smoke place trout on the planks. COOK for around 15 minutes -OR- until the trout is done.

The flesh should be opaque and flake easily. Remove the trout from the grill when done.

Serve right away!

Cedar Plank Arctic Char

Serves: 4

Go Fish Dry Rub:

2 tablespoons sea slat -OR- kosher salt

2 tablespoons paprika

4 teaspoons freshly ground black pepper

4 teaspoons light brown sugar

2 teaspoons dried grated lemon peel

2 teaspoon garlic powder

2 teaspoons dried basil

2 teaspoons dried tarragon

In a bowl, combine all the ingredients together and mix well. Use right away -OR- place in an air tight container (aka: jar) and store at room temperature until ready to use.

1 each Cedar BBQ Grilling Plank

4 Arctic Char Fillets (6 ounces), around 2" inches thick, skin removed

2 large fresh limes, cut into 4 wedges each

Soak 1 large cedar plank in water for at least 6 hours.

Sprinkle both sides of the fish with the dry rub. Press the rub into the flesh of the fish.

Refrigerate the fish fillets, uncovered 6-14 hours.

Preheat a gas -OR- charcoal grill to direct medium-high heat

Place the fillets on a cedar plank. Squeeze two lime wedges all over the fish fillets. Place the cedar plank on the grill rack. Reduce the grill heat to medium -OR- move the plank to a cooler spot on the grill rack, that is medium heat. Close the grill lid. Grill for around 9-11 minutes, depending on thickness of the fish fillet and the heat of the grill. COOK the fish until done.

Take the fish off the grill and serve right away with lime wedges.

Lime Tartar Sauce

Makes: around 1 1/2 cups

1 cup mayonnaise

4 tablespoons dill pickles, finely chopped

4 tablespoons green onions (scallions), finely chopped

2 tablespoons freshly grated lime zest

4 teaspoons fresh lime juice

In a bowl, combine all of the ingredients together and mix well. Place in the refrigerator, covered for at least 6 hours -OR- overnight before serving.

Capri Fresh Basil Tartar Sauce

Makes: around 1 1/2 cups

1 cup mayonnaise

2 tablespoons onion, finely chopped

2 tablespoons fresh basil, chopped

4 teaspoons capers, chopped

1/2 teaspoon freshly grated lime zest

In a bowl, combine all of the ingredients together, mix well. Cover and place in the refrigerator before use.

Grilled Jamaican Jerk Tilapia Packets

Serves: 4

4 Tilapia Fillets (6 ounces each)

1 cup white onions, chopped

1 cup green -OR- red bell peppers, cut into strips

1 jalapeno pepper, seeded, ribs removed and finely chopped

3 garlic cloves, crushed in a garlic press

3 tablespoons olive oil -OR- canola oil

3 tablespoons fresh cilantro leaves, chopped

3 tablespoons Jerk Seasoning

2 tablespoons fresh lime juice

kosher salt -OR- sea salt - to taste

freshly ground black pepper - to taste

4 each - large pieces of heavy-duty aluminum foil

Preheat a gas -OR- charcoal grill for direct medium-high heat

Place one piece of fish in each piece of foil. In a bowl, combine the garlic, oil, cilantro, lime juice and jerk seasoning, mix well. Brush both sides of fish with the oil mixture.

Grilled Seafood

Place equal amounts of onion, bell peppers and jalapeno pepper on top of each piece of fish. Season lightly with salt and pepper. Crimp the edges of the foil over and seal the packets very well. Place on the grill rack and COOK for 10 minutes, turn and COOK for a remaining 10 minutes. When the Tilapia no longer appears opaque and the vegetables become tender, remove from the heat.

Allow packets to rest for 5 minutes before opening. Serve right away!

Big Bob's Top 30 Greatest Ice Hockey Players All Time

Your Top 30 List:

#1. Wayne Gretzky

#2. Gordie Howe

#3. Bobby Orr

#4. Mario Lemieux

#5. Bobby Hull

#6. Phil Esposito

#7. Doug Harvey

#8. Patrick Roy

#9. Guy Lafleur

#10. Maurice "Rocket" Richard

#11. Bobby Clarke

#12. Mike Bossy

#13. Denis Potvin

#14. Terry Sawchuk

#15. Dominik Hasek

#16. Vladislav Tretiak

#17. Peter Stastny

#18. Tony Esposito

#19. Martin Brodeur

#20. Marcel Dionne

#21. Mark "the Moose" Messier

#22. Ray Borque

#23. Adam Oates

#24. Ken Dryden

#25. Borje Salming

#26. Doug Gilmour

#27. Valery Kaharlamov

#28. Yan Suchv

#29. Vsevolod Bobrow

#30. Jaromir Jagr

Big Bob's Greatest Ice Hockey Players at Each Position All Time

Your Greatest Players by Position:

Now this is a Hockey Dream Team!!!
Center: Wayne Gretzy
Right Wing: Gordie Howe
Left Wing: Bobby Hull

_____

_____

_____

Defensemen:
Bobby Orr
Doug Harvey

_____

_____

Goalie:
Patrick Roy

_____

Notes

CHAPTER #11

Pork

AUTO RACING

Titans Pork Chops

Serves: 4

Titan Marinade:

3/4 cup olive oil -OR- canola oil

1/2 cup fresh lime juice

2 tablespoons fresh tarragon, chopped

2 teaspoons freshly grated lime zest (peel), about 1 lime

2-3 garlic cloves, crushed in a garlic press

1/8 teaspoon salt, to taste

1/8 teaspoon ground black pepper, to taste

4 pork loin chops, around 1" inch, about 8 ounce each (2 pounds total)

In a bowl, combine the oil, lime juice, tarragon, lime zest, garlic, salt and pepper, mix well.

Place the pork chops into a large plastic resealable bag, pour the marinade over the chops in the bag. Seal the bag and turn to coat the chops with marinade. Place the chops in the refrigerator to marinate for 14- 24 hours (don't marinate for more than 24 hours), turn often.

Brush the grill rack with vegetable oil. Preheat a gas -OR- charcoal grill for direct medium heat W/ the grill lid closed.

Remove the pork chops from the marinade and throw out the marinade. Put the chops on the grill rack over medium heat and close the grill lid. Open all grill vents, grill for 10 minutes, - turning once, COOK until done. Chops are done when browned on the outside and no longer pink inside by the bone. Take off the grill, serve right away with homemade or store bought Salsa of your choice.

JG's Grilled Honey-Ginger Pork Chops

Serves: 4

4 center cut pork chops, 1 1/2" inches thick

Tennis Rack Marinade:

1/3 cup honey

4 tablespoon soy sauce

1 tablespoon olive oil -OR- canola oil

3 garlic cloves, crushed in a garlic press

1 teaspoon ground ginger

1 teaspoon sesame oil - to taste

In a bowl, whisk all the tennis rack marinade ingredients together, mix well. Place the chops in a resealable large plastic bag and pour the tennis rack marinade over the chops in the bag. Seal the bag, turn the bag to coat the chops and marinate in the refrigerator for at least 3-4 hours.

Lightly brush vegetable oil onto the grill rack.

Preheat a gas -OR- charcoal grill for direct medium heat

Take the pork chops out of the marinade and throw out the tennis rack marinade. Place the chops on the grill rack over medium heat and COOK for 20-25 minutes, turning only once.

When done cooking, take the chops off the grill.

Serve Right Away!!!

Joe's Grilled BEER-BBQ Pork Steaks

Serve: 4

4 Pork Steaks

1/2 can (6 ounces) beer (3/4 cup)

2 tablespoons butter

2 garlic cloves, crushed in a garlic press

salt - to taste

ground black pepper - to taste

1/2 store bought barbecue sauce - your favorite brand

Trim away all but a small amount of the fat from around the edges of the pork steak. Score the edges of the pork steaks in several places, to prevent the meat from curling up. In a saucepan, add a 1/2 can of beer over medium heat. Add butter, garlic, salt and pepper, allow the mixture to SIMMER for 15-20 minutes.

Lightly brush vegetable oil onto the grill rack.

Preheat a gas -OR- charcoal grill for direct medium-high heat.

Place the pork steaks on the grill rack over medium-high heat and grill for 15-20 minutes.

Turning often and basting with the sauce at each turn. Remove the steaks from the grill and brush both sides of pork steaks with barbecue sauce.

Serve right away!

Grilled Teriyaki Pork Tenderloin

Serves: 4-6

Mad Man Teriyaki Marinade:

2/3 cup Teriyaki sauce & marinade

1/4 cup good quality white wine

2 tablespoons fresh orange juice

2 tablespoons dark brown sugar

2 tablespoons green onions (scallions)

2 pounds pork tenderloins, trimmed

In a bowl, whisk together the teriyaki sauce, wine, orange juice, brown sugar and green onions, mix well. Place the pork tenderloins in a resealable large plastic bag, pour the marinade over the pork in the bag. Press the air out of the bag, seal the bag tightly. Turn the bag several times to coat the pork with the marinade. Place the pork into the refrigerator to marinate for 4 hours or overnight, turning often.

Preheat a gas -OR- charcoal grill for direct medium heat.

Take the pork out of the marinade, throw out the marinade. Place the pork on the grill rack over medium heat, close the grill lid. Grill for 17-23 minutes, turning often, don't burn. When the pork reaches the proper doneness, take the pork off the grill. Let the pork rest on a cutting board for 5-6 minutes before slicing.

Serve Right Away!

Gamecocks BBQ Pork ("A Little Spicy")

Serve: 4-6

Gamecocks Basting Sauce:

2 cups apple cider vinegar

2 tablespoons vegetable oil -OR- canola oil

1 tablespoon hot red (cayenne) pepper

1 tablespoon ground black pepper

2 pounds pork shoulder -OR- butt

3/4 - 1 cup store bought barbecue sauce (Your Favorite Brand)

*Serve your favorite store bought barbecue sauce, on the side!

In a bowl, combine the vinegar, oil, red pepper and black pepper, mix well. Allow the flavors to blend for at least 2 hours at room temperature.

Preheat a gas -OR- charcoal indirect medium-high heat.

After searing pork, move it and place a drip pan under the pork.

When the fire is set to go, position the grill rack 5" inches above the heat source. Place the pork on the grill rack over the part of the grill that is medium-high heat and SEAR (cooking over high heat to seal in flavor), it for 2 minutes on each side. When the pork has been seared, move the meat to the part of the grill set-up for indirect heat grilling. Baste it with the Gamecocks Basting Sauce and close the grill lid. After 12-15 minutes open the lid, turn pork, baste it and close lid. Continue turning and basting every 15 minutes, until the meat falls off the bone about 1 - 1 1/2 hours.

Transfer the pork to a cutting board, let rest for 5-7 minutes, then cut into bite-size pieces and serve right away!

Serve with store bought Honey/Smokey barbecue sauce!

The Secret

of Great

Barbecue

Is to Cook It

LOW & SLOW

Bob's BBQ Pork Sandwich

Makes: 12 BBQ Pork Sandwiches

2 pounds coarsely ground pork

5 garlic cloves, crushed in a garlic press

1 very large onion, finely chopped

2 cups store bought Smokey barbecue sauce (your favorite brand) dash hot red pepper sauce

12 hamburger buns, split, buttered and toasted

In a bowl, combine the pork, garlic and onion, mix well. In a heavy skillet, crumble the pork mixture and sauté over medium heat until the pork thoroughly cooked, drain very well. Place the pork back in the skillet and add the Smokey barbecue sauce. Stir in to combine well, then lower the heat SIMMER gently for 15 minutes, stir often. To serve place the split, toasted buns on serving plates and spoon the BBQ pork onto each bun, serve hot right away

RIBS

Pork Ribs W/ Rams Dry Rub

Serves: 5-6

Rams Dry Rub:

3/4 cup firmly packed brown sugar

1/3 cup sweet paprika

3 tablespoons chili powder

2 tablespoons garlic powder

2 tablespoons onion powder

1 1/2 tablespoons salt

3 3/4 teaspoons ground black pepper

3 teaspoons dry mustard

1 1/2 teaspoon dry thyme

5 pounds St. Louis Cut Pork Spare Ribs

Pork

*1cup store bought Smokey barbecue sauce

**You can serve your favorite store bought Smokey barbecue sauce on the side -OR- brush on ribs during the last few minutes of grilling.

In a bowl, combine the brown sugar; paprika, chili powder, garlic powder, onion powder, salt, pepper, dry mustard and dried thyme, mix well. Rub the ribs with dry rub until well coated.

Preheat the oven to 250 degrees F.

Wrap the ribs in 2 layers of heavy duty aluminum foil. Bake 2 hours at 250 degrees F. Always remember with PORK RIBS COOK THEM LOW AND SLOW. Remove ribs from the oven and unwrap.

Brush vegetable oil onto the grill rack.

Preheat a gas -OR- charcoal grill for direct medium heat

Place the pork spare ribs on the grill rack, over medium heat, grill for 30 minutes -OR- until desired doneness and tenderness, turn often. When done, take ribs off the grill and serve with a Smokey barbecue sauce on the side.

*Tip: When using a dry rub, always brush the grill rack with vegetable oil, before grilling the meat.

Turn-Up the Heat: Hot & Sweet Ribs

Serves: 7-8 hungry people

7 pounds pork spareribs

Hot & Sweet BBQ Sauce:

Juice from 2 fresh oranges

Juice from 2 fresh large lemons

5 garlic cloves, crushed in a garlic press

1 cup tomato sauce

1 cup ketchup

2 tablespoons honey

3 teaspoons prepared mustard

2 teaspoons fresh jalapeno pepper, finely chopped

1 teaspoon dried rosemary

1 teaspoon dried oregano

1 teaspoon onion powder salt - to taste

ground black pepper - to taste

2-4 cups wood chips soaked in water for at least 30 minutes & drained.

In 1-2 large pots, blanch the ribs in boiling water for 15 minutes. In a saucepan, combine all the hot & sweet BBQ sauce ingredients, mix well. Heat the BBQ sauce over low heat.

Brush the grill rack with vegetable oil. Preheat a gas grill to direct medium-high heat:

Place the wood chips in a smoker box -OR- a foil packet -OR- a pie pan with wood chips covered in foil, with holes poked in the top. Wait until you see smoke, baste ribs in BBQ sauce and place on hot grill. Close the grill lid. COOK for 30 minutes depending on the size of the ribs, basting and turning often.

Preheat a charcoal grill to (direct heat) hot coals: Brush the grill rack with vegetable oil

Place the soaked and drained wood chips on top of the charcoal. Wait for smoke, then baste the ribs in the BBQ sauce and place on a hot grill. Grill for around 30 minutes depending on the size of the ribs. Basting and turning often.

Take ribs off of the grill and serve right away!

Bobby's Chipotle Country Ribs

Serves: 4 hungry people

4 pounds country style ribs

Lizzies Rib Marinade:

1 1/2 cups red wine vinegar

1 cup olive oil -OR- canola oil

1 each (7 ounce) can chipotle chilies in adobo sauce

5 ea. scallions (green onions), chopped

4 garlic cloves, chopped

Pork

3 tablespoons fresh oregano leaves

1 jalapeno pepper, seeded, ribbed and chopped

1/2 teaspoon salt - to taste

ground black pepper - as needed

2 cups wood chips soaked at least 30 minutes & drained.

In a blender -OR- food processor combine the chipotles, scallions, garlic, oregano, jalapeno and salt. Blend until it just becomes smooth. While blending add red wine vinegar and oil. Season the pork ribs with ground black pepper. Place the ribs in a large resealable plastic bag and pour the Lizzies rib marinade over the ribs in the bag. Seal the bag, turn to coat the ribs and refrigerate overnight.

Brush vegetable oil onto the grill rack.

Preheat a gas grill to direct medium heat:

Gas Grill: Place the wood chips in a smoker box -OR- foil packet with holes on the top. Wait for smoke to form, remove the ribs from the Lizzies rib marinade and place on the grill rack over medium heat. Close the grill lid, grill for around 20 minutes -OR- until done, turning often. Don't let the ribs burn, when done take off the grill and serve right away.

Brush the grill rack with vegetable oil.

Preheat a charcoal grill to direct medium coals:

Charcoal grill: Place the soaked wood chips right on top of the charcoal. Wait for smoke to form, remove the ribs from the Lizzies rib marinade and place the ribs on the grill rack over medium coals. Close the grill lid and grill for 20 minutes -OR- until done, turning often. Don't burn the ribs. When done take the ribs off the grill and serve right away!

I have been told to figure 1 pound of raw ribs per person, when purchasing ribs.

Bobcat's Riblets

Serves: 4-8

4 pounds rib strips (rib tips)

NC Big Cat's Mop Sauce:

1 cup apple cider vinegar

1/4 cup brown sugar

1/4 cup unsalted butter

1 tablespoon red pepper flakes

kosher salt - to taste

ground black pepper - to taste

2-3 cups wood chips soaked at least 30 minutes & drained

1 each drip pan for indirect heat grilling

Preheat a gas -OR- charcoal grill for indirect medium heat

Season the rib tips with salt and pepper. In a saucepan melt the butter. Combine the vinegar, brown sugar and red pepper flakes to the melted butter. Stir the pan until the brown sugar dissolves over medium heat. Reduce the heat to low and SIMMER for around 10 minutes, stir often. If using a gas grill place a smoker box -OR- foil smoker packet on the heated side of the grill. If using a charcoal grill place the soaked wood chips right on top of the charcoal. Wait for the wood chips to start to smoke. Place ribs on the grill over medium hot heat. COOK until the outside of the ribs have browned. Move the riblets to the indirect heat cooler part of the grill over a drip pan. Mop the riblets with the sauce and grill until done, mop with sauce often. Keep the grill lid closed when you can. Take the riblets off the grill when done and serve with the remaining mop sauce on the side.

Texas Ranger Baby Back Ribs

Serves: 4

2-3 cups wood chips soaked in water for at least 30 minutes & drained

1 each drip pan for indirect heat grilling

4 pounds baby back ribs

Ground Ball Dry Rub:

2 teaspoons chili powder

2 teaspoon Hungarian paprika

2 teaspoons ground black pepper

1 teaspoon garlic powder

1 teaspoon ground thyme

Pork

2 cups store bought barbecue sauce (your favorite brand)

*Preheat a charcoal grill for indirect medium heat:

Place a pile of charcoal on one side of the grill, nothing should be under the food, except the drip pan. Once the charcoal is ready, throw some soaked wood chips on the charcoal. Wait for smoke to form before placing the food onto the grill rack over the drip pan.

**Preheat a gas grill for indirect medium heat

Only heat one side of a gas grill for indirect medium heat. Place a drip pan under the grill rack on the unheated side of the gas grill. Fill a smoker box -OR- a foil smoker packet with soaked wood chips. Place the smoker box -OR- foil smoker packet on the heated side of the gas grill.

Grilling the Ribs:

Remove the membrane from the ribs if the butcher has not already. In a bowl, combine all the ingredients for the ground ball dry rub, mix well. Cut the ribs with a sharp knife into 1/2 slabs.

Rub the ground ball dry rub into the ribs, let ribs stand at room temperature for 15 minutes before grilling.

Brush vegetable oil onto the grill rack for indirect grilling

Place the ribs on the grill rack over a drip pan on the unheated side of the grill. Close the grill lid.

Grill for 20-30 minutes, then brush with barbecue sauce. Close the grill lid and continue to COOK for an additional 30-35 minutes -OR- until done.

Serve Right Away!

Big Bob's Top 15 Greatest NASCAR Drivers All Time

Your Top 15 List:

#1. Richard Petty

#2. Glen "FIREBALL" Roberts

#3. Fred Lorenzen

#4. Jeff Gordon

#5. Bobby Allison

#6. David Pearson

#7. Tim Flock

#8. Cale Yarborough

#9. Darrel Waltrip

#10 Dale Earnhardt

#11. Herb Thomas

#12. Davey Allison

#13. Rusty Wallace

#14. Tim Richmond

#15. Jim Paschal

Big Bob's Top 10 Greatest Formula 1 Drivers All Time

Your Top 10 List:

#1. Jackie Stewart

#2. Alain Prost

#3. Ayrton Senna

#4. Michael Schumacher

#5. Juan Maneul Fangio

#6. Jacques Villeneuve

#7. Jim Clark

#8. Mika Hakkinen

#9. Niki Lauda

#10. Nigel Mansell

Pork

Big Bob's Top 10 Greatest Race Car Drivers of the 20th. Century

Your Top 10 List:

#1. A.J. Foyt

#2. Richard Petty

#3. Mario Andretti

#4. David Pearson

#5. Dale Earnhardt

#6. Al Unser Sr.

#7. Dan Gurney

#8. Rick Mears

#9. Cale Yarborough

#10 John Force

CHAPTER #12

Game

TENNIS

Iron Mike's Grilled Cornish Game Hens

Serves: 4-6

4 Cornish Game Hens (1 - 1 1/2 pounds each)

6 tablespoons olive oil -OR- canola oil

1/3 cup fresh lime juice

1/3 cup fresh lemon juice

2 tablespoons ground black pepper

1 teaspoon salt

Using a sharp knife split the game hens in half lengthwise. Rinse the hens under cold water and pat dry. In a bowl, combine the oil, lime juice, lemon juice, pepper and salt. Place hens in a resealable large plastic bag (put 2 hens in each bag) and pour the marinade over the hens in the each bag. Seal the bags, turn the bags to coat the hens and refrigerate for 3-5 hours (don't go over 5 hours when you marinate the hens).

Preheat a gas -OR- charcoal grill for indirect medium heat.

Lightly brush vegetable oil onto the grill rack.

Remove the hens halves from the marinade and place on the unheated side of a grill, already set-up for indirect medium grilling. Place the hens over a drip pan. Place the hens skin side up away from the direct heat. Baste with the remaining marinade during the grilling time. The hens should COOK for around 45-55 minutes. Test for doneness before removing from the grill.

When done take hens off the grill and place on a large platter.

Serve Right Away!

Grilled Wild Turkey Breast

Makes: 3-4 servings

1 each bone-in Wild Turkey Breast (around 1 1/2 pounds)

1 cup store bought Zesty Italian Dressing

2 tablespoons Dijon mustard

2 tablespoons honey

1-2 garlic cloves, crushed in a garlic press

Place the wild turkey breast in a resalable large plastic bag. In a bowl, whisk together the Italian dressing, mustard, honey and garlic, until well mixed. Pour the dressing mixture over the wild turkey in the bag. Seal the bag tightly and turn the bag to coat the wild turkey. Place the wild turkey in the refrigerator and marinate overnight.

Lightly brush vegetable oil onto the grill rack.

Preheat a gas -OR- charcoal grill for indirect medium heat

Place a drip pan under the Wild Turkey Breast.

Take the wild turkey out of the marinade and throw out the marinade. Place the turkey breast on the grill rack over a drip pan on the unheated side of the grill. Use indirect medium heat to grill the wild turkey for 50-55 minutes -OR- until the juices run clear. You can use a meat thermometer and COOK the wild turkey to a internal temperature of 170 degrees and above. When done take the wild turkey breast off the grill and place on a large platter.

Serve Right Away!

Grilled Quail W/ Pomegranate BBQ Sauce

Makes: 12 Quail Halves

Pomegranate Barbecue Sauce:

24 ounces (1 1/2 pounds) ketchup

1 cup bottled pomegranate juice

1/2 cup maple syrup -OR- dark syrup

3 tablespoons chili powder

3 tablespoons teriyaki sauce and marinade

1 tablespoon seasoned salt (aka: Lawry's)

2 teaspoons hot red pepper sauce (aka: Tabasco)

In a bowl, whisk together all of the ingredients, mix well. The Pomegranate BBQ Sauce needs no heating".

Grilled Quail:

6 each Quail, cleaned, rinsed, drained and cut in half

1 cup -OR- more olive oil -OR- canola oil

kosher salt - to taste

ground black pepper - to taste

Pomegranate Barbecue Sauce

Cut the quail in half with a sharp knife, season with salt and pepper.

Preheat a gas -OR- charcoal grill to direct medium heat

Place quail on the grill rack bone side down over medium heat, turning and basting with oil frequently. COOK for 16-20 minutes, meat should be opaque and no trace of pink at the bone.

During the last 5 minutes of grilling baste both sides of the quail with the pomegranate BBQ sauce. Continue turning quail until done (fork tender). Take off the grill and serve with the extra BBQ sauce, Serve Right Away!

Grilled Asian Honey-Peanut Pheasant

Serves: 4-6

Asian Honey-Peanut Marinade:

1 cup honey

1 cup creamy style peanut butter

1/2 cup chicken stock -OR- broth

5 garlic cloves, crushed a garlic press

1/4 cup soy sauce

1/4 cup apple cider vinegar

2 teaspoons olive oil -OR- canola oil

2 pheasants

In a pot, combine all of the Asian Marinade ingredients and Simmer for 5-9 minutes. Take off the heat and allow to COOL slightly. Place the two pheasants in a pan, brush 1/2 of the Asian Honey-Peanut Marinade, all over both pheasants, reserve the other 1/2 for basting. Cover the pan and refrigerate for 3-4 hours to marinate.

Brush vegetable oil onto the grill rack

Preheat a gas -OR- charcoal grill for direct medium-high heat

Place the pheasants on the grill rack over medium-high heat. Close the grill lid and grill for 55-60 minutes -OR- until the juices run clear. Baste the pheasants with the reserved marinade after 15 minutes and baste again at 30 minutes, COOK until done. Take pheasants off the grill when done, slice with a sharp knife and serve right away.

Bob's Barbecue Pheasant

Serves: 4-6

2 pheasants, cut into pieces

1/2 teaspoon salt

1/4 teaspoon freshly ground black pepper

1/4 teaspoon paprika

1/2 cup melted butter

1 cup store bought barbecue sauce (your favorite brand)

2-3 cups wood chips soaked in water for 30 minutes & drained

Lightly brush vegetable oil onto a grill rack Preheat a gas -OR- charcoal grill for direct medium-high heat.

For a gas grill use a smoker box -OR- a homemade foil smoker packet. When using a charcoal grill just place the soaked wood chips on top of the charcoal. Once the smoke forms place the pheasant pieces on the grill rack over medium-high heat. Sprinkle the pheasant pieces with salt, pepper and paprika. Brush with the melted butter on both sides. Grill for 15-22 minutes, turning often. Baste with the barbecue sauce often during the grilling process. Reduce the heat to medium heat for a gas grill -OR- move pheasant pieces to a cooler part of the grill, for a charcoal grill, try the edges of the grill. Grill for a additional 11-15 minutes. COOK, until done, take off the grill and serve right away.

Spicy Bacon Wrapped Grilled Duck Breast

Makes: 4 servings

2 each fresh jalapeno peppers

4 each duck breasts

8 slices smoked bacon

With a sharp knife hollow out jalapeno peppers and cut in half. Place 1 jalapeno pepper half in the center of each duck breast. Roll each breast around each pepper half. Roll 2 bacon strips around each of the 4 duck breasts

Preheat a gas -OR- charcoal grill to direct medium heat.

Place the duck breasts on the grill rack over medium heat -OR- coals. Grill to the desired doneness and the bacon should be very crispy. Take duck breasts off the grill and place on a platter and serve right away!

1st. Down Grilled Duck

Makes: 4 servings

4 duck breast halves

4 slices of smoked bacon

2 chicken bouillon cubes

1 cup water

1 tablespoon of grape jelly

1/2 teaspoon prepared mustard

2 tablespoons Good Quality Bourbon

1/8 teaspoon dried oregano

zest of one fresh orange (very outside layer of the orange)

Preheat a gas -OR- charcoal grill for direct high heat for searing

Wrap each breast with 1 slice of smoked bacon. Place duck breast on the grill rack over high heat -OR- coals for around 3 minutes for each side. The high heat will sear the outside of the duck breast and will help to keep in the juices. In a small pan with deep sides, dissolve the bouillon cubes in the water over medium-high heat. Add grape jelly, mustard, Bourbon, oregano and orange zest. Add the grilled duck breasts that you grilled to medium-rare. Reduce the heat to low, SIMMER on low to reduce the sauce. Keep basting the duck breasts as it reduces.

Serve Right Away!

Serve Hot Duck Breast W/ sauce over white rice -OR- wild rice!

MJ's Grilled Venison Steaks

Serves: 4

4 Venison Steaks

1- (12 ounce) can beer

1 cup Store Bought Italian Salad Dressing

Place the Venison Steaks in a large resealable plastic freezer bag, In a bowl, combine the beer and Italian dressing together, mix well. Pour the marinade over the Venison steaks in the bag.

Seal the bag tightly and turn to coat the steaks. Place the steaks in the refrigerator overnight to marinate.

Preheat a gas -OR- charcoal grill to medium-high heat. Lightly brush vegetable oil onto the grill rack.

Take the steaks out of the marinade and throw out the marinade. Place the Venison Steaks on the grill rack over medium-high heat -OR- coals and COOK to the proper doneness. When the steaks are cooked to the desired doneness, take them off the grill and let steaks rest for 5-6 minutes before serving.

Magic's Venison Steak Sauce

1/2 cup ketchup (I like Heinz Ketchup)

2 tablespoons Worcestershire Sauce

1/2 teaspoon garlic powder

In a bowl, combine the ketchup, Worcestershire sauce and garlic powder, mix well. Use right away -OR- refrigerate before serving.

Grilled BBQ Elk Burgers

Makes: 6 burgers

2 pounds ground Elk meat

1/3 cup ketchup

1/3 cup onions, finely chopped

3 garlic cloves, crushed in a garlic press

1 - 2 chipotle peppers in adobo sauce, finely chopped (adjust the heat)

1/2 teaspoon salt - to taste

vegetable oil for brushing on the grill rack

6 hamburger buns

6 large onion slices

6 large beefsteak tomato slices

6 romaine lettuce leaves

Mayo - to taste

In a bowl, combine the Elk meat, ketchup, onion, garlic, chipotles and salt, mix lightly, with your fingers. Form 6 patties of equal size and round shape.

Lightly brush the vegetable oil onto the grill rack. Preheat a gas -OR- charcoal grill for direct medium heat.

Place the Elk burgers on the grill rack over medium heat, COOK for 6-8 minutes per side, turning only once. Grill the burgers to the desired done. When burgers are done take off the grill and serve on buns with your favorite condiments.

Grilled Rosemary & Garlic Rabbit

Makes: 6-8 servings

2 (3 pounds, each) fryer rabbits

1/2 cup olive oil -OR- canola oil

8 garlic cloves, crushed in a garlic press

4 sprigs, fresh rosemary, chopped

With a sharp knife cut the rabbit into 8 pieces on a cutting board. Place the rabbit pieces in a large resealable plastic bag. In a bowl, combine the oil, garlic and rosemary, mix well. Pour the oil mixture over the rabbit in the bag, seal the bag tightly and turn the bag to coat the rabbit.

Place the bag in the refrigerator for at least 4 hours -OR- overnight to marinate.

Preheat a gas -OR- charcoal grill to direct medium heat

Place the meat on the grill rack over medium heat for 10-13 minutes per side, turning only once.

COOK rabbit to a internal temperature of 170 degrees F, using a instant read thermometer.

When the meat is done take off the grill and serve right away.

Grilled Wild Boar Chops

Makes: 8 servings

Wild Boar Marinade

juice of 6 fresh limes

2 1/4 cups olive oil -OR- canola oil

1/2 cup fresh rosemary, chopped

3 tablespoons fresh garlic, crushed in a garlic press

2 teaspoons kosher salt - to taste

2 teaspoons freshly ground black pepper

8 Wild Boar Chops

Place chops in a extra large resealable plastic bag. In a bowl, whisk together the lime juice, oil, rosemary, garlic, salt and pepper, mix well. Pour the marinade over the chops in the bag, seal the bag tightly and turn the bag to coat the chops with marinade. Place the bag in the refrigerator for 6 hours -OR- overnight to marinate, turning the bag every hour or so.

Preheat a gas -OR- charcoal grill to direct high heat.

Place the chops on the grill rack, sear over high heat for 2 minutes per side. Turn down the heat or move the chops to a cooler part of the grill for medium heat to finish the cooking process.

Close the grill lid and COOK for around 6-8 minutes on each side -OR- until cooked to the desired degree of doneness. Take the chops off of the grill and place on a serving platter.

Let the chops rest at room temperature for 10 minutes.

Serve Right Away!

Big Bob's Top 5 Greatest Men's Tennis Players All Time

Your Top 5 List:

#1. Pete Sampras

#2. Rod Laver

_____

#3. John McEnroe

_____

#4. Jimmy Connors

_____

TIE #5. Ivan Lendl

_____

TIE #5. Bjorn Borg

_____

Big Bob's Top 5 Greatest Women's Tennis Players All Time

Your Top 5 List:

#1. Martina Navratilova

_____

#2. Chris Evert

_____

#3. Steffi Graf

_____

#4. Margaret Smith Court

_____

#5. Billie Jean King

_____

Big Bob's Top 5's Tennis

Top 5 Winners of "The Grand Slam" in Singles: All four Majors in the same Calendar Year.

#1. Don Budge 1938

#2. Marueen Connolly 1953

#3. Rod Laver 1962 & 1969

#4. Margaret Smith Court 1970

#5. Steffi Graf 1988

Most Grand Slam Singles Titles: Women

#1. Margaret Smith Court 24

#2. Steffi Graf 22

#3. Helen Wills Moody 19

#4. Martina Navratilova 18

#5. Chris Evert 18

Game

Most Grand Slam Singles Titles: Men

#1. Pete Sampras 14
#2. Roy Emerson 12
#3. Rod Laver 11
#4. Bjorn Borg 11
#5. Bill Tilder 10

Big Bob's Top 5's Tennis

Most Career Singles Titles: Men

#1. Jimmy Connors 109
#2. Ivan Lendal 94
#3. John McEnroe 77
#4. Pete Sampras 64
TIE #5. Guillermo Vilas 62
TIE #5. Bjorn Borg 62

Most Career Singles Titles: Women

#1. Martina Navratilova 167
#2. Chris Evert 154
#3. Steffi Graf 107
#4. Margaret Smith Court 92
#5. Billy Jean King 67

Big Bob's Top 5's Tennis

Most Career Singles & *Doubles Titles : Men

#1. John McEnroe 154
#2. Jimmy Connors 128
#3. Ellie Nastase 108
#4. Tom Okker 108
#5. Stan Smith 100

*Doubles Titles count in the total, mixed doubles titles are not included.

Most Career Singles & *Doubles Titles: Women

#1. Martina Navratilova 341
#2. Chris Evert 189

#3. Billy Jean King 168
#4. Margaret Smith Court 127
#5. Rosie Casals 123

*Doubles Titles count in the total, mixed doubles titles are not included.

Big Bob's Top 20 Greatest Tennis Players All Time Men -OR- Women; Who is the greatest Tennis Player All Time?

Your Top 20 List:

#1. Martina Naratilova
#2. John McEnroe
#3. Pete Sampras
#4. Chris Evert
#5. Jimmy Connors
#6. Margaret Smith Court
#7. Rod Laver
#8. Steffi Graf
#9. Ivan Lendel
#10. Bjorn Borg
#11. Billie Jean King
#12. Vensus Williams & her Sister
#13. Ellie Nastase
#14. Guillermo Vilas
#15. Stan Smith
#16. Helen Willis Moody
#17. Roy Emerson
#18. Rosie Casals
#19. Tom Okker
TIE #20. Don Budge
TIE #20. Bill Tilder

Notes

CHAPTER #13

Side Dishes
BEER

Grilled Eggplant & Red Peppers W/ Roasted Garlic Oil

Makes: 6 servings

1 large eggplant (around 1 1/2 pounds) unpeeled, sliced crosswise 1/4" inch thick rounds

3 large red -OR- yellow bell peppers, quartered lengthwise

Olive Oil, as needed for brushing on vegetables

salt - to taste

ground black pepper - to taste

2 tablespoon -OR- more Roasted Garlic Oil

Preheat a gas -OR- charcoal grill for direct medium-high heat

Place the eggplant and bell peppers on a baking sheet, brush with oil and season with salt and pepper, do this to both sides. Place the eggplant and bell peppers on the grill rack over medium high heat, grill for 4 minutes on each side. Take the vegetables off the grill and place on a platter.

Drizzle with 2 tablespoons -OR- more of the Roasted-Garlic Oil. Season again with salt and pepper, if desired. Serve the grilled veggies warm -OR- at room temperature.

Roasted Garlic-Oil

7 large garlic cloves, peeled and halved

1 tablespoon olive oil

1 cup good quality extra virgin olive oil

Preheat your oven to 350 degrees F.

In a ovenproof skillet, add the garlic cloves & 1 tablespoon olive oil, stir to coat well.

Roast in the oven until the garlic is golden, shaking pan often, COOK, around 15 - minutes. Take the skillet out of the oven. Add the 1 cup of extra virgin olive oil, - COOK in the skillet. Pour the oil and garlic into a clean jar. Seal the top tightly and store the jar in the refrigerator for up to 2 weeks. Keep the garlic in the oil for more flavor and looks, however only use the oil in recipes.

Smoky Rum Baked Beans

Serves: 6-8 as a side dish

2 (15 ounce cans) pork & beans

1/2 onion, finely chopped

1 green pepper, finely chopped

1/2 cup brown sugar

1/4 cup Rum

2 garlic cloves, crushed in a garlic press

2 tablespoons liquid smoke

2 tablespoons soy sauce

1 tablespoon apple cider vinegar

2 teaspoons prepared yellow mustard

In a bowl, combine all the ingredients together, mix well. Pour into a glass baking dish, Bake at 350 degrees F. for 1 1/2 hours. Serve right away.

Bob's Beer Baked Beans

Serves: 10-12 as a side

5 strips bacon

1 medium onion, finely chopped

2 (28 ounces, each) cans baked beans

1/4 cup spicy brown mustard (I like Gulden's)

1/4 cup ketchup

3 tablespoons molasses

1 (12 ounces) bottled Lager Beer (your favorite lager beer)

Great Beer Baked Beans for your next Cook-Out -OR- Poker Night!

With a sharp knife cut each strip of bacon into 4 pieces. In a big pot, heat over medium, COOK the bacon until the fat is rendered, but the bacon is not yet crispy, set the bacon aside. Add the onion to the bacon fat, COOK over medium heat. Heat for 5-6 minutes, until soft, stir often.

Add the baked beans, mustard, ketchup, molasses and beer, stir to combine. Bring to a boil over medium-high heat, reduce heat to low heat and SIMMER for 10-12 minutes. Carefully pour into a 2 quart casserole dish. Bake in a preheated 400 degree F oven for 45 minutes - 1 hour -OR- until beans are desired thickness, stir often. Serve right away.

Cowboy Beer Baked Beans

Serves: 8 as a side dish

2 (15 ounce, each) cans pinto beans, drained, rinsed and drained

3/4 cup (6 ounces) beer

1/2 cup onion, finely chopped

1/2 cup (5 slices) crisp-cooked bacon, crumbled

1 (4 ounce) can diced green chili peppers

1/3 cup molasses

1/4 cup ketchup

1 tablespoon chili powder

In a 1 1/2 quart dish -OR- Dutch oven, combine the pinto beans, beer, onion, bacon, undrained green chili peppers, molasses, ketchup and chili powder, stir to mix well. Bean mixture can be covered and stored in the refrigerator for up to 24 hours -OR- cooked right away. Bake uncovered in a 350 degree F. oven for 1 to 1 1/2 hours -OR- until desired thickness.

BiBo's Fresh Tomato & Onion Salad

Makes: 6 serving

2 tablespoons olive oil

2 tablespoons balsamic vinegar

3 teaspoons fresh basil, chopped

1/2 teaspoon sugar

salt - to taste and ground black pepper - to taste

1 medium red onion, thinly sliced

1 pound ripe tomatoes, sliced (around 3-4 tomatoes)

1/3 cup crumbled Feta cheese -OR- Bleu cheese

In a bowl, whisk together the oil, vinegar, basil, sugar, salt and pepper. Place the -sliced onions on a serving platter. Place tomatoes in a single layer over the onions.

Pour the basil dressing mixture over the tomatoes. Sprinkle with Feta Cheese -OR-Bleu Cheese.

Serve right away!!!

Bob's Tomato & Watermelon Salad W/ Blue Cheese & Toasted Almonds

Feeds 8 or more hungry people

8 cups of 1-1/2" chunks, seedless watermelon (around 6 pounds)

6 cups ripe tomatoes, cut into 1-1/2" inch chunks (around 3 pounds))

1 teaspoon -OR- more kosher salt -OR- sea salt

5 tablespoons -OR- more olive oil

1 1/2 tablespoon red wine vinegar

4 tablespoons fresh mint, chopped

6 cups fresh arugula leaves

1 cup blue cheese, crumbled (around 5 ounces)

1/2 cup sliced almonds

In a big bowl, combine the watermelon and tomatoes. Sprinkle with 1 teaspoon of salt and toss to mix, let stand for 20 minutes at room temperature, covered. Add 4 tablespoons olive oil, vinegar and fresh mint to watermelon mixture. Season with salt and pepper. In a bowl, toss the arugula with remaining 1 tablespoon olive oil, toss.

Plating Salad:

Divide the arugula onto 6 plates, top each with the watermelon salad, sprinkle with the blue cheese and toasted almonds.

Serve right away!

Go Blue Coleslaw

Serves: 8

Great for Tailgating !!!!

3 pounds, green cabbage, shredded

4 carrots, peeled and shredded

1/2 cup sweet onion, finely chopped

2/3 cup apple cider vinegar

6 tablespoons sugar

2/3 cup good quality mayonnaise (I like HELLMANN'S)

2/3 cup sour cream

2/3 cup Bleu cheese, crumbled salt - to taste

pepper - to taste

In a big bowl, combine the cabbage, carrots and onion. In a saucepan, combine the cider vinegar and sugar, bring to a boil. Pour the hot vinegar mixture over the vegetables and toss, let stand for 15 minutes. Drain the vegetables well and combine with mayo, sour cream, crumbled bleu cheese, salt and pepper, mix lightly. Place in the refrigerator for at least 4 hours -OR- over- night to let the flavors blend well.

Tailgating Potato & Egg Salad

Serves: 6-8

This salad is great with grilled foods and will taste better outside!!!!

3 pounds potatoes, cooked until just tender, cut into cubes, COOLED

6 hard eggs, COOLED & coarsely chopped

1/2 cup red onion, chopped

1/2 cup celery, chopped

Dressing:

3/4 cup -OR- more of mayonnaise

2 tablespoons prepared mustard

salt - to taste

pepper - to taste

In a bowl, combine the potatoes, eggs, onions and celery. Stir in the mayonnaise, mustard, salt and pepper to taste. Stir the mayo and mustard in a little at a time, until you have the flavor and consistency you want.

Serve right away -OR- you can chill before serving.

German Potato Salad W/ Bacon

Serves: 6-8

Bacon is the perfect food, it makes all foods better!!!

4 cups potatoes, peeled, cubed

6 bacon slices, finely chopped

1/2 cup onion, chopped

1/2 cup green bell pepper, chopped

2 eggs, beaten

1/4 cup sugar

1/4 cup vinegar

1/4 teaspoon pepper - to taste

Fresh flat leaf parsley, chopped

COOK potatoes in a covered saucepan in an inch boiling salted water until tender, around 20 - 22 minutes. Drain well. In a big skillet, cook bacon until almost crisp. Add onion and bell peppers, COOK 3-4 minutes longer. In a bowl, combine the beaten eggs with vinegar, sugar and pepper, mix to blend well. Gradually add the egg mixture to the bacon mixture, stirring and cooking until the mixture thickens. Remove from the heat and toss gently with the potatoes. Spoon salad into a serving dish and garnish with the fresh chopped parsley.

Serve right Away!!!

Potato & Bacon Salad

Serves: 6

3 pounds small red bliss potatoes (buy potatoes all of the same size, so they cook together)

1/2 pound bacon, chopped

1 cup onions, chopped

3 tablespoons white wine vinegar

5 tablespoons olive oil

salt - to taste

freshly ground black pepper - to taste

1 cup green onions (scallions), chopped, including the green tops

1/2 cup flat leaf parsley, chopped

Scrub the potatoes and place them in a big pot of cold water to cover. Bring to a boil, lower the the heat and COOK until the potatoes are done, around 15-18 minutes after the water comes to a boil. While the potatoes are boiling, fry the bacon pieces in a small, heavy skillet 6"-7" inches.

When crisp and done. Drain the bacon on paper towels and pour off all but 4 tablespoons of bacon fat. In the bacon fat still in the skillet, fry the onions just until they wilt. When the potatoes are done, drain them. Using paper towels -OR- pot holders to handle the hot potatoes.

Quarter the potatoes directly into a serving bowl. Pour the onions, bacon and cooking fat over the potatoes. Add the vinegars, olive oil, salt and pepper. Gently toss with a wooden spoon.

When the salad COOLS add the green onions (scallions) and parsley. Taste before serving; the salad may need more olive oil and/or vinegar, as well as more salt and/or pepper.

Serve right away!

Big Bob's Top 25 Greatest Beers in America

Your Top 25 List:

#1. Samuel Adams Black Lager

#2. Great Lakes Holy Moses White Ale

#3. Bell's Expedition Stout

#4. Southhampton Double White

#5. Ommegang Hennepin

#6. Jolly Pumpkin Bam Biere

#7. Great Lakes Burning River Pale Ale

#8. Firestone Walker Pale Ale

#9. Dogfish Head 60 Minute IPA

#10. Stoudt's Pils

#11. Russian Temptation Ale

#12. Rogue Brutal Bitter

#13. Avery Mephistopheles Stout

#14. Anderson Vallery Boont Amber Ale

#15. Full Sail Session Lager

#16. Smuttynose Big A IPA

#17. Penn Weizen

#18. Sprecher Hefe Weiss

#19. Alaskan Amber

#20. Victory St. Victorious Doppelbock

#21. Deschutes Broken Top Block

#22. Lost Abbey Avant Garde

#23. New Glarus Yokel

#24. Allagash Interlude

#25. Alesmith Speedway Stout

Big Bob's Top 10 Best Imported Lagers

Your Top 10 List:

#1. Molson Golden

#2. Corona Extra

#3. Labatt Blue

#4. Fosters

#5. Becks

#6. Kirin

#7. Dos Equis

#8. St. Pauli Girl

#9. Heineken

#10. Pilsner Urquell

Big Bob's Top 7 Best Nonalcoholic Beers

Your Top 7 List:

#1. O'Douls

#2. Sharps

#3. Coors Cutter

#4. Kaliber

#5. Old Milwaukee

#6. Kingsbury

#7. Clausthaler

Big Bob's Top 15 Best Regular & Ice Beers

Your Top 15 List:

#1. Budweiser

#2. Red Dog

#3. Old Milwaukee

#4. Bud Ice

#5. Coors Original

#6. Michelob

#7. Molson Ice

#8. Stroh's

#9. Icehouse

#10. Busch

#11. Genesee Cream Ale

#12. Pabst Blue Ribbon

#13. Miller High Life

#14. Milwaukee's Best

TIE #15. Rolling Rock

TIE #15. Miller Genuine Draft

Big Bob's Top 5 Light Beers

Your Top 5 List:

#1. Coors Light

#2. Michelob Light

#3. Bud Light

TIE #4. Miller Lite

TIE #4. Amstel Light

#5. Natural Light

Notes

CHAPTER #14
Breads
BOWLING

Grilled Flat Bread

Makes: 4-6 servings

1 package (about 1 pound) refrigerated pizza dough

Flour for work surface

2 tablespoons olive oil, Plus 2 teaspoons olive oil

1 teaspoon kosher salt

1/2 teaspoon ground black pepper

2 tablespoons fresh rosemary, chopped

Let the pizza dough rest at room temperature for at least 20-30 to warm up to room temperature.

Divide the dough into equal portions. Roll each piece out into a rectangle approximately 1/4" inch thick. Brush one side of each rectangle with 1/2 tablespoon of olive oil and season with 1/4 teaspoon salt and 1/4 teaspoon pepper. Transfer the dough to the grill, place the oiled side down on the grill rack and close the grill lid. COOK until the dough begins to bubble on the top, around 3 minutes. Working fast, brush each rectangle with 1/2 tablespoon of olive oil and season with the remaining kosher salt and pepper. Turn and COOK until golden and crisp on the bottom, 2-3 minutes more. Brush each piece of the flat bread with the remaining olive oil and sprinkle with chopped fresh rosemary. Place flat bread on a cutting board and with a sharp knife cut into pieces.

Serve right away!!!

Grilled Cheese & Cilantro Bread

Makes: 12 servings

1 cup shredded Cheddar cheese -OR- Jack cheese

1/2 cup softened butter

3 tablespoons fresh cilantro, chopped

1 teaspoon paprika

1/2 teaspoon garlic powder - to taste

1 (1-pound) loaf Italian bread -OR- French bread, sliced diagonally 3/4" inch thick

Heavy-Duty aluminum foil

Preheat a gas -OR- charcoal grill for indirect medium heat

In a bowl, combine the cheese, butter, cilantro, paprika and garlic powder, mix well

Spread the cheese mixture onto the cut-sides of the bread. Arrange bread back into a loaf. Wrap bread in heavy-duty foil; tightly seal the top and ends. Place bread on the unheated side -OR- cool side of the grill. Grill over indirect heat for 13-21 minutes, turning once. Grill until the cheese is melted, take off the grill and remove the foil, carefully.

Serve Right Away!!!

4th. & 1 Grilled Bread

Makes: 12 servings (2 slices per person)

Lizzies Dressing for Bread:

1 (8 ounce) bottle; Store Bought Italian Dressing

3 garlic cloves, crushed in a garlic press

2 tablespoons fresh flat leaf Italian parsley

1 large loaf French Bread (around 24" inches long), cut into 24 slices (1" thick slices)

Preheat a gas -OR- charcoal for direct medium heat

In a bowl, combine the Italian dressing, garlic and parsley, mix well. Spread the Lizzies dressing generously onto each side of the bread slices. Place bread slices on the grill rack and grill for 3-4 minutes on each side -OR- until golden brown on both sides, don't burn. When done take the bread off the grill.

Serve right away!!!

3rd. & 3 Grilled Cheese Bread

Makes: 12 servings

1 1/2 cups shredded Mozzarella cheese

1/2 cup softened butter

3 tablespoons fresh basil, chopped

1 teaspoon paprika

1/4 teaspoon garlic powder - to taste

1 loaf Crusty Italian -OR- French Bread, cut into 3/4" inch slices

Preheat a gas -OR- charcoal grill for Indirect medium heat

In a bowl, combine the cheese, butter, basil, paprika and garlic powder, mix well. Spread the cheese mixture between the bread slices. Reform the bread slices back into a loaf shape. Wrap the bread in heavy-duty foil, tightly sealing tops and sides. Place the bread on the cool side of the unheated side of a grill set-up for indirect medium heat. Close the grill lid and grill for 14-20 minutes, turning over after 7 minutes. Cook until the cheese melts and the bread is heated.

Take off the grill, don't burn.

Serve right away!!!

Bob's Buttermilk Cornbread

Makes: 9 servings (3" inches, each)

1 cup yellow cornmeal

1 cup all-purpose flour

1 1/2 teaspoon double-acting powder

1/2 teaspoon baking soda

2 large eggs

1 1/4 cups buttermilk

1/2 stick (2 ounces) unsalted butter, melted & COOLED

Preheat the Oven to 425 degrees F.

Grease a 9" inch square pan generously. In bowl, whisk together the dry ingredients; cornmeal, flour, baking powder, baking soda and salt. In another bowl, whisk together the eggs, buttermilk, and the melted unsalted butter, add the buttermilk mixture to the cornmeal mixture and stir the batter until it is just combined. Heat the greased pan in the oven for 4-5 minutes, or until it is very hot. Add the batter, spreading it evenly and bake the cornbread in the middle of the oven.

Use the middle rack of the oven. Bake for 14-16 minutes or until the top is a pale golden brown and the sides begin to pull away from the edges of the pan. Take the pan out of the oven, COOL the cornbread fro 5 minutes. Turn the cornbread out of the pan onto a cooling rack and let it COOL completely. Cut the cornbread into 9 squares (3X3).

Serve right Away!!!

Skillet Cornbread w/Bacon

Makes: 4-6 servings

1/2 pound bacon, chopped

2 tablespoons fresh crushed garlic

4 jalapeno peppers, seeded, ribbed and finely chopped

3 cups cornmeal

1 teaspoon baking powder

1 teaspoon baking soda

2 teaspoons salt

1/2 teaspoon freshly ground black pepper

3 cups buttermilk

2 large eggs, lightly beaten

10 tablespoons melted unsalted butter

Preheat the oven to 450 degrees F.

In a 10" inch cast iron skillet -OR- any heavy skillet, brown the chopped bacon. Add the garlic and jalapeno peppers, sauté until softened. In a bowl, combine the cornbread, baking powder, baking soda, salt and pepper, mix well. In a bowl, combine the buttermilk, eggs and melted butter. Add the dry ingredients and stir to combine. Quickly pour the cornbread batter into the skillet. Bake of 25-30 minutes -OR- until firm and golden brown on top, bake in the middle of the oven. Take the cornbread out of the oven, let stand for 5 minutes, then turn out onto a clean cutting board. Cut with a sharp knife into wedges.

Serve hot with lots of butter on the side!!!

In a Flash Cornbread

Makes: 12 servings

A great cornbread to serve with your favorite Chili!!!

1 cup cornmeal

1 cup all purpose flour

1 tablespoon baking powder (I like CALUMET)

1/2 cup sugar

1 cup fresh corn kernels -OR- frozen, thawed

3/4 cup Shredded Cheddar Cheese

1/2 cup red bell pepper, chopped

1 egg

1/4 cup melted butter

1 cup buttermilk

Preheat your oven to 400 degrees F.

In a bowl, combine the cornmeal, flour, baking powder and sugar. Stir in the corn, cheese and red bell pepper. In a bowl, beat the egg. Add the melted butter and buttermilk; stir in the corn mixture until combined. Pour into a greased 8" inch square baking pan. Bake 25-30 minutes or until light golden brown and a toothpick inserted in the center should come out clean.

Take the cornbread out of the oven, place on a cooling rack to COOL for 5-10 minutes. With a sharp knife cut cornbread into 12 pieces.

Serve cornbread with lots of butter !!!

Beer & Mustard Biscuits

Makes: around 2 dozen

4 cups all purpose flour

4 teaspoons baking powder

1 1/2 teaspoon salt

1/2 cup cold shortening

1/2 cup cold butter

1 cup Beer (8 ounces)

2 tablespoons, Plus 2 teaspoons prepared mustard

2 tablespoons milk

Preheat your oven to 425 degrees F.

In a bowl, combine flour, baking powder and salt. Cut in the shortening & butter, until the mixture looks like coarse crumbs. In a bowl, combine the beer and mustard, pour into crumb mixture, stirring the whole time, just until blended. Turn onto a floured surface; knead gently around 8 times. Still on the floured surface, pat dough to a 1/2" inch thickness. Cut out biscuits using a 2" inch round biscuit cutter. Always reroll scraps and cut out additional biscuits. Place 1" inch apart on a greased baking sheet. Combine remaining mustard with the milk and brush over tops. Bake 13-15 minutes -OR- until browned. Take out of the oven let COOL 5 minutes on a cooling rack.

Serve biscuits warm with lots of butter & honey & enjoy!!!

Cowboy Biscuits

Makes: around 18 biscuits

4 cups Biscuit/Baking Mix

8 teaspoons Dry Ranch Salad Dressing Mix

1 1/3 cups milk

4 tablespoons butter

2 teaspoons dried parley flakes

1/4 teaspoon garlic powder

In a bowl, combine the biscuit mix, ranch salad dressing mix and milk, stir just until blended.

Drop 2 inches apart onto a greased baking sheet. Bake at 425 degrees F. for 10-15 minutes or until golden brown. Take the biscuits out of the oven, place on a rack to COOL. In a bowl, combine the butter, dried parsley and garlic powder; brush the butter mixture onto the warm biscuits.

Serve right away !!!

Players Choice Soft Beer Pretzels

Makes: 1 Dozen Soft Pretzels

3 1/4 cups all purpose flour

1 (0.25 ounces) Package Rapid Rise Yeast

1 teaspoon salt

2/3 cups Beer

1/2 cup water

2 tablespoons vegetable oil -OR- canola oil

6 cups water

2 tablespoons baking soda

1 egg, beaten

Kosher Salt

In a very big bowl, combine 3 cups flour, yeast and salt. In a saucepan heat the beer, water and oil to 120 degrees F., using a thermometer, don't go over 120 degrees F. Add the beer mixture to the flour mixture, beat until moistened. Stir in enough remaining flour, 1 tablespoon at a time, to form a soft dough. turn dough onto a lightly floured surface, knead the dough for 5-6 minutes or until smooth and elastic. Place in a oiled bowl, cover and let rise in a warm place for 15-18 minutes. Place the dough on a floured cutting board, using a sharp knife. Divide the dough in half, then divide each half into 6 equal pieces. Lightly flour your hands, roll each piece into a 14" inch rope with tapered ends. (Make sure you cover the remaining dough while working prevent it from drying out). Form a pretzel by creating a U shape, then cross one end over the other to form a circle, leaving around 3" inches at the end of the rope. Twist the rope at base of circle and fold ends over circle to form a pretzel shape. Always make large exaggerated loops, when shaping the pretzels, so they won't close when boiling. Place on greased baking sheets. Cover and let rise in a warm place 15-18 minutes.

Preheat oven to 400 degrees F.

In a big non-aluminum pot bring 6 cups of water to a boil and stir in the baking soda. Working in batches gently lower the pretzels into boiling water, COOK for 30 seconds, turning once. Using a slotted spoon, remove pretzels from the water, place on a wire rack, that is coated with non-stick cooking spray (aka: PAM).

Lightly brush the pretzels with beaten egg and sprinkle with kosher salt. Bake on a ungreased baking sheet for 10-11 minutes -OR- until golden brown. COOL on a wire rack.

Serve warm pretzels with your favorite mustard.

Life is good, sit down in your favorite chair to watch Baseball, eat a warm pretzel and drink a cold drink !!!

Breads

Big Bob's Top 20 Greatest PBA Bowlers All Time

Your Top 20 List:

#1. Earl Anthony

#2. Walter Ray Williams Jr

#3. Dick Weber

#4. Mark Roth

#5. Pete Weber

#6. Parker Bohn 3rd.

#7. Don Johnson

#8. Mike Aulbey

#9. Wayne Webb

#10. Brain Voss

#11. Norm Duke

#12. Marshall Holman

#13. Johnny Petraglia

#14. Dick Ritger

#15. Dave Davis

#16. Billy Hardwick

#17. Amleto Monacelli

#18. Steve Cook

#19. Carmen Salvino

TIE #20. Wayne Zahn

TIE #20. Dave Soutar

Big Bob's Top 30 Greatest Women Bowlers All Time

#1. Marion Ladwig

#2. Donna Adamek

#3. Lisa Wagner

#4. Betty Morris

#5. Dotty Fothergill

#6. Wendy Macpherson

#7. Patty Costello

#8. Robin Romeo Mossonte

#9. Carolyyn Dorin-Ballard

TIE #10. Tish Johnson

TIE #10. Kim Adler

#11. Helen Duval

#12. Aleta Rzepecki

#13. Floretta McCutheon

#14. Millie Martorella Ignizio

TIE #15. Anne Marie Duggan

TIE #15. Liz Johnson

#16. Aleta Sill

#17. Nikki Gianulius

#18. Leanne Barrette

#19. Judy Souter

TIE #20. Shirley Garms

TIE #20. Carol Gianotti-Block

#21. LaVerne Carter

#22. Cindy Coburn-Carroll

#23. Dana Miller-Mackie

#24. Sylvia Wene Martin

#25. Vesma Grinfelds

#26. Emma Jaeger

#27. Val Mickiel

#28. Cheryl Daniels

#29. Paula Carter

#30. Dorothy Miller

Your Top 30 List:

_____

Notes

CHAPTER #15

Grilled Fruit

TOP 35 SPORTS BOOKS

TOP 35 GRILLING SONGS

TOP 40 SPORTS MOVIES

Grilled Blueberry & Raspberry Cobbler

Serves: 6

5 tablespoons melted butter

1 cup all purpose flour

1 teaspoon baking powder dash of salt

2/3 cup sugar

3/4 cup milk dash of vanilla

1 cup fresh blueberries

1 cup raspberries

1/3 cup sugar

Preheat a gas -OR- charcoal grill for indirect medium heat

Coat the inside sides and bottom of a 8" inch round disposable foil cake pan with the melted butter. In a bowl, combine the flour, baking powder, salt, 2/3 cup sugar, milk and vanilla, mix well. Pour the batter into the melted buttered cake pan, level the top of the batter. Arrange the fresh blueberries and fresh raspberries on top of the batter, sprinkle with 1/3 cup sugar. Cover the pan tightly with heavy-duty foil. Place the pan on the COOL side of a grill set-up for indirect medium heat/coals for around 30-40 minutes. The cobbler is done when a toothpick inserted into the center of the clobber comes out clean. Take off the grill, serve with ice cream and/or whipped cream.

Grilled Apple Crisp

Makes: 8 servings

1 (21 ounce) can store bought apple filling

1/3 cup brown sugar, packed

1/2 teaspoon cinnamon

1/4 teaspoon nutmeg

2 tablespoons fresh lime juice

1/2 package (box) yellow cake mix (18.5 ounce) appox. (2 cups)

1/2 cup butter; cut into slices

vanilla ice cream and/or whipped cream

Preheat a gas -OR- charcoal grill for indirect medium heat & close the grill lid.

Spray the sides and bottom of a grill safe 9" baking pan with PAM. Pour pie filling into the baking pan. Sprinkle with the brown sugar, cinnamon, nutmeg and fresh lime juice. Then sprinkle the cake mix over the apple filling to cover and dot with butter slices. Place the baking pan on the cool side of the grill and close the grill lid. Bake for 50-65 minutes or until browned and bubbly. Take the crisp off the grill and let stand until it is warm. Serve in bowls with ice cream and/or whipped cream.

*Tip: You might have to double pan the crisp and/or cover the top tightly with heavy-duty foil.

Grilled Honey Apricots

Serves: 6

8 each fresh ripe apricots, halved and pitted

4 tablespoons unsalted butter

3 tablespoons sugar

1/4 teaspoon cinnamon

3 tablespoons honey

4 fresh lime wedges

Your Favorite Vanilla Ice Cream

Lightly brush vegetable oil -OR- olive oil onto the grill rack

Preheat a gas -OR- charcoal grill to direct medium heat

In a saucepan, combine the melted butter and sugar together, heat over medium heat. Turn heat off, right away add apricots and coat with butter mixture. Place the apricots on the grill rack, cut side down. Grill for 5-7 minutes, turning often, until done. When cooked, take off the grill, place apricots on dessert plates. Drizzle with honey and fresh lime juice, serve warm with ice cream.

Serve right away!!!

Kim's Grilled Plums W/ Ricotta & Honey

Serves: 4-6

vegetable oil -OR- olive oil for brushing on the grill rack.

4 each ripe plums, halved and pitted

Fresh Ricotta Cheese

honey, for drizzling

toasted almonds

Lightly brush the grill rack with vegetable oil -OR- olive oil Preheat a gas -OR- charcoal grill to direct high heat

Place the plums on the grill rack, cut side down, until marked tender and softened. COOK, 3-4 minutes -OR- until done grilling. Take off the grill and COOL, until warm. Serve warm plums on dessert plates with a dollop of ricotta, drizzle of honey and sprinkle with toasted almonds.

Serve right away!!!

Grilled Nectarines

Serves: 6

6 nectarines, halved and pitted

2 tablespoons honey

Vanilla Ice Cream

Brush cut sides of nectarine halves with honey.

Lightly brush the grill rack with vegetable oil

Preheat a gas -OR- charcoal grill for direct medium-low heat

Place the nectarines on the grill cut side down over medium-low heat, COOK until warm and has grill marks, but still firm around 5 minutes. Take the nectarines off the grill and serve hot with a scoop of your favorite vanilla ice cream.

Grilled Peaches

Makes: 4 Servings

4 large, ripe peaches, halved and pitted

4 tablespoons unsalted butter, melted

3 tablespoons packed brown sugar

Vanilla Ice Cream

In a big bowl, place the peach halves, drizzle with the butter and sprinkle with the brown sugar, toss to make sure it is mixed well. Cover and let stand for 1 hour at room temperature.

Lightly brush vegetable oil onto the grill rack. Preheat a gas -OR- charcoal grill to direct medium-low heat.

Place peaches on the grill rack, cut side down over medium-low heat. COOK for 10 minutes -OR- until tender and light brown, with grill marks. Baste the peaches with the butter-brown sugar mixture and only turn over once.

Serve hot -OR- warm with favorite vanilla ice cream!!!

Grilled Fresh Figs W/ Mascarpone, Walnuts & Balsamic Syrup

Serves: 6

3/4 cup Balsamic Vinegar

1 1/2 tablespoons light molasses

1 1/2 pints fresh figs (12-18), stems trimmed & cut in 1/2 lengthwise

6 tablespoons Mascarpone Cheese

toasted walnuts

In a heavy saucepan, combine the balsamic vinegar and molasses, bring to a boil over medium heat. Keep boiling until reduced to 3 3/4 tablespoons, around 10 minutes. Let COOL.

Lightly brush vegetable oil onto the grill rack. Preheat a gas -OR- charcoal grill to direct high heat, close the grill lid.

Place the fresh figs on the grill rack, cut side down. COOK, with the grill lid closed, 2-3 minutes or until golden, turning once. Use tongs or a spatula to take the figs off the grill and onto a platter. COOL slightly, place 2-3 figs on each dessert plate. Top figs with around 1 tablespoon of mascarpone cheese. Drizzle with the balsamic syrup and sprinkle with toasted walnuts.

Serve right away!!!

Grilled Cinnamon Bananas

Serves: 6

6 large bananas, cut on the diagonal into 1" inch slices juice of 2 fresh limes

2 tablespoons brown sugar

3 tablespoons dark rum

1 1/2 teaspoons ground cinnamon

vanilla bean -OR- chocolate ice cream

6 each 12" inch squares of heavy-duty foil

In a big bowl, toss the banana slices with lime juice, brown sugar, rum and cinnamon. Divide the bananas among 6 foil squares. Bring the edges of the foil together and scrunch tightly to form a good seal.

Preheat a gas -OR- charcoal grill to direct medium-low heat

Place foil packets on the grill rack, over medium-low heat. COOK for 16-21 minutes, until hot through. Serve hot -OR- warm with a scoop of your favorite vanilla bean -OR- chocolate ice cream.

Grilled Pineapple W/ Margarita Ice Cream

Serves: 4

1 unpeeled medium size fresh ripe pineapple, quartered

1 tablespoon Tequila

2 tablespoons fresh lime juice

2 tablespoons honey

With a sharp knife cut away the core form the pineapple quarters. In a bowl combine the Tequila, lime juice and honey, whisk to dissolve, this mixture will be used as a glaze.

Lightly brush vegetable oil onto the grill rack.

Preheat a gas -OR- charcoal grill to direct medium-low heat

Brush the cut sides of the pineapple with the glaze. Place the pineapple on the grill rack cut side down over medium-low heat. COOK for 6-11 minutes per side -OR- until hot and has grill marks on all sides. Serve hot -OR- warm with any leftover glaze and a scoop of Margarita Ice Cream on each pineapple quarter.

Margarita Ice Cream

Serves: 4

Margarita Ice Cream:

1 pint Vanilla Ice Cream, softened

2 tablespoons fresh lime juice

1 tablespoon fresh lemon juice

1 tablespoon Tequila

1/8 teaspoon salt, to taste

In a big bowl, combine the softened vanilla ice cream, lime juice, lemon juice, Tequila and salt, stirring well to combine. Freeze to desired consistency. Serve the cold ice cream with warm or hot grilled pineapple.

Grilled Pears W/ Toasted Hazelnuts

Serves: 6

1/3 cup brown sugar, packed

2 tablespoons softened unsalted butter

1/4 teaspoon nutmeg

1/2 teaspoon cinnamon

2 tablespoons honey

3 cups cored and sliced fresh pears

Your Favorite Vanilla Bean Ice Cream

4 tablespoons honey to drizzle on ice cream

1/3 cup toasted hazelnuts, COOLED, to sprinkle on ice cream

Grilled Fruit

6 each 18" inch aluminum foil squares

In a bowl, combine brown sugar, butter, nutmeg, cinnamon and honey, mix well. Make 6 each

18" inch aluminum foil squares. Place sliced pears into the center of each foil square. Spoon the brown sugar mixture into the pears and seal the edges of foil. Make sure to leave space to allow for the steam to build.

Preheat a gas -OR- charcoal grill to direct medium heat

Place the packets onto the grill rack, over medium heat. Allow to COOK for 12-15 minutes -OR- until done. Remove the packets carefully from the grill. Place the warm pears on a dessert plate plate, place a scoop of ice cream on each plate. Drizzle each with honey and sprinkle each with the toasted hazelnuts.

Serve right away!!!

Big Bob's Top 35 Greatest Sports Books of All Time

Book: Title	Author:	Your Top 35:
#1. The Sweet Science	A.J. Liebling 1956	
#2. Friday Night Lights	H.G. Bissinger 1990	
#3. A Season on the Brink	John Feinstein 1986	
#4. The Boys of Summer	Roger Kahn 1971	
#5. Ball Four	John Bouton 1970	
#6. Semi Tough	Dan Jenkins 1972	
#7. Paper Loin	George Plimpton 1965	
#8. The Game	Ken Dryden 1983	
#9. Bang the Drum Slowly	Mark Harris 1956	
#10. Fever Pitch	Nick Hornby 1991	
#11. Seabiscuit	Laura Hillenbrand 2001	
#12. Loose Balls	Terry Pluto 1990	
#13. Levels of the Game	John McPhee 1969	
#14. The Breaks of the Game	David Halberstam 1981	
#15. The Summer Game	Roger Angel 1972	
#16. Everybody's All American	Frank De Ford 1981	
#17. Instant Replay	Jerry Kramer & Dick Schaap 1968	
#18. The Long Season	Jim Brosnan 1960	
#19. The City Game	Pete Axthelm 1970	
#20. North Dallas Forty	Peter Gent 1973	
#21. Ben Hogan's Five Lessons	Ben Hogan & Herbert Warren Wind 1957	
#22. The Natural	Bernard Malamud 1952	
#23. When Pride Still Mattered	David Maraniss 1999	
#24. Babe: The Legend Comes to Life	Robert Creamer 1974	
#25. About Three Bricks Shy of a Load	Roy Blount Jr. 1974	
#26. A FAN'S NOTE	Frederick Exley 1968	
#27. JOE DIMAGGIO: The Hero's Life	Richard Ben Cramer 2000	
#28. The Game They Played	Stanley Cohen 1977	
#29. The Bronx Zoo	Sparky Lyle & Peter Goldenbock 1979	

#30. Shoeless Joe	W.P. Kinsella 1982	_____
#31. VEECK as in WREAK	Bill Veeck & Ed Linn 1962	_____
#32. A False Spring	Pat Jordan 1975	_____
#33. End Zone	Don Delillo 1972	_____
#34. COSELL	Howard Cosell 1973	_____
#35. Harvey Penick's Little Red Book	Harvey Penick & Bud Shrake 1992	_____

Big Bob's Top 35 Best Summer Grilling Songs All Time

#1. Cheeseburger in Paradise - Jimmy Buffet
#2. Margaritaville - Jimmy Buffet
#3. Rock Lobster - the B-52s
#4. School's Out - Alice Cooper
#5. Born to Run - Bruce Springsteen
#6. Boys of Summer - Don Henley
#7. Brown-Eyed Girl - Van Morrison
#8. California Girls - Beach Boys/David Lee Roth
#9. 99 in the Shade - Bon Jovi
#10. Summer in the City - the Lovin' Spoonful
#11. Dancing in the Streets - Martha & the Vandellas
#12. Wipeout - the Surfaris
#13. Under the Board Walk - the Drifter's
#14. Hot Fun in the Summertime - Sly and the Family Stones
#15. I Can See Clearly Now - Johnny Cash
#16. In the Summertime - Mungo Jerry
#17. Let's Go Crazy - Prince
#18. Saturday in the Park - Chicago
#19. Walking on Sunshine - Katrina and the Waves
TIE #20. Locomotion - Little Eva
TIE #20. Low Rider - War
#21. Groovin' - The Young Rascals
#22. Soak up the Sun - Sheryl Crow
#23. Love Shack - B-52s
#24. Dance the Night Away - Van Halen
#25. Don't Worry Baby - The Beach Boys
#26. All Summer Long - The Beach Boys
#27. 2 Pina Coladas - Garth Brooks
#28. Mary's Place - Bruce Springsteen and the E Street Band
#29. Summertime-Summertime - Jamies
#30. Cabo Wabo - Van Halen
#31. Warm California Sun - The Rivieras
#32. It's 5:00 Somewhere - Alan Jackson/Jimmy Buffet

#33. Master Blaster - Stevie Wonder
#34. Iko, Iko - The Belle Stars
TIE #35. Summer Lovin' - Grease
TIE #35. Those Lazy Hazy Days of Summer - Nat King Cole

Big Bob's Top 40 Sports Movies All Time

This is a list of my All Time favorite Sports Movies !!!

Your Top 40 List:

#1. Rocky, Rocky 3 & Rocky 2 _____
#2. Raging Bull _____
#3. Hoosiers _____
#4. Brain's Song _____
#5. North Dallas Forty _____
#6. Caddy Shack _____
#7. Sea Biscuit _____
#8. Jerry Maguire _____
#9. Bull Durham _____
#10. Field of Dreams _____
#11. Slap Shot _____
#12. The Natural _____
#13. The Longest Yard _____
#14. Bang the Drum Slowly _____
#15. Tin Cup _____
#16. When We Were Kings _____
#17. The Hustler _____
#18. Hoop Dreams _____
#19. Chariots of Fire _____
TIE #20. Breaking Away _____
TIE #20. Rudy _____
#21. Remember the Titans _____
#22. Eight Men Out _____
#23. The Bad News Bears _____
#24. A League of Their Own _____
#25. Pride of the Yankees _____
#26. Heaven Can Wait _____
#27. White Men Can't Jump _____
#28. The Color of Money _____
#29. Rounders _____

#30. Friday Night Lights

#31. Any Given Sunday

#32. ALI

#33. HURRICANE

#34. The Legend of Bagger Vance

#35. Dead Solid Perfect

#36. 61

#37. Happy Gilmore

#38. Major League

#39. THE REPLACEMENTS

TIE #40. THE SANDLOT

TIE #40. Follow the Sun

CHAPTER #16
Dinner Hot Off The Grill!!!
THE GREATEST

MENU

Hot Off The Grill !!!

Thanksgiving Dinner

Cranberry Sauce

Big Bob's Grilled Turkey with Gravy

Grilled Sweet Potato Slices

Grilled Yellow Squash

B.B. Bread Stuffing

Classic Green Bean Casserole

Airing It Out Cornbread

Pumpkin Head Pie

Grilled Apples with Vanilla Ice Cream

Chocolate & Bourbon Pecan Pie

Big Bob's Grilled Whole Turkey W/ Gravy

Makes: 12 Servings

1 fresh -OR- frozen whole turkey (10-12 lbs.) THAWED

1/4 cup melted butter

BB Turkey Rub:

3/4 teaspoon kosher salt

1/2 teaspoon garlic powder

1/2 teaspoon onion powder

1/2 teaspoon dried thyme

1/4 teaspoon ground black pepper

1/8 teaspoon ground ginger

In a bowl, mix all the ingredients together, Use right away -OR- will store for months in a air tight container in a dry place.

Preheat a gas -OR- charcoal grill to indirect medium heat

1 each drip pan

Remove and discard neck and giblets from turkey. Rinse turkey with cold running water. Season the cavity of turkey with 2 teaspoons of BB turkey rub. Fasten neck skin with skewers. Turn wings back and tuck tips under shoulder joints. Refasten drumsticks with metal skewer or tuck under band of skin at tail. Rub the entire surface of the turkey with melted butter. Place a drip pan over the burner on the unheated side of the grill. Place the turkey on the grill rack, breast side up, over the unheated side of the grill directly over the drip pan. Close the grill lid; COOK, turkey with indirect medium heat for 2 1/2 - 3 1/2 hours or until the meat thermometer reaches 180 - 185 F. degrees and legs move easily when moved or twisted. Avoid opening the grill lid until ready to check the thermometer. (You do not have to baste or turn the turkey). Let the turkey stand at room temperature for 20 minutes on the cutting board before carving.

Serve right away!

*Tip: Never thaw a turkey at room temperature. To thaw a 10-12 lb. turkey allow 2-3 days in your refrigerator. A quicker way to thaw a turkey, is to immerse in cold water, keep it in it's original wrapped. Allow 5-6 hours for a frozen 10-12 lb. turkey. Change the cold water frequently.

**Note: If you want extra BB turkey rub for another day, make sure you 2X the rub recipe.

*Tip: Just buy your favorite Store Bought Turkey Gravy in a packet, can -OR- jar, follow the heating directions.

Grilled Sweet Potato Slices

Makes: 12 Servings

4 1/2 pounds unpeeled clean sweet potatoes, sliced 1/2" inch thick

6 garlic cloves, crushed in a garlic press

1 cup olive oil -OR- canola oil

kosher salt -OR- sea salt

Cook potato slices in boiling salted water until tender, but still firm, COOK for 4-5 minutes. Drain. In a bowl, combine the garlic and oil, mix well.

Preheat a gas -OR- charcoal grill for direct medium heat.

Place the potato slices on the grill rack, baste potato slices with garlic oil and sprinkle with salt.

COOK for 4-5 minutes, turn over baste with garlic oil and sprinkle with salt, grill over direct medium heat for 4-5 minutes more -OR- until lightly charred, don't burn.

Grilled Yellow Squash

Makes: 12 Servings

12 yellow squash, washed, cut in half lengthwise

1 1/4 cups Store-Bought Italian Salad Dressing

On a cutting board, using a sharp knife cut the yellow squash in half lengthwise. Place the squash halves in 1-2 large resealable plastic bags. Pour the Italian dressing into one -OR- both bags, seal tight, turn to coat the squash and place in the refrigerate to marinate for at least 1 hour.

Preheat a gas -OR- charcoal grill for direct medium heat.

Lightly brush the grill rack with vegetable oil.

Remove squash from marinade, place the squash on the grill rack, place cut side down, close the grill lid. Grill over medium heat for 5-8 minutes -OR- until tender, with grill marks, don't burn.

You can baste with the leftover marinade during the grilling time. Take grilled squash off the and place on a platter.

Serve right away!!!

B.B. Bread Stuffing

You can purchase 2 boxes of (aka); Stove Top Stuffing -OR- Make B.B. Bread Stuffing

1 1/2 sticks (6 ounces) unsalted butter, plus extra butter to spread on the casserole dish

3 3/4 cups store-bought canned turkey -OR- chicken broth

1-2 onions, finely chopped (2 cups)

9 stalks celery, trimmed and chopped (4 1/2 cups)

3/4 cup fresh flat leaf parsley, chopped

4 tablespoons fresh sage leaves, cut into strips

1 (16 ounce bag) Store-Bought Plain bread stuffing

freshly ground black pepper - to taste

1 tablespoon salt to taste

Place oven rack in center of oven, preheat oven to 400 degrees F.

Lightly butter a big casserole dish

In a saucepan, combine the unsalted butter, broth, onions, celery, parsley, salt to taste and sage, bring to boil over medium heat. Cook, until the celery is translucent and tender, 9-13 minutes. In a bowl, add the dry plain bread stuffing. Pour the warm (hot) mixture from the saucepan over the bread stuffing. With a big spoon mix the stuffing mixture, until well combined.

When COOL, enough blend completely. Season with the pepper, mix well. Pack the stuffing mixture into a buttered casserole dish. COOK for 30 minutes -OR- until done (hot).

Use right away -OR- cover with foil, it will stay warm for at least 1/2 hour -OR- so!!!

Classic Green Bean Casserole

Makes: 12 Servings

8 slices bacon, cook until crisp

1 cup chopped onions

3 cans French-Style green beans

2 each (10 3/4 ounce) cans condensed Cream of Mushroom Soup

salt - to taste

pepper to taste

1 (8 ounce) can sliced Water Chestnuts, drained

1 (2.8 ounce) can Fried Onion Rings, crumbled

COOK the bacon in a big skillet until crisp; remove, crumble and set aside.

Preheat your oven to 350 degrees F.

Drain off excess bacon drippings, leaving 2 tablespoons of fat in the skillet. Sauté onions in bacon drippings until tender; drain. Combine onions, green beans and mushroom soup; blend well. Add salt and pepper to taste.

Spoon half of the green bean mixture into a greased 12"X8"X2" inch baking dish. Arrange water chestnuts over the layer; sprinkle half of the crumbled bacon over the water chestnuts. Top with the remaining green bean mixture. Cover and bake at 350 degrees F. for 30 minutes, Uncover. Combine crumbled onion rings with the remaining bacon and water chestnuts. Arrange over the top of the casserole. Return green bean casserole to the oven and bake for 7-9 minutes longer until hot.

Serve right away!!!

Cranberry Sauce

2 cups water

2 cups sugar

4 cups fresh cranberries

In a Dutch Oven, combine the water and sugar, stir well to dissolve. Heat slowly to a boil over medium heat, BOIL rapidly 5-6 minutes longer. COOL, cover and refrigerate for at least 10 hours or longer.

Airing It Out Cornbread

Yield: 18 Servings

Makes: 2 each 8" X 8" pans

2 1/2 cups all purpose flour

1 1/2 cups cornmeal

1/2 cup sugar

2 cups buttermilk

8 teaspoons baking powder

2 teaspoons salt

1/2 cup vegetable oil -OR- canola oil

8 egg whites

Preheat your oven to 350 degrees F.

Grease 2 each - 8" X 8" inch pans

In a really big bowl, combine the flour, cornmeal, sugar, buttermilk, baking powder, salt, oil and egg whites, mix well till moistened. Pour half of the cornmeal mixture into each of the 2 - 8" X 8" inch pans, make sure you have a equal amount into each pan. Bake for 25-30 minutes at 350 degrees F. When done take the pans out of the oven and COOL on a rack, when cool turn out of pan, cut each cornbread into 9 square pieces each.

Serve right away with lots of butter!!!

Pumpkin Head Pie

Makes: 8 Servings

1 unbaked 9" inch frozen deep dish pie shell, THAWED

4 cups sugar

1 teaspoon ground cinnamon

1/2 teaspoon salt

1/2 teaspoon ground ginger

1/4 teaspoon ground cloves

2 eggs, large

1 can (15 ounces) 100% Pure Pumpkin (I like Libby's)

1 can (12 ounces) Evaporated Milk (I like Carnation)

Preheat your oven to 425 degrees F.

In a bowl, combine the sugar, cinnamon, salt, ginger and cloves, mix well. In a big bowl, beat the eggs. Stir the pumpkin and the sugar-spice mixture into the egg mixture. Slowly stir in the Evaporated Milk.

Pour the pumpkin mixture into a 9" inch deep dish pie shell.

Bake in your oven at 425 degrees F. for 15 minutes. Reduce the oven temperature to 350 degrees F. and bake for 45-50 minutes -OR- until a knife/toothpick inserted in the center comes out clean. COOL, on a wire cooling rack for 2-3 hours.

Serve right away at room temperature -OR- refrigerate before serving.

Pumpkin Pie is great served with Whipped Cream.

Grilled Apples w/Vanilla Bean Ice Cream

Makes: 12 Servings

6 each, ripe apples, cored and cut in half

1 1/2 cups white wine

4 tablespoons sugar

3 cinnamon sticks (about 2 inches each)

1 1/2 teaspoons nutmeg

Spray one very large grill safe baking dish -OR- 2-medium size grill safe baking dishes with cooking oil spray. On a cutting board with a sharp knife cut the apples in half from the top and remove all the seeds. Place the apples cut side down in the grill safe baking dish and cover with the remaining ingredients. Cover the grill safe baking dish with a lid -OR- heavy-duty foil tightly.

Place baking dish on a pre-heated medium grill and COOK for around 15 minutes. COOK, until most of the liquid is gone and the apples can be easily pierced with a fork and are very tender.

Take the apples off the grill and serve hot -OR- warm with your favorite Vanilla Ice Cream and Store-Bought Caramel Sauce.

Chocolate & Bourbon Pecan Pie

Makes: 8 Servings

1 each - 9" inch unbaked frozen pie shell, THAWED

3 eggs

2/3 cup sugar

1/2 teaspoon salt

1/3 cup melted butter

2 squares (1 ounce) unsweetened chocolate, melted

3/4 cup corn syrup

1/4 cup Good Quality Bourbon

1 cup pecan halves

Preheat your oven to 375 degrees F.

Thaw a frozen pie shell -OR- make your own single-crust pie pastry.

In a bowl, beat the eggs, sugar, salt, butter, melted chocolate, corn syrup and Bourbon with a hand beater, until well mixed. Stir in the pecans. Pour into unbaked pastry-lined pie pan. Bake until set, around 45-50 minutes. COOL slightly on a wire cooling rack. Serve right away warm or refrigerate and ready to use. Chocolate & Bourbon Pecan Pie should be served with Sweetened Whipped Cream -OR- Cool Whip.

Homemade Sweetened Whipped Cream

Makes: 2 1/3 cups

1 cup chilled whipping cream

3 tablespoons powdered sugar

1 teaspoon vanilla

In a well chilled bowl, Beat the chilled-whipping cream, powdered sugar and vanilla until stiff. Use right away for best results !!!

MENU

Dinner Hot Off The Grill !!!

EASTER DINNER

Grilled Lime-Yogurt Leg of Lamb

Grilled Orangemen Herb Chicken

Grilled Lettuce W/ Bacon & Blue Cheese

Curly's Grilled Potato Salad

Bug's Grilled Carrots

Grilled Lemon & Garlic Asparagus

Grilled Pound Cake w/Berry Sauce

Grilled Lime & Yogurt-Marinated Leg of Lamb

Lime & Yogurt Marinade:

1 1/2 cups plain yogurt

2/3 cup fresh lime juice

2 each red onions, thinly sliced

2 each fresh garlic cloves, crushed in a garlic press

2 tablespoons fresh marjoram

2 teaspoons crushed oregano

1 each (pounds) butterflied boneless leg of lamb

In a bowl, stir together all the ingredients of the Lime & Yogurt Marinade, mix well. Place the lamb in a pan and coat it well with the Lime & Yogurt Marinade. Cover and refrigerate for 12 -24 hours to marinate, turning lamb occasionally. Don't marinate for more than 24 hours. Take the lamb out of the refrigerator and let it come up to room temperature before grilling.

Preheat a gas -OR- charcoal grill to direct medium heat.

Place the lamb on the grill rack over medium heat and grill lamb for 11-14 minutes on each side. COOK the lamb to the desired doneness and take the lamb off the grill. Let the lamb rest for 5 minutes before slicing.

Serve Right Away!!!

Grilled Orangemen Herb Chicken Breast

Orange Herb Marinade:

1 cup fresh orange juice

3 3/4 tablespoon vinegar

1 1/2 tablespoon soy sauce

1/2 teaspoons fresh rosemary, finely chopped

1/2 teaspoon freshly grated orange zest

1/2 teaspoon fresh thyme, finely chopped

4 fresh garlic cloves, crushed in a garlic press

freshly ground black pepper to taste

2 pounds boneless, skinless chicken breast

In a bowl, whisk together all the ingredients of the orange herb marinade, mix well. Place the chicken breast in a resealable large plastic bag and pour the orange herb marinade over the chicken. Seal the bag tightly and turn to coat the chicken. Place the bag in the refrigerator and marinate overnight. Take the chicken breast out of the refrigerator and let it come up to room temperature before grilling.

Lightly brush vegetable oil onto the grill rack

Preheat a gas -OR- charcoal grill for direct high heat !!!

Take the chicken breast out of the marinade. Place the chicken on the grill rack over high heat for 4 minutes on each side, turning and basting often. *Tip: For basting heat the orange herb marinade to a boil over medium-high heat, stirring often. Take the marinade off the heat. Brush the marinade on the chicken during the grilling. COOK the chicken to the desired doneness.

Take the chicken off the grill and serve right away.

Grilled Boston Lettuce w/Warm Bacon & Blue Cheese Dressing

Serves: 8

Blue Boy Salad Dressing:

1 cup heavy cream

1/2 cup bleu cheese, crumbles

6 bacon slices, chopped & fried crisp, then drained

salt to taste

freshly ground pepper to taste

In a saucepan, bring the heavy cream to a boil. Reduce the heat right away to medium heat and add the bleu cheese, stir often. SIMMER for 5 minutes, then add the cooked bacon, salt and pepper. Take off the heat and set aside, keep warm.

Grilled Boston Lettuce:

4 heads Boston Lettuce, rinsed and dried

4 tablespoons olive oil

salt to taste

freshly ground pepper to taste

Cut each head of lettuce in half. Toss the leaves with olive oil until all sides are coated and season with salt and pepper.

Preheat a gas -OR- charcoal grill to direct medium-high heat

Place the lettuce on the grill rack and grill for 45 seconds on each side. Place the grilled lettuce on salad plates and ladle on the warm bacon & bleu cheese dressing.

Serve right away !!!

Curly's Grilled Potato Salad

Serves: 8 as a side salad

8 each medium size red potatoes

2 each large red onions

3/4 cup olive oil

1/4 cup balsamic vinegar

1/4 cup fresh basil, chopped

2 tablespoons prepared mustard

1/2 - 1 tablespoon dill weed to taste

salt to taste

pepper to taste

Lightly brush vegetable oil onto the grill rack

Preheat a gas -OR- charcoal grill to direct high heat

On a cutting board with a sharp knife cut the potatoes in half. Place potato halves in the microwave for 3 minutes or until they start to COOK. Cut the onions into 1/2" inch slices and place on a hot grill with the potatoes. Grill the onions and potatoes over high heat until tender. COOL to touch, Cut potatoes and onions with a sharp knife into 1/4" inch chunks.

In a bowl, combine the olive oil, vinegar, basil, mustard and dill, mix well. Pour the olive oil mixture over the potatoes and onions, toss well to coat the potatoes and onions. Season with salt and pepper, place in the refrigerator for at least 2-3 hours.

Serve right away cold!!!

Bug's Grilled Carrots

Serves: 8

8 medium carrots

olive oil, as needed

salt to taste

pepper to taste

Preheat a gas -OR- charcoal grill to direct medium-high heat

On a cutting board with a sharp knife cut the carrots in 1/2 lengthwise. Brush the carrots all over with olive oil. Place the carrots on the grill rack over medium-hot coals. Turn the carrots every few minutes until tender. Take the carrots off the grill when done.

Serve right away !!!

Grilled Lemon & Garlic Asparagus

Serves: 8

2 pounds fresh asparagus

6 tablespoons olive oil

5 fresh garlic cloves, crushed in a garlic press

2 teaspoons freshly grated lemon zest

1/2 teaspoon paprika

salt to taste

freshly ground black pepper to taste

Preheat a gas -OR- charcoal grill to direct medium heat

Trim the fresh asparagus. In a bowl, combine the oil, garlic, lemon zest and paprika, mix well.

Lay the asparagus side by side and pierce on 2 skewers to form rafts. Place the rafts on the grill rack over medium heat. Brush often with the olive oil mixture. Grill to the desired doneness and tenderness. Season with salt and pepper, take off the grill.

Serve right away !!!

Grilled Pound Cake W/Warm Raymond Berry Sauce

Makes: 8 Servings

4 heaping cups (24 ounces) mixed frozen berries (I like blueberries & raspberries)

Juice of 1 fresh large lime (2 tablespoons)

4 tablespoons granulated sugar

1/2 teaspoon pure vanilla extract

1/2 cup water, Plus 2 tablespoons water

3 teaspoons corn starch

2 Store-Bought pound cake, slice 3/4" inch thick

1/2 cup unsalted butter, melted

In a saucepan over medium-low heat, combine the berries, lime juice, 2 tablespoons sugar, vanilla and 1/2 cup of water. COVER, COOK until the berries are softened, around 10 minutes.

Stir the sauce, crush some of the berries. Taste test, add the remaining sugar, stir to dissolve.

In a bowl stir 2 tablespoons of water into the cornstarch, then stir the white wash mixture into the sauce. Continue to COOK, uncovered, until thick around 3 minutes or more, stir often.

Remove the saucepan from the heat, cover to keep warm.

Preheat a gas -OR- charcoal grill for direct medium-low heat

Brush the pound cake slices with the melted butter. Place the pound cake on the grill rack.

Grill until the pound cake is toasted, around 2-3 minutes on each side, don't burn. Take the grilled pound cake slices off the grill rack. Spread the warm berry sauce onto 8 dessert plates, then place 2 cake slices on each plate. Top each serving of cake with the additional sauce.

You can add a scoop -OR- more of vanilla ice cream -OR- some whipped cream.

Serve right away!!!

MENU

Hot Off The Grill !!!

Lizzies Favorite Dinner

Daddy's Famous London Broil

Grilled Corn on the Cob w/Lime

Grilled Garden Fresh Tomatoes

Classic Root Beer Float

Daddy's Famous London Broil

Serves: 4 hungry people

1 cup Teriyaki Sauce and/or Marinade (aka: Lawry's, A1 marinade, Grill Mates -OR- Kikkoman's)

1/3 cup pineapple juice (aka: Dole 100% juice)

juice of 2 fresh limes (about 2 tablespoons)

juice 1 fresh lemon (about 1 tablespoons)

2 fresh garlic cloves, crushed in a garlic press

1 each steak (2 - 2.25 pounds) Beef TOP ROUND London Broil

*Note: When it's in the budget try to buy certified Angus Beef for great flavor & quality. Choice Angus Beef is sold in most Supermarkets.

In a large resealable plastic freezer bag, combine all the ingredients for the marinade in the bag as follows; Teriyaki Sauce, pineapple juice, lime juice, lemon juice and garlic. Seal the bag tightly, shake the bag to thoroughly mix all of the ingredients.

Place the London broil on a cutting board and pierce both sides all over with a fork. This will tenderize the beef and the marinade inside the meat. Place London broil into the resealable bag and seal bag tightly. Turn the bag to coat the beef with the marinade. Place the bag in the refrigerator for 12-24, don't marinate over 24 hours. Turn the bag to move the marinade around to coat the meat every 4 hours or so.

Remove the meat from the refrigerator, scrape off marinade, pierce again with a fork on all sides. Allow the meat to stand at room temperature for 45 minutes.

Preheat a gas -OR- charcoal grill to direct medium-high heat

Place the meat on the grill rack over medium-high heat. COOK for 10 minutes on each side, turning only once -OR- to desired doneness. Grill this type meat to Rare, Medium-Rare don't COOK past medium doneness. Heat the marinade to a boil, then take it off the heat. Baste with the marinade often during the grilling. Take off the grill and place on a cutting board to rest for 10 minutes, slice thin diagonal slices with a sharp knife.

Serve right away!!!!

Grilled Corn on the Cob w/Lime

Serves: 4

4 ears fresh corn on the cob

4 tablespoons melted butter, salt to taste, freshly ground black pepper to taste

4-8 fresh lime wedges extra butter, cold, to serve with the hot corn

COOK corn in unsalted boiling water (you can add sugar to the water) for 2 minutes. Shock in cold ice water to stop the cooking process. Drain corn, brush the corn with butter and sprinkle with salt and pepper.

Preheat a gas -OR- charcoal grill direct medium-high heat

Place corn on the grill rack over medium-high heat, turning often. Grill until lightly charred, about 5-6 minutes, cook until done, don't burn.

Serve the hot ears with slices of butter & fresh lime wedges.

Grilled Garden Fresh Tomatoes

Serves: 4-6

6 ripe fresh tomatoes, cut in half with a sharp knife

3 tablespoons or more, olive oil -OR- canola oil salt - to taste, ground black pepper - to taste

Sprinkle each hot grilled tomato half with chopped fresh chives.

Preheat a gas -OR- charcoal grill for direct medium-high heat. Brush vegetable oil onto the grill rack

Place tomato halves skin side down onto the grill rack. Brush on oil, sprinkle with salt and pepper. Grill over medium-high heat until lightly charred on the outside but still firm. COOK about 3 minutes for each side, take tomatoes off the grill when done. Place tomatoes on a platter and sprinkle chopped fresh chives onto each grilled tomato half. Serve hot -OR- at room temperature

Great Grilled Tomatoes Come Ripe From Your Garden -OR- Buy Vine Ripe Tomatoes.

Classic Root Beer Float

Serves: 4

4 scoops of Scoops Premium Vanilla Ice Cream

One 2-liter bottle of Root beer

Pour about 1/2 cup of root beer into each of 4 extra-large glasses. With care add 1 large scoop of ice cream to each extra-large glass. Then fill each glass with more root beer to the top.

Serve right away and enjoy !!!

MENU

Hot off the Grill !!!

Super Bowl

Home Tailgate Bash

Colts Grilled Potato Chips w/Saints Onion Dip

Cowboys Grilled Nachos w/Cardinals Salsa

Grilled Buffalo Wings w/Blue Cheese Dip & Celery Sticks

Eagles Burgers

Chicago Bears Spicy Dogs

Broncos Chili

Patriots Cole Slaw

Packers Grilled S'mores

Colts Grilled Potato Chips

1 pound large potatoes

1/4 cup olive oil -OR- canola oil

1 teaspoon or more of kosher salt -OR- sea salt

Preheat a gas -OR- charcoal grill to direct medium-high heat

Use a mandoline to cut potatoes lengthwise into very thin slices. Place in a big bowl and coat with oil and salt. Place a grill pan on the grill rack and allow it to heat. Place the potatoes on grill pan forming a single layer. COOK for 4-5 minutes per side, don't let them burn. Repeat the process with rest of the potato slices. Serve with the Saints French Onion Dip.

Saints French Onion Dip

1 package Lipton onion soup mix

1 large carton sour cream

1/4 teaspoon fresh lime juice

In a bowl, combine all of the ingredients, mix well. Chill and refrigerate until use.

Cowboys Grilled Nachos

4 dozen tortilla chips

2 cups grated Monterey Jack Cheese -OR- grated Cheddar Cheese

1/2 cup fried & crumbled bacon

1 medium red onion, chopped

4 jalapeno peppers, seeded, ribbed & chopped

Serve with:

Cardinal Salsa

Store Bought Sour Cream

Store Bought Guacamole

Preheat a gas grill to direct high heat with the grill lid down.

Arrange nacho chips in a flat grilling pan. Cover with the cheese, bacon, onion and jalapeno peppers. Place the grill safe pan on the grill rack and turn off the grill. Close the grill lid, COOK for about 5-10 minutes -OR- until the cheese melts. Watch the grill carefully to make sure that the cheese melts without burning.

Serve right away with sides!!!

Cardinal Salsa:

1 (24 ounce) jar Store Bought chunky red salsa

3 tablespoons fresh cilantro leaves, chopped

3 each green onions (scallions) white & green parts, chopped

2 teaspoons Taco seasoning mix (from a 1.25 ounce packet)

In a bowl, combine the salsa, cilantro, green onions and Taco seasonings, mix lightly. Cover and refrigerate for at least 2 hours to let the flavors blend together. Serve with the Grilled tortilla chips.

Grilled Buffalo Bills Wings

Makes: 12 Servings

4 1/2 pounds, chicken wings, separated at joints, discard the tips

1 1/2 cups Louisiana style red hot sauce

2 1/4 cups (18 fluid ounces) Coke -OR- any brand Cola

1/4 teaspoon -OR- more red (cayenne) pepper - to taste

1/4 teaspoon ground black pepper

1 1/2 tablespoons soy sauce

Preheat a gas -OR- charcoal grill to direct medium heat

In a big pot, combine the hot sauce, cola, ground red pepper, black pepper and soy sauce, mix well. Add the wings to the sauce. Place the pot to one side of the grill, so the sauce comes to a simmer, stir often. Use a long pair of tongs to get the wings out of the sauce. Place all the wings on the grill rack and COOK for 9-11 minutes, turn often. Then return the wings to sauce to a simmer. Repeat the same process for around 50 minutes. The sauce will thicken. When the wings are tender and pull away from the bone. For sloppy wings, dip the wings one last time in the sauce -OR- serve wings right off the grill for dryer wings. Serve the grill wings with Blue Cheese Dressing and fresh celery sticks.

Eagles Burgers

Makes: 12 Burgers

3 pounds ground chuck

2 egg yolks

1/2 cup grated onion

3 garlic cloves, crushed in a garlic press

1 teaspoon oregano

2 teaspoons basil

kosher salt - to taste

ground black pepper - to taste

12 slices provolone cheese

12 hamburger buns/ketchup/mayonnaise

In a bowl. combine the beef, egg yolks, onion, garlic, oregano, basil, salt and pepper. Lightly mix the meat mixture, using your hands. Shape into 12 round patties.

Lightly brush vegetable oil onto the grill rack. Preheat a gas -OR- charcoal grill for direct medium-high heat

Grill to desired doneness. Top with provolone, let the cheese melt. Serve on hamburger buns with ketchup and mayonnaise.

Chicago Bears Spicy Dogs

Makes: 12 Spicy Dogs

12 each Vienna Beef Spicy Polish Sausage

3 cups sliced green bell peppers

3 cups sliced red -OR- yellow bell peppers

6 cups sliced white onions

3/4 cup -OR- more of canola oil -OR- olive oil

12 each Ciabatta Rolls

12 tablespoons Store bought Chipotle mayonnaise

24 slices jack cheese -OR- pepper jack cheese

Preheat a gas -OR- charcoal grill for direct medium-high heat. Lightly brush the grill rack with vegetable oil

With a sharp knife split the sausages lengthwise down the middle. Char-grill on both sides. In a big pot, heat the oil. Add the green peppers, red -OR- yellow peppers and onions. Sauté vegetables until soft, adding more oil, if needed to prevent sticking. Toast the rolls on outside edges of the grill, with the cut sides down. Spread chipotle mayo over both sides of the rolls.

Place hot dog, skin side down, on bottom half of rolls, top with cheese and sautéed bell peppers and onions. Cover over with top half of the rolls .

Serve right away !!!

Broncos Chili

Makes: 15 servings

3 pounds ground beef

1-1/2 (46 ounce) cans tomato juice

1-1/2 (29 ounce) cans tomato sauce

1-1/2 (15 ounce) cans kidney beans, drained & rinsed

1-1/2 (15 ounce) cans pinto beans, drained & rinsed

2-1/4 cups onions, chopped

1/4 cup, plus 2 tablespoons green bell pepper, chopped

1/4 teaspoon ground red (cayenne) pepper

3/4 teaspoon granulated sugar

3/4 teaspoon dried oregano

3/4 teaspoon ground black pepper

1-1/2 teaspoons salt

2-1/4 teaspoons ground cumin

1/4 cup, Plus 2 tablespoons chili powder

In a big deep skillet, COOK ground beef over medium-high heat until evenly brown. Drain and crumble.

In a big pot over high heat, combine the ground beef, tomato juice, tomato sauce, kidney beans, pinto beans, onions, bell peppers, ground red pepper, sugar, oregano, black pepper, salt, cumin, and chili powder. Bring to a boil, then reduce heat to low. SIMMER for 90 minutes.

*Note: If using a slow cooker (Crock Pot), set on low, add all the ingredients and cook for 8-10 hours.

Patriots Cole Slaw

Makes: 16 servings

2 small heads green cabbage, shredded

1/2 small head red cabbage, shredded

6 carrots, shredded

2 bunches green onions (scallions), sliced

1-1/2 cups mayonnaise

1 cup buttermilk

2/3 cup granulated sugar - to taste

4 tablespoons fresh lemon juice

4 tablespoons white wine vinegar

2 teaspoons salt - to taste

1 teaspoon celery seed

1 teaspoon paprika

1/2 teaspoon freshly ground black pepper - to taste

In a big bowl, toss the cabbage, carrots and green onions. In a bowl, whisk together the remaining ingredients until smooth. Pour into the cabbage mixture and toss to coat. Cover and refrigerate for 8-36 hours, tossing often. Serve chilled.

Packers Grilled S'mores

Makes: 12 Servings

1 box graham crackers

1 bag large marshmallows

6 large chocolate bars

Preheat a gas -OR- charcoal grill to direct medium heat

Stack 1 large marshmallow, cut in half and 1 section of a candy bar on half of a graham cracker.

Place another half of a graham cracker on top. Place as many S'mores you can fit into a foil pan and set on the grill rack for around 1-3 minutes -OR- until the chocolate melts and begins to ooze out.

Serve right away!!!

MENU

Dinner Hot off the Grill !!!

Board Game Night

Grilled Beer Cheeseburgers
Big Daddy's Grilled Fries
NAPA Cabbage Coleslaw
Classic Chocolate Milkshake

Grilled Beer Cheeseburgers

Makes: 6 burgers

2 pounds ground chuck

1 each onion, finely chopped (1/3 cup)

1/3 cup Regular -OR- Nonalcoholic Beer

1 1/2 tablespoon Worcestershire Sauce

1 1/2 teaspoon kosher salt - to taste

1/3 teaspoon ground black pepper

3 garlic cloves, crushed in a garlic press

6 Kaiser Rolls, split

6 slices American Cheese

6 large ripe tomatoes, ketchup, thin sliced hamburger pickles

6 lettuce leaves

6-12 slices red onion/mayonnaise

Make Grilled burgers more FUN than going out !!!

Hot coals -OR- A gas grill for direct medium heat

In a bowl, combine the beef, onion, beer, Worcestershire sauce, salt, pepper and garlic, mix well. Shape the beef mixture into 6 equal patties, about the size of the rolls.

Lightly brush vegetable oil onto the grill rack!!!

Place the patties on the grill rack over medium heat for 13-15 minutes, close the grill lid, turning only once, a meat thermometer inserted in the center of a pattie should read 160 degrees F. and patties are no longer pink in the center. During the last few minutes of grilling put 1 slice of cheese on top of each burger, COOK until the cheese melts. Also at the end place the rolls around the edges of the grill, cut sides down, until toasted.

Serve the cheeseburgers on rolls, with the items you like on them!!!

Big Daddy's Grilled Fries

Serves: 6

Got to Have it DRY RUB:

2 tablespoons paprika

2 teaspoons kosher salt

2 teaspoons freshly ground black pepper

1 teaspoon onion powder

1 teaspoon garlic powder

1 teaspoon chili powder

1/2 teaspoon packed brown sugar

*Tip: You can make the dry rub well in advance and store in a airtight container it keeps for weeks!!!

6 large Russet Potatoes, well scrubbed with a veggie brush but unpeeled

canola oil -OR- olive oil -OR- vegetable oil as needed

Grated cheddar cheese at room temperature ketchup -OR- your favorite barbecue sauce

Preheat a gas -OR- charcoal grill to direct medium-low heat

To prepare the Got to Have it DRY RUB:

In a bowl, combine the paprika, salt, pepper, onion powder, garlic powder, chili powder and brown sugar, stir well. Cut the potatoes lengthwise in half and then slice in half into long wedges 1/2" inch thick. Coat the potatoes wedges with oil and sprinkle them generously with dry rub.

Brush the grill rack with vegetable oil!!!

Grill the potatoes uncovered over medium-low heat for 30-35 minutes -OR- until the proper doneness, turning often every 6-10 minutes brushing them lightly with additional oil once -OR- twice.

The potatoes are ready when the outsides are brown and crisp and the insides are soft and tender.

For CHEESE FRIES:

Top the hot potato wedges with cheese as soon as they come off the grill.

Serve Big Daddy's Grilled Fries HOT with ketchup -OR- BBQ sauce.

*Note: For a English Twist serve HOT FRIES with Malt Vinegar!!!

NAPA Cabbage Coleslaw

Serves: 4

3 cups Napa cabbage, shredded

1 cup Bok Choy, shredded

1/4 cup sweet pepper, finely chopped

1/4 cup rice vinegar

1 tablespoon sesame oil

In a bowl, toss the cabbage, bok choy and peppers together. Combine the vinegar and sesame oil. Pour vinegar mixture over the cabbage mixture and toss to coat. Serve right away -OR- refrigerate 2-4 hours to let the flavors blend together, then toss again before serving.

Classic Chocolate Milkshake

Serves: 2

1 1/2 cups milk

1 teaspoon vanilla extract

6 tablespoons Chocolate Syrup (I like Hershey's Syrup)

1 cup -OR- more of Vanilla Ice Cream

2 teaspoons sugar

Combine all the ingredients in a blender and blend until mixed and smooth.

*Tip: To make a dessert Milkshake, top with canned whipped cream (aka: Reddi Whip).

Get
YOUR
Grill - On
XXXXXXXXXXXXXXX
Don't
Touch
MY
GRILL

MENU

Hot off the Grill !!!

Tuscan Grill

Grilled Marinated Chicken

Artichoke & Chickpea Salad

Grilled Zucchini

Grilled Eggplant

Italian Bread w/Herb Olive Oil

Gelato

or

Fresh Strawberries w/Balsamic Vinegar

Grilled Italian Marinated Chicken Breast

Serves: 4-6

6 boneless chicken breast

1 cup Store Bought Italian Salad Dressing

2 fresh garlic cloves, crushed in a garlic press

1/8 teaspoon crushed red pepper flakes - to taste

In a bowl, whisk together the Italian Dressing, garlic and red pepper flakes, mix well. Place the chicken breast in a large resealable plastic bag, pour the Italian dressing over the chicken in the bag. Seal the bag tightly and turn the bag to coat the chicken with marinade. Place the chicken in the refrigerator for 8-12 hours to marinate.

Preheat a gas -OR- charcoal grill to direct medium heat

Take the chicken out of the marinade. Place the chicken breast on the grill rack over medium heat, Grill for 14-20 minutes on each side. When the chicken is done, take it off the grill.

Serve right away!!!

Artichoke & Chickpea Salad

Serves: 4

1 (6 ounce) jar marinated artichoke hearts reserved artichoke liquid

1/4 cup fresh basil, chopped

2 tablespoons extra virgin olive oil

2 tablespoons white wine vinegar

1 large garlic clove, crushed in a garlic press

1/2 teaspoon dried oregano

1/4 teaspoon salt - to taste

1/4 teaspoon ground black pepper - to taste

2 (19 ounce) cans chickpeas, drained and rinsed

1/4 cup grated parmesan cheese

Drain the artichoke hearts, reserving the liquid. Slice the artichokes thinly and set aside. In a big bowl, whisk together the reserved artichoke liquid, basil, oil, vinegar, garlic, oregano, salt and pepper, mix well. Add the artichoke hearts, chickpeas and parmesan cheese. Toss the salad ingredients lightly to combine.

Serve right away!!!

Grilled Zucchini

Serves: 4

1 pound fresh zucchini

2 tablespoons olive oil

1 teaspoon oregano

freshly ground black pepper - to taste

2 tablespoons fresh lime juice salt - to taste

On a cutting board with a sharp knife cut the zucchini in 1/2 lengthwise, rub with olive oil, sprinkle with the oregano and season with freshly ground black pepper.

Preheat a gas -OR- charcoal grill to direct medium-high heat

Place the zucchini on the grill rack, cut side down, over medium hot coals. Grill until well browned. COOK until tender, take off the grill. To serve; sprinkle with fresh lime juice and season with salt.

Serve right away!!!

Grilled Eggplant

Makes: 4 servings

1 large eggplant (about 1 1/2 pounds), cut into 1/2" inch slices

olive oil, as needed

salt to taste/freshly ground black pepper - to taste

Preheat a gas -OR- charcoal grill to direct medium heat

Lightly brush the 1/2" inch thick eggplant slices with olive oil and season with salt and black pepper. Place the eggplant slices on the grill rack, oil side down, brush the top side of the eggplant with olive oil and season with salt and black pepper. Grill over medium heat for 3 minutes on each side -OR- until tender. Take the eggplant off the grill and place on a platter.

Serve right away!!!

Italian Bread w/ Herb Olive Oil

1 Freshly Baked Loaf of Crusty Italian Bread

Herb Olive Oil:

1/2 cup olive oil

1 teaspoon dried basil

1 teaspoon dried oregano

2 teaspoons fresh garlic

In a small skillet heat the olive oil, basil, oregano and fresh garlic, sauté for 2-3 minutes. Pour onto bread plates.

Serve with freshly baked crusty Italian bread.

Dessert:

Gelato or Fresh strawberries drizzled with balsamic vinegar

Wine: ECCO DOMANI: aka; PINOT GRIGIO any year (I like 2003)

MENU

Dinner Hot off the Grill !!!

Pizza Night

Grilled Cheese Steak Pizza

Grilled Wings of Fire

Fennel Slaw

Java & Cola Float

Grilled Cheese Steak Pizza

Makes: 4 servings

1 Store bought 12" inch pre-baked pizza crust

1 pound ground beef

1 small green -OR- red bell pepper, cut into thin strips

1 small onion, sliced thin & separated into rings

1/2 teaspoon kosher salt - to taste

4 tablespoons or more of mayonnaise

2 cups mozzarella cheese, shredded

There is nothing better than Grilled Pizza & a Ice Cold Beer!

Preheat a gas -OR- charcoal grill to direct medium heat

In a big non-stick skillet brown the ground beef over medium heat for 5-6 minutes, stir often. Add the bell peppers and onion. COOK until beef is no longer pink and veggies are crisp and tender.

Crumble the beef into small pieces, season with salt to taste. Drain, pour off only the fat, set the skillet aside.

Place the pizza crust on a flat surface, evenly spread the mayo on the pizza crust. Top the pizza crust with the beef mixture, then evenly top with the cheese. Place pizza on grill rack over medium heat and close grill lid. Grill, rotating often. COOK on the grill rack, covered for 8-10 minutes, or until all the cheese is melted, don't burn. Take off grill, cut on cutting board or pizza pan with a sharp knife -OR- pizza wheel.

Serve right away!!!

Grilled Wings of Fire

Serves: 4-6 hungry people

3 pounds chicken wings (around 16 wings)

3 tablespoons olive oil -OR- canola oil

3 tablespoons fresh lime juice

5 fresh garlic cloves, crushed in a garlic press

2 teaspoon ground cumin

2 teaspoon paprika

1 teaspoon peeled and grated ginger

1 teaspoon kosher salt - to taste

1/2 - 1 teaspoon ground hot red (cayenne) pepper - to taste

1/2 teaspoon cinnamon

Rinse the chicken wings under cold running water and pat dry with clean paper towels. Cut off the wing tips at the joints and throw out the tips -OR use the wing tips to make a chicken stock.

In a large resealable plastic bag, combine all the remaining ingredients, close bag and shake to blend them all well. Add the chicken wings to the bag, seal the bag tightly, turn the bag to coat the wings in the marinade. Press out any air and place in refrigerator for 4-8 hours to marinate.

Brush grill rack with vegetable oil!!! Preheat a gas -OR- charcoal grill to direct medium heat

Place wings on grill rack over medium heat. COOK for 18-25 minutes, close the grill lid, turn over wings after 10 minutes. Grill until juices run clear and center meat of wings is no pink at thickest part when cut. Chicken should have a internal temperature of 165 degrees F. -OR- higher when done.

Serve Wings with Store Bought Blue Cheese Dressing & Celery Sticks!

Fresh Fennel Slaw

Makes: 4-6 Servings

juice of 1 fresh lime (around 1 tablespoon)

3 teaspoons fresh oregano, finely chopped

1 teaspoon kosher salt -OR- sea salt - to taste

1/2 teaspoon freshly ground black pepper - to taste

1/4 cup olive oil -OR- canola oil

3 bulbs fresh fennel (3 pounds)

2 red -OR- yellow bell peppers, cored, seeded and julienne (cut into strips)

In a bowl, whisk together the lime juice, fresh oregano, salt and pepper, mix well. Slowly drizzle in the oil, whisking constantly until emulsified.

On a cutting board with a sharp knife carefully trim the stalks of the fennel down to bulb and and throw out the stems. Cut the bulbs into quarters and trim away the small triangle of core at the base. Still using a sharp knife slice the fennel bulbs as thinly as possible.

To Serve:

In a salad bowl, toss the fennel, red -OR- yellow bell peppers and the dressing together until evenly coated with dressing. Serve right away -OR- cover and refrigerate up to 2 hours before serving to blend the flavors together. Bring back up to room temperature and toss slaw again before serving.

Enjoy!!!

Java & Coke Float

Serves: 4

2/3 cup light cream -OR- half and half

2 1/2 cups strong coffee (pick your favorite coffee)

4 scoops coffee -OR- vanilla ice cream

1 bottle of Coke -OR- your favorite Cola

Mix the cream and coffee, pour into 4 large glasses (half full). Add one scoop of ice cream to each large glass, then top off each large glass with Coke. For a great dessert touch add some whip cream to the top of each float.

It's your after dinner coffee & dessert in one glass!!!

MENU

Hot off the Grill!!!

BURGER NIGHT

First Team Burgers

Whoa Sweet Potato Chips

Summer Classic Cole Slaw

Lemon Iced Tea

First Team Burgers

Makes: 6 burgers

2 pounds ground chuck

2 teaspoons kosher salt - to taste

6 - toasted Kaiser Rolls

6 - large beefsteak tomato slices

6 - large Vidalia onion slices

6 - lettuce leaves

ketchup, mayo, mustard, pickles

In a big bowl, lightly mix together the ground chuck and salt, using your clean hands. Shape into 6 equal round patties, each about the size of the rolls. Chill patties for around 1-2 hours after that time, remove from the refrigerator. Let stand and come back up to room temperature before grilling.

Brush grill rack with vegetable oil Preheat a gas -OR- charcoal grill to direct medium-high heat

Place the patties on the grill rack over medium heat. COOK for 5 minutes on each side -OR- until the burgers reach desired doneness. Place the rolls on the outer edges of the grill rack, cit side down and toast until done, don't burn.

Serve burgers on toasted rolls with lettuce, tomato and onion. Also serve with ketchup, mayo, mustard and pickles on the side.

Great Burgers to serve w/sweet potato chips, cole slaw & lemon iced tea!

WHOA Sweet Potato Chips

Makes: 6-8 servings

4 large sweet potatoes

Peanut oil -OR- Canola oil for frying

Cajun Seasoning -OR- Sea Salt - to taste

Wash and scrub the sweet potatoes, then peel the sweet potatoes. Cut crosswise into very thin slices. Heat oil to 350 degrees F. Fry the very thin slices, in batches, for around 4-5 minutes or until light brown and crispy, don't burn. Drain on clean paper towels and sprinkle right away with Cajun seasoning -OR- Sea salt, chips must be hot. Serve right away!!!

Summer Classic Cole Slaw

Serves: 6

3/4 cup distilled white vinegar

9 tablespoons sugar

3 teaspoons Dijon mustard

3/4 - large white cabbage (around 6 cups), shredded

1 1/2 large red onion, sliced thin

1 1/2 large green -OR- red bell peppers

In a saucepan, combine the vinegar, sugar and mustard. Stir over low heat until the sugar dissolves. Remove the saucepan from the heat and set aside. In a big bowl, mix together the cabbage, red onion and bell pepper. Add the vinegar mixture (dressing) and toss to coat. Cover and refrigerate for at least 4 hours tossing often.

Serve cold.

Lemon Iced Tea

Makes: 8 servings (1 1/2 cups - each)

6 cups boiling water

12 each tea bags

3 medium lemons

1 cup sugar - to taste

1 1/2 trays ice cubes (around 21 cubes - you can use more)

Pour boiling water on tea bags, let steep 4-5 minutes -OR- until desired strength. COOL, down to room temperature. Hold each lemon using a sharp paring knife cut each peel in a continuous motion to form a spiral. Squeeze the juice for the lemons, remove and discard the seeds. Mix the lemon peel, lemon juice, sugar and ice cubes in a big pitcher; stir in the tea.

Serve right away in ice-filled glasses!!!

MENU

Dinner Hot off the Grill !!!

BASEBALL NIGHT

Yankee's Grilled Soft Shell Crabs

Grilled Corn on the Cob

World Series Cole Slaw

South of the Border Sweet Ice Tea

Yankee's Grilled Soft Shell Crabs

Serves: 4-6

8 fresh soft shell crabs, cleaned

2 cups whole milk

1/4 teaspoon chili pepper sauce

1/8 teaspoon smashed coriander seeds

In a shallow pan, place the soft shell crabs. In a bowl, combine the milk, chili pepper sauce and smashed coriander seeds, pour the mixture over the soft shell crabs. Cover and put in the refrigerator for at least 1-2 hours.

Lightly brush vegetable oil onto the grill rack!!! Preheat a gas -OR- charcoal grill to direct high heat.

When the coals are very very hot. Carefully lift each soft shell crab out of the milk mixture, give the crab 1 good shake. Place the crabs on the grill rack over high heat. Grill for 1 or more minutes on each side and serve right away.

Best Grilled Soft Shell Crabs to serve with World Series Cole Slaw.

World Series Cole Slaw

Serves: 8

1 1/3 cups Store Bought Mayonnaise

3 tablespoons apple cider vinegar

1 1/2 teaspoons sugar

1 teaspoons celery seeds

1 head green cabbage (2 1/2 pounds), cored and thinly sliced (8 packed cups)

3 medium carrots, shredded

3 green onions (scallions) white & green parts, trim & chop

2 tablespoons fresh parsley, chopped

salt - to taste

ground black pepper - to taste

This Cole Slaw hits it out of the ballpark!!!

In a big bowl, combine the mayo, vinegar, sugar and celery seeds, mix well. Add the cabbage, carrots, green onions and parsley, mix well. Then season well with salt and pepper. Cover and refrigerate for at least 4 hours -OR- overnight to let the flavors blend.

Serve well chilled!!!

Grilled Corn on the Cob

Servings: 6

6 ears corn on the cob

lots of butter for corn

Carefully peel back the husks from the corn, leaving them attached to the stalk. Remove the silk from each corn and throw out the silks. Smooth the husks back onto the corn and tie a piece of string on corn to keep the husk in place (closed). Soak corn covered in cold water for 1 hour.

Lightly brush vegetable oil onto the grill rack. Preheat a gas -OR- charcoal grill to direct medium heat. Grill the corn until done.

South of the Border Sweet Ice Tea

Makes: 1/2 gallon of sweet tea

3 cups boiling water

3 regular-size tea bags

3/4 cup sugar - to taste

5 cups cold water

A lot of Ice Cubes

Pour the boiling water over the tea bags. Set aside and let steep for 5-6 minutes. Remove the tea bags. In a large pitcher, add the sugar and pour the warm tea over the sugar, stirring, until the sugar dissolves. Add the 5 cups of cold water and stir until well mixed. COOL tea and serve in glasses over ice.

MENU

Dinner Hot Off The Grill

BOB'S MUSSELS NIGHT

Grilled Garlic-Wine Mussels

All Star Grilled Cabbage

Players Choice Grilled Garlic Bread

Sharks White Wine Sangria

Grilled Garlic-Wine Mussels

Serves: 4

1/3 cup olive oil -OR- canola oil

4 tablespoons (1/2 stick) unsalted butter

1/4 cup shallots, chopped

5 fresh garlic cloves, crushed in a garlic press

3/4 cup good quality dry white wine

3 tablespoons flat leaf parsley, finely chopped

1/8 teaspoon crushed red pepper flakes

4 pounds, mussels, cleaned

What A Great Meal; Grilled Mussels, Grilled Cabbage & Grilled Garlic Bread.

Preheat a gas grill on direct high heat for 10 minutes -OR- Build a charcoal fire in a outdoor grill, burn until the coals are covered with white ash

Place a new 15"X10" inch aluminum foil baking pan (*Tip: new pan - no holes) on the grill. Add the oil and melt the butter over high heat. Add the shallots and garlic, COOK, stir often. Use oven mitts -OR- oven gloves to protect your hands. When shallots are soft, about 2-3 minutes, add wine, parsley and red pepper flakes and bring to a boil. Carefully take the foil pan off the grill. Place the mussels into the foil pan and cover loosely with foil. Carefully return the pan to grill, COOK until the mussels open up around 5-8 minutes. If some mussels don't open hit them a couple times on the shell with a metal serving spoon -OR- tongs. Using a large serving spoon or tongs, put the cooked mussels into 4 soup bowls. Pour the juices in the pan over the mussels.

Serve right away!!!

All Star Grilled Cabbage

Serves: 4

olive oil -OR- canola oil -OR- vegetable oil

1 head cabbage, quartered & cored

8 strips bacon (partially cooked)

1 onion, chopped

1/4 cup -OR- more butter

salt - to taste

freshly ground black pepper - to taste

Preheat a gas -OR- charcoal grill to direct low heat.

Brush oil onto 4 big squares of aluminum foil. On each square place 1/4 of the cabbage, crisscross two strips of bacon, 1/4 of the onion and a pat of butter (cut the butter into small pieces).

Season each with salt and pepper to taste. Fold edges of the foil to seal tightly. Grill the foil packets of cabbage over low heat, until done to your liking. Turn often on the grill, so they won't burn. Take packets off the grill when done and open each packet carefully.

Serve right away!!!

Players Choice Grilled Garlic Bread

Serves: 4-6

2 large bulbs (heads) fresh garlic, grilled

2 tablespoons olive oil -OR- canola oil -OR- vegetable oil

kosher salt -OR- sea salt - to taste

freshly ground black pepper - to taste

12 thin slices from a long Italian bread -OR- French bread

Preheat a gas -OR- charcoal grill to direct medium heat

Peel and take off loose paper like covering from the garlic bulbs (head), however don't separate cloves. Cut 2 - 18" X 12" inch pieces of heavy duty foil. On each piece of foil, place a garlic bulb (head). Brush bulbs (heads) generously with oil. Season with the salt and pepper to taste.

Wrap the foil tightly around each garlic bulb (head). Place the foil wrapped garlic heads on the grill rack over medium heat, close the grill lid. COOK for 30-35 minutes -OR- until very soft.

Add the bread slices to the grill for last 4-5 minutes of grilling, turn over once, until golden brown.

Don't burn the bread.

To Serve:

Squeeze out the garlic pulp from the papery skin onto the bread slices and spread with a knife.

Serve right away!!!

Sharks White Wine Sangria

1 (750 ml. bottle) dry white wine

1/2 cup fruit brandy fruit juice of your choice - to taste sugar - to taste sliced fresh fruit (berries, melon, mango, seedless grapes etc...)

1 - 2 cups of 7-up, sprite, club soda -OR- seltzer

Ice Cubes

In a large clean pickle jar; add the wine, brandy and fruit.

In a large clean pickle jar; fruit juice, sugar, fruit and soda.

Allow both mixtures to set for 1 hour. Combine the 2 mixtures together, add ice and set for 30 minutes. Serve the Sharks Sangria over ice in big wine glasses. *To fill a wine glass, add the glass half full of ice. Pour some Sangria over the ice, add some marinated slices of fruit and add some fresh berries. Top off glass with more Sangria and serve right away!

MENU

Dinner Hot off the Grill!!!

FAMILY NIGHT

Tony's Grilled Pizza Margherita

Joey's Grilled Caesar Salad

Fresh Squeezed Lemonade

Tony's Grilled Pizza Margherita

Makes: 4 servings

1- Store bought 12" inch pre-baked pizza crust

1 cup Store bought Tomato & Basil Sauce

6 ounces fresh mozzarella cheese, thinly sliced

Olive Oil

Fresh basil leaves, chopped

lightly brush vegetable oil onto the grill rack Preheat a gas -OR- charcoal grill to direct medium heat

Place pizza crust on a flat surface, evenly spread sauce on pizza crust, then top with cheese.

Put the pizza on grill rack over medium heat, close the grill lid, rotating the pizza often. COOK, covered for 8-10 minutes -OR- until all the cheese is melted. Take off the grill, place pizza on a cutting board -OR- pizza pan. Cut with a sharp knife -OR- pizza wheel. Drizzle with olive oil and sprinkle with the chopped basil leaves.

Serve right away!!!

Joey's Grilled Caesar Salad

Serves: 4-6

3 - medium size heads Romaine lettuce

12 each Italian bread slices, cut on the diagonal (bias)

2 tablespoons olive oil around 3/4 cup Club Caesar Dressing

1 chunk (around 8 ounces) Parmesan Cheese for shaving onto the salad

freshly ground black pepper - to taste

Soak 2 cups wood chips -OR- chunks (Oak is best) covered in water for 1 hour, drained

Remove any blemished -OR- wilted leaves from the heads of Romaine. On a cutting board cut each head in half lengthwise with a sharp knife, leave the stem end attached. Place the cut end under cold running water, separate the leaves from the stem gently using your fingers. Under cold running water rinse each leave front and back. Make sure the leaves are clean. Hold each lettuce half and give it a gently shake over the sink, place the lettuce halves in a salad spinner and spin dry. *Tip: If you don't have a salad spinner, pat each leaf dry with a dry clean piece of paper towel.

Preheat a gas -OR- charcoal grill to direct high heat

To Form Smoke:

Charcoal grill: Toss the soaked chips -OR- chunks directly onto the coals.

Gas grill: Put the wood chips -OR- chunks in a smoker box -OR- a foil homemade smoker pouch. Run the gas grill on high heat until you see smoke.

Brush vegetable oil onto the grill rack.

Place the romaine halves on the grill rack with cut side up and brush oil onto both sides of the bread slices and place on the grill rack. Grill Romaine over high heat until wilted and the inside is still crisp and the outside is a deep golden brown, don't burn. COOK for around 1-2 minutes or until cooked to the desired doneness. Take the romaine halves off the grill and place on a platter -OR- plate. cut side up. Put a slice of grilled bread on either side of each romaine half.

Using a vegetable peeler shave big thin slices of the parmesan cheese over the salad. Sprinkle with the freshly ground black pepper to taste. Ladle Caesar dressing lightly over each salad.

Serve right away!!!

In a hurry you can buy Store Bought Creamy Caesar Salad Dressing or Make Club Caesar Dressing

Club Caesar Dressing

1 cup mayonnaise

1/4 cup egg substitute

1/4 cup grated parmesan cheese

2 tablespoons water

2 tablespoons olive oil

1 1/2 tablespoons fresh lime juice

1 tablespoon anchovy paste

2 fresh garlic cloves, crushed in a garlic press

2 teaspoons sugar

1/2 teaspoon freshly ground black pepper

1/4 teaspoon salt - to taste

1/2 teaspoon fresh flat leaf parsley, finely chopped - to taste

In a bowl, combine all of the ingredients, beat with a electric hand mixer for 1-2 minutes. It should be a smooth and slightly thick mixture, Cover and refrigerate for at least 3-5 hours -OR- more, to let the flavors blend.

Freshly Squeezed Lemonade

8 cups very cold water

1/4 cup freshly squeezed lemon juice

6 very thin lemon slices

1/2 cup sugar

1 teaspoon freshly grated lemon zest lemon wedges, to garnish each glass

Lots of Ice, for the glasses

In a big glass pitcher, combine the very cold water, lemon juice, lemon slices, sugar and fresh lemon zest. Mix well with a long handled wooden spoon until all the sugar is dissolved. Serve in big glasses with a lot of ICE. Garnish each glass with a lemon wedge.

Serve right away!!!

MENU

Dinner Hot off the Grill !!!

MOVIE NIGHT
Dinner, Popcorn and a Movie !

Tin Cup Cheesy BBQ Popcorn

Porky's Pork Burgers w/Spicy Chili Mayo

Lucky's Jicama Slaw

Potato Chips w/Blue Cheese & Scallions

Rudy's Grilled S'Mores

Boys of Summer Mint Lemonade

Tin Cup Cheesy Barbecue Popcorn

Makes: 8 cups

2 tablespoons melted butter

1/2 teaspoon chili powder

1/2 teaspoon garlic salt

1/4 teaspoon onion powder

8 cups freshly popped corn

1/4 cup grated parmesan cheese

In a big bowl, combine the melted butter, chili powder, garlic salt and onion powder, mix well.

Lightly mix in all the popcorn until well coated. Sprinkle with the cheese, mix lightly.

Porky's Pork Burgers w/Spicy Chili Mayo

Makes: 4 burgers

1 pound ground pork

1 tablespoon jalapeno pepper, finely chopped (wear gloves, when working with hot peppers)

2 tablespoons teriyaki sauce and/or marinade

3 tablespoons fresh cilantro, finely chopped

1/2 cup smoked cheddar cheese, diced

1/2 cup yellow onion, diced

2 teaspoons fresh flat leaf parsley, finely chopped

1/8 - 1/4 teaspoon or more of ground cumin - to taste

Serve with:

Spicy Chili Mayo

Ketchup

4 tomato slices

4 large onion slices

4 lettuce leaves pickles

4 toasted hamburger buns

Preheat a gas -OR- charcoal grill to direct medium-high heat.

*Tip: When using a charcoal grill white ash on the coals, will be medium-high heat !

In a big bowl, crumble the ground pork into the bowl. Add jalapeno peppers, teriyaki sauce, fresh cilantro, cheddar, onion, fresh parsley, and cumin, mix well. Make sure to break up the ground pork, evenly distribute all the ingredients. Using your clean hands shape the pork into 4 round patties all of the same size.

Place the patties on the grill rack over medium-high heat, turning only once. COOK for 4-5 minutes on each side, until the juice run clear. Take burgers off the grill when cooked to the desired doneness. Place the buns on the outer edges of the grill rack and toast until done 1-2 minutes.

Serve burgers on toasted hamburger buns with spicy chili mayo!

Spicy Chili Mayo

1 cup mayo

chili powder - to taste

hot red pepper sauce -to taste

1 tablespoon fresh cilantro, finely chopped - to taste

In a small bowl, combine the mayo, chili powder, red pepper sauce and fresh cilantro, mix well.

Serve right away -OR- cover and refrigerate before using.

Lucky's Jicama Slaw

1 ear grilled cooked corn (1/2 cup of corn kernels)

1 large jicama, peeled

1/2 cup sour cream

1/4 cup fresh green onions (scallions), chopped, both white & green parts

1/4 cup red wine vinegar

2 tablespoons fresh cilantro, chopped

sea salt -OR- kosher salt - to taste

freshly ground black pepper

Grill the corn, COOL, using a sharp knife remove the corn from the cob. Shred the Jicama.

In a big bowl, combine the grilled corn, sour cream, green onions, vinegar, cilantro, salt, and pepper, mix well. Add the shredded Jicama and toss well to coat with the dressing.

Cover and refrigerate for at least 2-4 hours before serving.

Serve chilled -OR- at room temperature !!!!

Homemade Potato Chips w/Blue Cheese & Scallions

4 large Russet potatoes, around 2 pounds

Peanut oil -OR- canola oil, for frying kosher salt -OR- sea salt

3/4 - 1 pound Blue cheese, finely crumbled

4-6 green onions (scallions), chopped

*White Truffle Oil - if desired

*Sub: You can Sub chopped fresh chives for the chopped fresh scallions, if you like!

Peel the potatoes and slice them into thin 1/8" inch using a mandolin -OR- a sharp knife. Rinse the slices in many changes of cold water until the water runs clear. Drain the slices and pat them dry. In a large deep pot, put around 3" inches of oil, the oil should not come up more than half way. Heat the oil up to 325 degrees F over medium-high heat. Working in batches, carefully add the potato slices, a dozen at a time. Give them a stir so they don't stick together. Fry the potato slices until they are a light golden brown. They should fry for around 3-4 minutes. Remove the slices and drain them well on paper towels, season with the salt. Repeat and fry with the remaining potato slices. Preheat the oven to 450 degrees F. On a baking pan arrange a single layer of chips and sprinkle with some of the blue cheese and scallions. Place another single layer of chips on top of that and some more cheese, scallions and very lightly sprinkle with white truffle oil, if desired. Keep going until you have used up all the chips, cheese, scallions and sprinkled every other layer with white truffle oil, if desired.

Place the baking pan in the center of the oven at 425 degrees F for around 5 minutes -OR- until the cheese has melted.

Serve right away!!!

Rudy's Grilled S'mores

Makes: 6 S'mores

6 each Chocolate Graham Crackers -OR- Whole Honey Graham Crackers

6 sheets (12" X 8" inch each) heavy duty aluminum foil

3/4 cup semi-sweet chocolate chunks

6 each large marshmallows

Preheat a gas -OR- charcoal grill to indirect medium heat

Center each of 6 of the graham squares on sheets of foil, top each with a 1/6th. of the chocolate chunks and 1 marshmallow. Cover each the remaining graham cracker squares to make a total of 6 s'mores. Bring up the foil sides on each s'more, then double fold the top and both ends to seal each packet, leaving room for heat circulation inside. Place S'mores on the unheated side of the grill, close the grill lid. Grill using indirect heat for 4-5 minutes -OR until the marshmallows are melted. Carefully open the foil packets and remove the S'mores.

Serve right away!!!

Boys of Summer Mint Lemonade

4 lemons, washed, sliced thin and seeds removed

1 cup fresh mint leaves, wash, loosely packed

1 cup -OR- more sugar

6 cups water

3/4 cup fresh lemon juice

Serve with:

Whole Fresh Mint Leaves

Fresh Lemon Slices

In a blender -OR- food processor, pulverize the lemon slices and mint with 1/2 cup of the sugar until the lemons release most of their juice and flavor. Pour this mixture through a fine mesh sieve into a big glass pitcher, use a long handle wooden spoon to press down on the solids to release more juices. Add the water, the remaining 1/2 cup sugar and lemon juice to the pulp left inside the sieve, again press down on the solids to release as much juice as you can. Throw out the mixture left in the sieve. Serve lemonade in a big glass over ice. Put lemon slices and mint in each glass.

Serve right away!!!

MENU

Hot off the Grill !!!

BBQ NIGHT

Easy Does It BBQ Chicken

Grilled Cajun Corn on the Cob

Endless Summer Baked Beans

Kings Asian Slaw

King of the Hill Grilled Plums

Motor City Mocha Latte Shake

Easy Does It BBQ Chicken

Serves: 6

Fast Paced BBQ Sauce:

3 cups ketchup

3/4 cup molasses

3 tablespoons brown sugar

3 teaspoons garlic powder

3 teaspoons chili powder

3 teaspoons cider vinegar

2 teaspoons onion powder pinch crushed red pepper flakes - to taste

3 pounds fresh chicken pieces

4 fresh garlic cloves, crushed in a garlic press

crushed red pepper flakes - to taste

salt - to taste and ground black pepper

2 cups wood chips -OR- chunks soaked in water for 30 minutes & drained.

If using a gas grill use a smoker box -OR- throw the soaked chips right on top of the charcoal.

Always wait for the smoke before placing the food on the grill rack.

Fast Paced BBQ Sauce: In a saucepan, combine all of the ingredients, mix well. COOK, over medium heat until bubbly. Use the BBQ sauce to baste chicken on the grill rack, during the last few minutes of grilling and also serve the BBQ sauce on the side. Makes around 3 cups.

Wash the chicken in cold water and pat dry with clean dry paper towels. Then season the chicken with crushed garlic, red pepper flakes, salt and black pepper. Clean the grill rack with a grill brush and a clean towel.

Lightly brush the grill rack with vegetable oil.

Preheat a gas -OR- charcoal grill for direct medium-low heat.

Place the chicken on the grill rack, skin side up and close the grill lid. Grill for 1 - 1 1/2 hours, turning often. The chicken is done when meat is fork tender and the juices run clear. During the end of the grilling baste the chicken with Fast Paced BBQ Sauce. Turn the chicken once so the BBQ sauce can dry and cook into the meat. Take the chicken off the grill and place on a serving platter.

Serve right away with the extra BBQ sauce on the side!!!

Awesome BBQ Chicken to serve with Corn on the Cob, Baked beans & Asian slaw.

Grilled Cajun Corn on the Cob

Serves: 4-6

1/4 cup + 1 tablespoon butter, melted

1 1/4 tablespoons store bought Cajun seasoning

2-3 drops hot red pepper sauce

6 ears corn leave the husks on.

Preheat a gas -OR- charcoal grill for direct medium heat

(Heat coals to a white ash.)

In a bowl, mix 1/4 cup butter, Cajun seasoning and red pepper sauce. Reserve (set aside) 1 tablespoon of the butter mixture.

With care pull back the husks on each ear of corn; remove only the silk. Brush the butter mixture generously over the ears of corn. Put the husks back over the ears of corn; tie the husks in place with a thin piece of husk or string. Place the corn on the grill rack over medium heat, close the grill lid. COOK for 20-25 minutes, turn often, until corn is tender. With long handle tongs remove the corn carefully from the grill. Remove husks, brush corn with reserved 1 tablespoon of butter mixture.

Serve right away!!!

Endless Summer Baked Beans

Serves: 6 hungry people

1/2 pound smoked bacon, thick slices and chopped into 1/2 inch pieces

2 - (32 ounces each) cans baked beans

1/2 cup ketchup (I like Heinz Tomato Ketchup)

1/3 cup brown sugar

3 tablespoons honey

1-2 tablespoons hot red pepper sauce

This is a good dish to make on the side burner of a gas grill!!!!

In a dutch oven -OR- heavy pot, add the 1/2" inch chopped smoked bacon and COOK over medium heat. COOK until the fat begins to come out as liquid (render), around 4-5 minutes. Add the baked beans, ketchup, brown sugar, honey and hot red pepper sauce (to taste). Over medium-low heat bring to a SIMMER. Adjust to maintain a SIMMER for 30 minutes -OR- until thick and all the flavors are combined, stir often.

Serve right away!!!

Kings Asian Slaw

Serves: 4

1/4 cup rice vinegar

1 1/2 tablespoons soy sauce

1 tablespoon water

1 tablespoon olive oil -OR- canola oil -OR- vegetable oil

3/4 teaspoon sugar

1/2 teaspoon fresh ginger, peeled & minced

1/8 teaspoon five spice powder

2 cups shredded cabbage with carrots (Store-Bought Coleslaw Mix)

1/2 large cucumber; peeled & chopped

1/2 medium apple, cored & shredded

1 1/2 tablespoon fresh cilantro leaves

To make the dressing: Use a jar with a screw top, add vinegar, soy sauce, water, oil sugar, ginger and five spice powder. Cover the jar and shake very well. Set to the side.

To make the slaw: In a bowl, combine coleslaw mix, cucumber, apple and fresh cilantro. Shake the dressing in the covered jar again; drizzle the dressing over the slaw, use it all. Toss the slaw lightly to combine all the ingredients.

Serve right away!!!

King of the Hill Grilled Plums

Makes: 6 serving

6 each large ripe plums

molasses as needed

lightly brush the grill rack with vegetable oil

Preheat a gas -OR- charcoal grill for direct medium heat

With a sharp knife cut the center of the plum and remove the pit. Then lightly brush the plums with molasses on both sides. Place the plums on the grill rack, cut side down. Grill until the fruit begins to get a little bit charred, then flip the plums over. Shut the grill lid & give them a few minutes until they reach the desired doneness and are soft, don't burn.

Serve right away, great with ice cream!!!

Motor City Mocha Latte Shake

1 1/2 cups cold strong coffee

1 1/2 cups cold milk

15 ice cubes

1/2 package of instant chocolate pudding mix

3 tablespoons cocoa powder

Hazelnut Creamer - to taste and sugar - to taste

In a blender, combine all the ingredients, blend until ice is crushed and the shake is thick.

Serve right away!!!

MENU

Dinner Hot off the Grill!!!

Fan Meets Grill

Lime & Garlic Beef Steaks
Grilled Red Potatoes
Grilled Romaine Lettuce
Tiny's Grilled Sweet Peaches
Sonny's Lemonade

Lime & Garlic Beef Steaks

Serves: 4-6

3 -Bottom Round (Western Griller) Steaks, 1"-1 1/4" inches thick & 12-16 ounces each

2/3 cup fresh lime juice

5 tablespoons green onion (scallions), finely chopped

5 tablespoons water

4 tablespoons olive oil -OR- canola oil -OR- vegetable oil

2 tablespoons fresh garlic, crushed in a garlic press

1 teaspoon salt - to taste

Serve with:

Mango-Jalapeno Salsa or Your favorite Steak Sauce

Season the Steak W/ salt & pepper before serving with salsa -OR- steak sauce.

Place the 3 steaks in a extra-large resealable freezer plastic bag, with no holes in it.

For Marinade: In a bowl, combine the lime juice, scallions, water, oil, garlic and salt, mix well. Pour the marinade over the steaks and seal the bag tightly. Turn the bag to coat the steak and place in the refrigerator for 12 - 24 hours (don't marinate for more than 24 hours), turning if you can every 4 hours. Take steaks out of the refrigerator and let them come back to room temperature before grilling time.

Grilling the Steaks: Take the steaks out of the marinade and throw out the marinade.

Preheat a gas grill for 10 minutes on direct high heat; reduce to direct medium heat for grilling.

Charcoal grill: Heat coals to a white ash direct medium coals

Place the steaks on the grill rack over direct medium heat, turning only once. Grill for 10 - 12 minutes for medium-rare (145 degrees F) -OR- 12 -15 minutes for medium (160 degrees F).

Take steaks off of the grill and let rest for at least 5 minutes before serving.

Don't ever cook this cut of steak past medium doneness.

To Serve: On a clean cutting board with a sharp knife slice each steak very thinly-across the grain. If you want season the steaks with salt and pepper to taste. Serve the steaks with Salsa -OR- Steak Sauce.

Lime & Garlic Steaks go good w/Grilled Potatoes, Grilled Lettuce & Lemonade.

Grilled Red Potatoes

Serves: 6 hungry people

2 pounds red bliss potatoes, 1 1/2" inches in diameter each, well scrubbed & cut into 1/4ers.

3 tablespoons olive oil -Or- canola oil

3 teaspoons fresh rosemary, snipped

1/2 teaspoon kosher salt - to taste

1/2 teaspoon ground black pepper - to taste

In a big bowl, combine potatoes, oil, fresh rosemary, salt and black pepper, mix well.

Lightly brush vegetable oil onto the grill rack!!!

Gas grill: Preheat a gas grill for 10 minutes on high heat, reduce to direct medium heat.

Charcoal grill: Preheat coals for direct medium coals.

Gas Grill: Place potatoes on the grill rack over direct medium heat and close the grill lid. COOK for 15-20 minutes -OR- until tender and brown on all sides. Turn the potatoes by scooping them up with a big spatula and turning them over every 5 minutes or so. When done take potatoes off the grill and serve hot or warm right away.

Charcoal Grill: Place potatoes on grill rack over direct medium coals , UNCOVERED. COOK for 15-20 minutes -OR- until tender and brown on all sides, flip over potatoes by scooping them up with a big spatula and turning over every 5 minutes or so. Serve hot or warm right away!!!

Grilled Romaine Lettuce

Serves: 4-6 hungry people

3 tablespoons olive oil

2 heads Romaine lettuce, salt - to taste, freshly ground black pepper - to taste

2 tablespoons Balsamic vinegar

Lightly brush olive oil -OR- vegetable oil onto the grill rack.

Preheat a gas -OR- charcoal grill to direct medium-high heat.

Rinse the 2 heads of Romaine lettuce under cold running water and pat dry with paper towels.

With a sharp knife cut each head into 1/4ers. On a long platter place all the 1/4 ers of Romaine with 2 tablespoons of olive oil and season with salt and pepper to taste. Place Romaine on the grill rack over direct medium-high heat. Grill for 5-6 minutes, until crisp-tender and brown grill marks, turn often. When done grilling Romaine rough chop, Toss in a bowl with the remaining 1 tablespoon of oil and the vinegar. Season the salad to your taste with salt and freshly ground black pepper.

Serve the salad warm right away !!!

Sonny's Lemonade

Makes: 5 servings at 1-1/2 cups each

6 cups very cold water*Serve over a lot of ice*

2 cups fresh lemon juice - no seeds (around 8 lemons)

1 cup sugar

In a big glass -OR- plastic pitcher mix cold water, fresh lemon juice and sugar. Stir very well, serve over a lot of ice.

Tiny's Grilled Sweet Peaches

Makes: 4 servings

1 each (16 ounce) package frozen peaches

1/2 cup honey

2 tablespoons cinnamon

Serve with Vanilla Ice Cream

Preheat a gas -OR- charcoal grill to direct medium heat

Place peaches onto 2 large pieces of heavy duty aluminum foil. Drizzle the honey over peaches and sprinkle with the cinnamon. Close up the foil and seal very tightly. Place the foil packets on the grill rack over direct medium heat. COOK for 8-10 minutes -OR- until done, turning only once. Take the foil packets off the grill, carefully open the packets and serve right away with Vanilla Ice Cream!!!

MENU
Dinner Hot off the Grill !!!!

All American Dinner

Barbecue Marinated Pot Roast w/Horseradish Sauce

Safe at Home Baked Potatoes

JR's Grilled Romaine w/Bacon & Blue Cheese

Grilled Banana Splits

Rick Berry Iced Tea

BBQ Marinated Pot Roast W/ Double Play Horseradish Sauce

Serves: 4-6

2 1/2 pounds Boneless Chuck Roast

1/2 cup ketchup

1/4 cup Worcestershire Sauce

4 tablespoons red wine vinegar

4 tablespoons canola oil -OR- olive oil -OR- vegetable oil

2 fresh garlic cloves, crushed in a garlic press

1 teaspoon ground ginger

1 bunch green onions (scallions), thinly sliced - green & white parts

Place the meat on a clean dry flat surface. Pierce both sides all over with a fork, this will tenderize and let the marinade inside the meat. Place the meat in a extra large resealable plastic bag. In a bowl, combine the ketchup, Worcestershire Sauce, vinegar, oil, ground ginger, fresh garlic and scallions. Pour the marinade over the meat in the bag. Seal the bag and turn the bag to coat the meat with marinade. Place the meat in the refrigerator for 12-24 hours to marinate, don't go over 24 hours. Turn the bag every 4 hours -OR- so to keep the meat covered in marinade.

Remove the beef from the refrigerator, SCRAPE off marinade. Pierce again with a fork on all sides. Allow to stand at room temperature for 45 minutes before grilling.

Preheat a gas grill -OR- charcoal grill to direct medium-high heat

On a cutting board with a sharp knife cut the meat in half. Place meat halves on the grill rack over medium-high heat. COOK for 45 minutes to 1 hour, turn over every 10 minutes. Heat the marinade to a boil over medium heat, BASTE with marinade often during grilling. When done grilling the roast, let it rest on a cutting board for 10 minutes. Carve roast into very thin diagonal slices with a sharp knife.

Super Pot Roast serve w/horseradish sauce, grilled baked potatoes, grilled lettuce & iced tea!

Double Play Horseradish Sauce

1/2 cup Store Bought mayonnaise

1/2 Store Bought sour cream

4 tablespoons prepared white horseradish, drained - to taste

In a bowl, whisk together all the ingredients. Chill before serving.

Safe at Home Grilled Baked Potatoes

Serves: 4

4 medium size baking potatoes kosher salt -OR- rock salt

Preheat a gas grill -OR- heat coals for direct medium heat

Gently scrub potatoes (use a vegetable brush, if you have one) under cold water. Pierce potatoes all around with a fork, this will allow the stream to escape during baking. In a 2 each - 8" X 4" inch disposable foil loaf pans, pour in a 1" inch layer of kosher salt -OR- rock salt.

Place 2 potatoes in the salt in each pan; then pour kosher -OR- rock salt over the potatoes until covered totally in salt. Carefully place the pans on the grill with the potatoes in the salt for about 1 hour -OR- until the grilled potatoes are fork tender. When the potatoes are fully cooked, carefully take the pans off the grill and remove the potatoes from salt. Serve right away with plenty of butter and sour cream.

Enjoy!!!

Jr's Grilled Romaine w/Bacon & Blue Cheese

Jr's Salad Dressing:

1/4 cup extra virgin olive oil

3/4 cup shallots, finely chopped

1/2 pound smoked bacon, chopped

1/2 cup balsamic vinegar

In a saucepan, heat 1 tablespoon olive oil over high heat, Add shallots and bacon, COOK until the bacon is crisp. In the same saucepan, add balsamic vinegar and 1 tablespoon of olive oil, mix well. Remove from the heat and set aside.

3 heads fresh Romaine lettuce, cut in 1/2 lengthwise

1/2 cup blue cheese, crumbled freshly ground black pepper

Lightly brush the grill rack with Vegetable oil -OR- Olive oil.

Preheat a gas -OR- charcoal grill to direct high heat

Brush the remaining 2 tablespoons of olive oil onto the Romaine lettuce. Place Romaine cut side down on the grill rack over high heat, for around 1 - 1 1/2 minutes, just to sear. Take off the grill right away!!!

Serve the Romaine lettuce, cut side up and drizzle with the JR's salad dressing. Then sprinkle with blue cheese and serve with freshly ground black pepper to taste.

Grilled Banana Splits

Makes: 6 servings

6 large bananas, unpeeled and stems removed

2 cups semi-sweet chocolate chips

1 each (10.5 ounce) package mini marshmallow

6 - large sheets of heavy-duty aluminum foil can cooking spray - as needed

Preheat a gas -OR- charcoal grill to direct medium-high heat spray 6 sheets of heavy-duty aluminum foil, large enough to wrap the bananas in, with can cooking spray. Cut the peel of the banana from the stem to the bottom, cut the banana inside lengthwise. Carefully open the banana peel just enough to place the chocolate chips and mini marshmallows inside the peels of the bananas. Stuff with as many chocolate chips and mini marshmallows as you would like. Close the peels tightly and wrap the bananas in the sheets of foil.

Place the foil wrapped bananas on the grill rack over medium heat. Grill for around 4-6 minutes - or until the chocolate chips and the mini marshmallows melt. Take off the grill when done, carefully unwrap the bananas and open up the peels.

Serve right away with a spoon. Enjoy!!!

Rick Berry Iced Tea

6 cups water

6 bags raspberry tea

3 bags blackcurrant tea

6 tablespoons honey - to taste

6 orange slices -OR- lemon slices

A lot of Ice

Bring the water to a boil. Add the tea bags. Steep for 10-15 minutes, take tea bags out. Sweetened the tea with the honey, stir to dissolve the honey. Serve with ice and fruit slices.

Big Bob's Top 50 Greatest Sportswomen All Time

Your Top 50 List:

#1. Babe Didrikson Zarharias Track/Golf _____

#2. Jackie Joyner Kersee Track & Field _____

#3. Martina Navratilova Tennis _____

#4. Bonnie Blair Speed Skating _____

#5. Sonja Henie Figure Skating _____

#6. Wilma Rudolph Track & Field _____

#7. Chris Evert Tennis _____

#8. Billie Jean King Tennis _____

#9. Mia Hamm Soccer _____

TIE #10. Olga Korbut Gymnastics _____

#10. Nadia Comaneci Gymnastics _____

#11. Florence Griffith Joyner Track & Field _____

#12. Janet Evans Swimming _____

#13. Peggy Fleming Figure Skating _____

#14. Tracy Caulkins Swimming _____

TIE #15. Cheryl Miller Basketball _____

TIE #15. Nancy Lopez Golf _____

#16. Julie Krone Horse Racing _____

#17. Mary T. Meagher Swimming _____

#18. Steffi Graf Tennis _____

#19. Margaret Court Tennis _____

TIE #20. Joan Beniot Samuelson Running _____

TIE #20. Ann Meyers Basketball _____

#21. Dawn Frazier Swimming _____

#22. Teresa Edwards Basketball _____

#23. Mickey Wright Golf _____

#24. Dorothy Hamill Figure Skating _____

#25. Mary Decker Slaney Track & Field _____

#26. Maureen Connolly Tennis _____

#27. Grete Waitz Running _____

#28. Althea Gibson _____

#29. Katarina Witt Figure Skating _____

#30. Ruffin Horse Racing _____

#31. Kathy Whitworth Golf _____

#32. Pat McCormick Diving _____

#33. Picabo Street Skiing _____

#34. Susan Butcher Dogsledding _____

TIE #35. Lisa Fernandez Softball _____

TIE #35. Amy Van Dyken Swimming _____

#36. Michele Akers Soccer _____

#37. Wyomia Tyus Track & Field _____

#38. Nancy Lieberman-Cline Basketball _____

#39. Rosi Mittermaier Skiing _____

TIE #40. Mary Lou Retton Gymnastics _____

TIE #40. Shirley Muldowney Auto Racing _____

#41. Sheila Young Speed Skating/Cycling _____

#42. Camille Duvall Waterskiing _____

#43. Marion Ludewig Bowling _____

#44. Donna de Varona Swimming _____

#45. Jenny Thompson Swimming _____

#46. Cammi Granato Hockey _____

#47. Sheryl Swoopes Basketball _____

#48. Sarah Hughes Figure Skating _____

#49. Lisa Anderson Surfer _____

TIE #50. Manon Rheaume Hockey _____

TIE #50. Marion Jones Track & Field _____

Big Bob's Top 35 Best Coaches of All Time Pro -OR- College Sports

Coach: Your Top 35 List:

#1. John Wooden

#2. Vince Lomabardi

#3. Bear Bryant

#4. Red Auerbach

#5. Dean Smith

#6. Paul Brown

#7. Pat Summit

#8. Dan Gable

#9. Scotty Bowman

#10. Joe Paterno

#11. Mike Krzyzewski

#12. Toe Blake

#13. Joe Torre

#14. Don Shula

#15. Casey Stengel

#16. Tom Landry

#17. Phil Jackson

#18. Bill Walsh

#19. Chuck Noll

#20. Bobby Knight

#21. Knute Rockne

#22. Eddie Robinson

#23. Sparky Anderson

#24. John McGraw

#25. Frank Leahy

#26. Morgan Wooten

#27. Bill Bowerman

#28. John Madden

#29. Connie Mack

#30. Chuck Daly

#31. Lenny Wilkens

#32. "POP" Warner

#33. Bill Parcels

#34. Woody Hayes

TIE #35. Pat Riley

TIE #35. Joe Gibbs

Big Bob's Top 12 Greatest Women's Basketball Players All Time

Your Top 12 List:

#1. Cheryl Miller

#2. Ann Meyers

#3. Teresa Edwards

#4. Nancy Lieberman

#5. Sheryl Swoopes

#6. Cynthia Cooper

#7. Chamique Holdsclaw

#8. Dawn Staley

#9. Lisa Leslie

#10. Diana Taurasi

#11. Ruthie Bolton

#12. Lauren Jackson

Big Bob's Top 50 Greatest Sports Heroes All Time

Your Top 50 List:

#1. Jackie Robinson

#2. Babe Ruth

#3. Muhammad Ali

#4. Johnny Unitas

#5. Joe Di Maggio

#6. Lou Gehrig

#7. Ted Williams

#8. 1980 U.S. Olympic Hockey Team

#9. Billy Jean King

#10. Vince Lombardi

#11. Larry Bird & Magic Johnson

#12. Rex Kern & Woody Hayes

#13. Jim Brown

#14. Johnny Bench & Pete Rose

#15. Jesse Owens

#16. Jim Thorpe

#17. Roger Staubach

#18. Bart Starr

#19. Joe Louis

TIE #20. Rudy from Notre Dame _____

TIE #20. Seabiscuit _____

#21. Jackie Joyner Kersee _____

#22. Bonnie Blair _____

#23. Carl Lewis _____

#24. Mia Hamm _____

#25. Mark Spitz _____

#26. Jack Nicklaus _____

#27. Tiger Woods _____

#28. Michael Jordan _____

#29. Lance Armstrong _____

#30. Steve Largent _____

#31. Thurman Munson _____

#32. Ernie Banks _____

#33. Gale Sayers _____

#34. Chris Evert _____

TIE #35. Bill Russell _____

TIE #35. Wayne Gretky _____

#36. Joe Montana _____

#37 Joe "Willie" Namath _____

#38. Arthur Ashe _____

#39. Bo Jackson _____

TIE #40. Jimmy Connors _____

TIE #40. Gordie Howe & Bobby Orr _____

#41. Terry Bradshaw & Franco Harris _____

#42. Bill Mazeroski _____

#43. Willie Stargell & Roberto Clemente _____

#44. Ben Hogan _____

TIE #45. Jerry West & Dave Bing _____

TIE #45. Wilt Chamberlain _____

#46. John Havlichek _____

#47. John "Jack" Twyman _____

#48. Babe Didrikson Zaharias _____

TIE #49. George Foreman _____

TIE #49. Joe Greene _____

#50. Pistol Pete Maravich _____

Top 10 Favorite Sports Hero's

Your Top 10 List:

#1. Lance Armstrong

#2. Michael Jordan

#3. Muhammad Ali

#4. Babe Ruth

TIE #5. Tiger Woods

TIE #5. Jackie Robinson

#6. Mia Hamm

#7. Wayne Gretky

#8. Cal Ripken Jr.

#9. Joe Montana

TIE #10. Pele

TIE #10. Magic Johnson & Larry Bird

TIE #10. Bruce Jenner

_____

_____

_____

_____

_____

_____

_____

_____

_____

_____

_____

_____

_____

Big Bob's Top 35 Greatest Athlete's/Sportsperson All Time

Your Top 35 List:

#1. Lance Armstrong

#2. Muhammad Ali

#3. Pele

#4. Michael Jordan

#5. Jack Nicklaus

#6. Babe Didrikson Zaharias

#7. Jim Thorpe

#8. Carl Lewis

#9. Mark Spitz

#10. Jesse Owens

#11. Secretariat

#12. Jim Brown

#13. Jackie Joyner-Kersee

#14. Jackie Robinson

#15. Wayne Gretky

#16. Tiger Woods

#17. Bill Russell

#18. Sugar Ray Robinson

#19. Johnny Unitas

TIE #20. Martina Navratilova

TIE #20. John McEnroe

#21. Joe Montana

#22. Oscar Robertson

#23. Jerry Rice

#24. Lawrence Taylor

#25. Mia Hamm

#26. Rocky Marciano

#27. Willie Shoemaker

#28. Kareem Adbul Jabbar

#29. Vince Lombardi

#30. Jerry West

#31. Magic Johnson

#32. Wilt Chamberlain

#33. Bonnie Blair

TIE #34. Larry Bird

TIE #34. SHAQ

TIE #35. Bruce Jenner

TIE #35. Bo Jackson

TIE #35. Billy Jean King

Big Bob's Top 10 Greatest NFL Teams All Time

Team: Your Top 10 List:

#1. 1972 Dolphins

#2. 1978 - 1979 Steelers

#3. 1962 Packers

#4. 1985 Bears

#5. 1992 - 1993 Cowboys

#6. 1989 49ers.

#7. 1976 Raiders

#8. 1986 Giants

#9. 1998 Broncos

#10. 1990 Bills

Top 17 Sexist Athletes from the Past

To be on this list you have to be retired!!!

                                         Your Top 17 List:

#1. Gabrielle Reece

#2. Katarina Witt

#3. Summer Sanders

#4. Gariela Sabatini

#5. Manon Rheaume

#6. Chris Evert

#7. Steffi Graf

#8. Carling Basset

#9. Florence Griffin Joyner

#10. Laura Baugh

#11. Peggy Fleming

#12. Mary Lou Retton

#13. Anne White

#14. Dorothy Hamill

#15. Janet Evens

#16. Sonja Henie _____

#17. Tonya Harding _____

Big Bob's Top 12 Greatest College Basketball Teams All Time

Team:	Your Top 12 List:
#1. 1968 UCLA 29-1	_____
#2. 1976 Indiana 32-0	_____
#3. 1972 UCLA 30-0	_____
#4. 1956 San Francisco 29-0	_____
#5. 1957 UNC 32-0	_____
#6. 1996 Kentucky 34-2	_____
#7. 1954 Kentucky 25-0	_____
#8. 1992 Duke 34-2	_____
#9. 1960 Ohio State 25-3	_____
#10. 1982 UNC 32-2	_____
#11. 1974 NC State 30-1	_____
#12. 1990 UNLV 35-5	_____

Big Bob's Top 10 Greatest Pro Basketball Teams All Time

Team:	Your Top 10 List:
#1. 1964-1965 Boston Celtics	_____
#2. 1971-1972 L.A. Lakers	_____
#3. 1986 -1987 L.A. Lakers	_____
#4. 1969-1970 N.Y. Knicks	_____
#5. 1985-1986 Boston Celtics	_____
#6. 1988-1989 Detroit Pistons	_____
#7. 1966-1967 Philadelphia 76ers	_____
#8. 1982-1983 Philadelphia 76ers	_____
#9. 1995-1996 Chicago Bulls	_____
#10. 1991-1992 Chicago Bulls	_____

Big Bob's Top 15 Greatest Major League Baseball Teams All Time

Team:	Your Top 15 List:
#1. 1927 N.Y. Yankees	_____
#2. 1998-2000 N.Y. Yankees	_____
#3. 1906 Chicago Cubs	_____
#4. 1939 New Yankees	_____
#5. 1975-1976 Cincinnati Reds	_____
#6. 1955 Dodgers	_____
#7. 1944 St. Louis Cardinals	_____
#8. 1972-1974 Oakland A's	_____
#9. 1902 Pittsburgh Pirates	_____
#10. 1929 Philadelphia Athletics	_____
#11. 1936 N.Y. Yankees	_____
#12. 1968 Detroit Tigers	_____
#13. 1954 Cleveland Indians	_____
#14. 1984 Detroit Tigers	_____
#15. 1995 Cleveland Indians	_____

Big Bob's Top 35 Greatest Sports Players Nicknames All Time

Nickname: Your Top 35 List:

#1. The Great One (Gretzy)

#2. The Galloping Ghost (Grange)

#3. The Splendid Splinter (Williams)

#4. The Yankee Clipper (di Maggio)

#5. The Golden Bear (Nicklaus)

#6. Mr. October (Reggie)

#7. Basketball Jesus (Bird)

#8. The Iron Horse (Gerhig)

#9. Shoeless Joe (Jackson)

#10. The Assassin (Jack Tatum)

#11. Magic (Johnson)

#12. The Barber (Sal Maglie)

#13. His Heinous (Laimbeer)

#14. Refrigerator (William Perry)

#15. Round Mound of Rebound (Barkley)

#16. Mr. Hockey (Howe)

#17. Hibachi (Arenas)

#18. M.J. (Jordan)

#19. the Microwave (Vinny Johnson)

#20. The Babe (Ruth)

#21. Sugar Ray Robinson

#22. Big O (Robinson)

#23. Charlie Hustle (Rose)

#23. Sweetness (Payton)

#24. Mr. Clutch (West)

#25. Mr. May (Winfield)

#26. Big Papi (Ortiz)

#27. He Hate Me (XFL Player)

#28. The Admiral (Robinson)

#29. The Ice Man (Gervin)

#30. The Big Unit (Johnson)

#31. The Dream (Olajuwon)

#32. The Mailman (Malone)

#33. The Bear (Bryant)

#34. Night Train (Lane)

#35. POP (Warner)

Big Bob's Top 10 Greatest Unit Nicknames All Time

Unit Nicknames: Your Top 10 List:

#1. Purple People Eaters (Vikings)   _____

#2. Big Red Machine (Cincy)   _____

#3. Bad Boys (Pistons, Late 1980's)   _____

#4. Steel Curtain (Steelers 1970's D)   _____

#5. Fab Five (Michigan 1990's)   _____

#6. Phil Slamma Jamma (Houston)   _____

#7. The Hogs (Redskins O-Line)   _____

#8. Monsters of the Midway (Bears)   _____

#9. The 4 Horsemen (ND 1922-24 BF)   _____

#10. Bronx Bombers (N.Y. Yankees)   _____

Big Bob's Top 17 Really Great Cigars

I don't really smoke cigars, but I like the smell & taste of a great cigar!

Your Top 17 List:

#1. Montercristo #2 (1993)   _____

#2. Cohiba Robusto (1994)   _____

#3. Partagas Series Du Connoisseur #1 (1998)   _____

#4. Bolivar Lonsdale (1997)   _____

#5. La Gloria Cubana Medaille D' & #2 (1998)   _____

#6. Romeo Y Julieta Petit Corona (1995)   _____

#7. Sancho Panza Sancho   _____

#8. Bolivar Royal Corona (2005)   _____

#9. Romeo Y Julieta Short Churchill   _____

#10. El Rey De Mundo Lonsdale (2001)   _____

#11. Romeo Y Julieta 1875 Bully   _____

#12. San Cristobal De la Habana Mercaderies   _____

#13. Gispert Maduro Churchill   _____

#14. Cuaba Salamone   _____

#15. Flor De Rafael Gonzalez Lonsdale   _____

#16. Padron 1926 40th. Anniversary Natural   _____

#17. Pardon Millennium Seris Maduro 2000   _____

I received no money for this -OR- any list; it's my opinion based on no true facts.

Big Bob's Top 10 Luxury Auto's

Where is my 2000 Honda Accord on this list, it's a great car !

Your Top 10 List:

#1. Ferrari F99 GTB Fiorano

#2. Lamborghini Gallardo

#3. Jaguar XK

#4. Bentley Continental Flying Spur

#5. Mercedes-Benz S550

TIE #6. Cadillac Escalade

TIE #6. BMW X5

#7. Lexus GS430

#8. Land Rover Range Rover Sport

#9. Audi Q7

#10. Infiniti G35

_____
_____
_____
_____
_____
_____
_____
_____
_____
_____

*Note: I was paid no money to form this list of luxury vehicles - it's just my own opinion!!!

Dinner Hot off the Grill!! Menus

The Greatest:

College Football Player
Red Grange

College Football Coach
Frank Leahy

College Football Team
Nebraska 1971

College Football Rivalry
Ohio State and Michigan

Pro Football Player
Jim Brown

Pro Football Coach
Vince Lombardi

Pro Football Team
1972 Dolphins

Pro Football Quarterback
Johnny Unitas

Pro Football Running Back
Jim Brown

Women's Basketball Player
Cheryl Miller

Men's College Basketball Player
Lew Alcindor

Men's College Basketball Coach
John Wooden

Men's College Basketball Team
1968 UCLA

Men's Pro Basketball Player
Michael Jordon

Men's Pro Basketball Coach
Red Auerbach

Men's Pro Basketball Team
Boston Celtics 1964-1965

Major League Baseball Player
Babe Ruth

Major League Baseball Manager
Sparkey Anderson

Major League Baseball Team
1927 New York Yankees

Major League Baseball Pitcher
Walter Johnson

Baseball Movie
Bull Durham

Baseball Radio Announcer
Ernie Harwell

Ice Hockey Player
Wayne Gretzky

Pro Boxer
Muhammad Ali

Female Soccer Player
Mia Hamm

Male Soccer Player
PELE

Male Golfer
Jack Nicklaus

Female Golfer
Mickey Wright

Golf Movie
Tin Cup

Dinner Hot off the Grill!! Menus

Female Tennis Player
Martina Navratilova

Male Tennis Player
Pete Sampras

Female Bowler
Marion Ludwig

Male Bowler
Earl Anthony

NASCAR Driver
Richard Petty

Overall Race Car Driver
AJ Foyt

Jockey
Willie Shoemaker

Race Horse
Secretariat

Athlete / Sports Person
Lance Armstrong

Sports Woman
Babe Didrikson

Sports Hero
Jackie Robinson

Coach Any Sport Pro -OR- College
John Wooden

Sports Players Nicknames
The Great One (Gretzky)

Sports Unit Nicknames
Purple People Eaters

American Beer
Sam Adams Black Lager

Sports Movie
Rocky

Summer Grilling Songs
Cheeseburger in Paradise

Sports Books
The Sweet Science